D1269911

Race, Class, and Party

— From the Raleigh News and Observer, 4 July 1900.

This cartoon was used in the campaign for the ratification of the North Carolina disfranchising constitution. It pictures the ogre "Negro domination" rising out of a third-party ballot-box, illustrating the Southern fear of a Negro balance of power in the event of white disharmony. See Chapter V, section IV.

Race, Class, and Party

A HISTORY OF NEGRO SUFFRAGE AND WHITE POLITICS IN THE SOUTH

BY Paul Lewinson

The Universal Library

GROSSET & DUNLAP
NEW YORK

UNIVERSAL LIBRARY EDITION, 1965

BY ARRANGEMENT WITH RUSSELL & RUSSELL, INC.

LIBRARY OF CONGRESS CATALOG CARD NUMBER: 15168

PRINTED IN THE UNITED STATES OF AMERICA

To

My Mother and Father
without whose patient sacrifices
this work could never
have been undertaken

"POSTSCRIPT, 1964"

This book, when it first appeared more than three decades ago, dealt with an aspect of one of the most durable problems in our history, but at a time when that problem was in a relatively quiescent stage. I am frankly glad to see it re-appear now, when the problem has again become an active one. History is an intellectual discipline, but it has practical and moral uses. For that reason, a historical work like this one cries to be supplemented, revised, adapted, when it bids for renewed attention.

But to bring it exhaustively up to date would be a major task, beyond the scope of a postscript, and one which ought probably be postponed until the present eddy of forces has settled down into a flow of events whose direction is more clearly discernible.

Some setting of the problem in its now longer background may, however, be attempted here. It will be speculative; based on much thought but not on research. But first I must make clear that this postscript, like this book, is about (1) Negro suffrage (not race relationships generally), (2) white politics (in relationship thereto), and (3) the South (not Harlem, Rochester, or Philadelphia). Race relationships generally, political history generally, and the general history of our country figure in it, of course.

What, then, has been happening to Negro suffrage in the South since 1930?

In 1930 it was "negligible" except in a few localities (v.p. 106 below). In 1940, Myrdal's "American Dilemma" estimated the number of Negro voters in eight Deep South States at 80,000 to 90,000. This summer the Southern Regional Council estimated Negro voters' registrations in eleven Southern States at about 1,400,000 in 1960 and about 1,935,000 in

1964. Most recently, the Associated Press estimated that the Negro vote in the same States was "almost double" its 1960 strength: "more than two million, as compared with 1.1 million four years ago . . . Negroes now make up 13 per cent of the Southern electorate." Clearly Negro voting has not only been increasing, but has been increasing at a rising rate, with a sharp rise in the rate of increase after 1940, and another some time around 1960.

What has brought this change about? It is too great to have resulted from the dropping of the poll-tax prerequisite for voting by five (Fla., Ga., La., S.C., Tenn.) out of the ten States in which it was still required in 1930. In other respects Southern election laws have changed little. The Supreme Court's decision finally forbidding "white primaries" (Smith v. Allwright, 1944) is believed to have had some effect that may have spilled over into registration and voting in general elections. Till the second spurt in registrations, some time around 1960, the Court has taken no other new line on the constitutional law of suffrage; nor has there been any Federal legislation or executive action on suffrage, except the anti-poll tax amendment ratified only nine months ago. I ascribe this change to a growth in Negro self-confidence based on improving economic and educational conditions, to the advent of a new type of Negro leadership, to a more resolute and widespread activism among the Negro rank and file, to a change in the national attitude towards segregation and discrimination, to the growing political power of the Negro in the North, and to Southern white acquiescence.

That the increase in Negro voting registration stems, to begin with, from growing Negro activism and self-confidence is self-evident; no one can register or vote without putting himself forward for the purpose. Equally self-evident is white acquiescence: as any Southern Negro will tell you, registration and voting is not a unilateral action. This acquiescence is not of all white Southerners everywhere. The 1964 "summer of violence" in Mississippi, arising out of a Negro voter-education campaign, is the most recent evidence of this; a group of

Democratic congressmen, in an open letter to President Johnson, "noted that in McComb alone, 17 bombings, 32 arrests, nine beatings, and four church burnings have been reported since June," and that "law and order is clearly not being maintained" (New York *Times,* Oct. 5, 1964). Since at least 1955, the year of the first organized demonstrations under Dr. Martin Luther King in Alabama, there has been an upsurge of racist organizations in the South – the old Klan, the new White Citizens Councils, for example; educational desegregation has been resisted by violence or threats of violence, most sensationally in Little Rock in 1957, in Athens, Ga., in 1961, and in Oxford, Miss., in 1962; and Negro demonstrations elsewhere, on a variety of grievances, have been met by violent counter-demonstrations, as notably in Birmingham in 1963, and by police repression.

Nevertheless it must be true that an increasing number of white Southerners have acquiesced in change; otherwise there could have been no such rise in Negro voter registration as has actually taken place. A changing Southern white attitude over the years is also reflected in other developments: the growth of biracial organizations to promote inter-racial adjustment, the condemnation of discrimination and even of segregation by Southern (as well as Northern) religious bodies, an overall decrease in lynching (until the late 1950s, at any rate), the election and appointment of a few Negroes to State and municipal offices, a certain amount of desegregation of such public facilities as libraries and parks and the admission of a few Negroes to graduate and professional schools in Southern universities (without judicial intervention), the employment of Negro policemen and firemen, and some effort to raise Negro public schools closer to white standards. These changes no doubt reflect to a degree the increase in Negro suffrage itself.

On the national level, both as reflecting a change in national sentiment and as influencing Southern attitudes, weight must be given to a series of Supreme Court decisions after 1930 that have struck at the legality of discrimination and of segregation: in public transportation (Henderson v. U. S., 1950; Gale v. Browder, 1956), in education (Missouri ex rel. Gaines v. Canada, 1938; Sipuel v. University of Georgia, 1948; Sweatt v. Painter, 1950; Brown v. Board of Education, 1954), in eligibility for jury duty (Avery v. Georgia, Norris v. Alabama, 1953), and in declaring racially-restrictive real-estate covenants unenforceable (Shelly v. Kramer, 1948). Weight must also be given to the increasing influence of the Federal government exercised through various kinds of grants-in-aid to local authorities and through contracts for construction, purchases, and research, all statutorily hedged against discriminatory practices. And much weight must be given to the growth of the political power of the Negro in the North, in both parties but particularly in the Democratic Party in the cities of the North.

Additional light will be thrown on the national and Southern change of attitude by considering the causes of the specially sharp rise in Negro voting registration from 1940 to 1960 (according to the Southern Regional Council, something under 1, 200,000—an average of 60,000 per year), and the even sharper rise from 1960 to 1964 (about 535,000—an average of about 134,000 per year). The first sharp rise may reflect the social consciousness of the New Deal, and some of its mechanisms (Negroes voted fairly widely in the Federally-supervised AAA crop referenda, e.g.). It very probably reflects the democratic ideology fostered by World War II, the inter-racial contacts in the armed forces, reinforced by a considerable measure of desegregation in the defense departments' policy, and the "fair employment" practices enforced federally first as a manpower device during the war and later extended to cover all work done under federal contracts or with federal aid.

The second spurt, beginning around 1960, I connect with the Supreme Court's climactic school-desegregation decision (Brown v. Board of Education) of 1954, the demonstrations in Montgomery, Ala., under Dr. Martin Luther King in 1955, and the passage of the Federal Civil Rights Acts of 1957 and 1960. Only the Civil Rights Acts bore directly on suffrage.

These three events dramatized the racial problem. The Supreme Court's 1954 school decision ranged the judiciary against segregation as a form of discrimination, dealt with one of the most articulate grievances of the Southern Negro, and – as shown in Little Rock, Athens, and Oxford – provided a fulcrum for Federal executive intervention such as had not existed since the lapse of the Reconstruction codes after 1876. The Montgomery demonstrations – resulting in the first instance from a bus segregation incident – showed the Negro how he might bring his struggle into the open, and has been followed by demonstrations elsewhere, by the formation of new and more militant Negro organizations like the Congress on Racial Equality and the Students Non-Violent Coordinating Committee, and by increasing the militancy of the older organizations like the NAACP and the Urban League.

Of the two Civil Rights Acts, that of 1960 was the more far-reaching. Both set up a commission to make reports and recommendations. The substantive innovation of the first Act was to authorize the Federal government to bring civil suits for injunctions against voting officials for the denial of the right to vote, an action that had hitherto been available only to aggrieved individuals. Because Alabama officials evaded this provision by destroying their records and resigning, the 1960 Act declared the acts of registrars to be acts of the States, provided that the Attorney General of the United States could seek injunctions against the States, required that records be kept for 22 months after any election, and gave the Attorney General access to them. In addition, it provided that where any "pattern or practice" of disfranchisement was found, Federal courts could appoint referees and on their recommendation require that aggrieved persons be permitted to vote.

I feel that these three events raised the curtain on a new period of "Negro Suffrage and White Politics in the South," with which future historians will have to deal, as also the beginning of a new period in race relationships generally and on a national scale. Its first episode was the passage of the Civil Rights Act of 1964, which may put the Federal government back actively in the entire field of civil – including suffrage – rights enforcement for the first time since the end of the Reconstruction era. Briefly, the eleven titles of this Act forbid discrimination in education, in employment, in the administration of Federally-assisted programs, in access to places of public resort (including business establishments), and in voting rights. On voting rights specifically it requires that tests must be administered in a non-discriminatory way, safeguarding especially the administration of literacy tests; and it gives the Justice Department new authority to speed up and simplify the enforcement of provisions in the 1957 and 1960 Acts. Preventive relief may be sought in civil actions by aggrieved persons, with the assistance of the Justice Department if the case is of general public importance, or by the Justice Department itself where a "pattern of discrimination" exists. The life of the Commission on Civil Rights, first established by the 1957 Act, is extended for four years, and the Commission is given enlarged investigatory powers especially in the fields of equal protection of the laws and voting rights in Federal elections. Enforcement and court tests of this Act have already begun.

For the South, Negro activism on the present scale, white acquiescence in racial adjustment to the extent I have indicated, and the new pressures in national law and sentiment represent a considerable change since 1930, when this book was finished. But I must emphasize that the change in Negro voting is spotty and localized.

The Southern Regional Council's study of Negro voting registration, cited above, shows that in March 1964 in eleven Southern States the highest percentage of voting-age Negroes registered was 67.2 (in the Border State of Tennessee); the lowest was 6.7 (Mississippi). The following table ranks these

States in the order of percentage of voting-age Negroes registered, from highest to lowest, and presents certain other relevant percentages.

NEGRO VOTERS' REGISTRATION IN THE SOUTH, 1964

State	*% Eligibles Reg'd.* *Negro*	*White*	*Negro Registrants as % of All Regts.*	*Negro Eligibles as % of All Eligibles*
Tenn.	67.2	72.9	13.0	14.9
Texas	57.7	62.2	12.5	11.8
Fla.	51.1	72.6	10.0	15.0
N.C.	45.0	92.6	10.0	20.9
Ark.	41.5	65.1	12.3	18.4
Ga.	39.1	65.8	16.0 - 18.0	25.3
S.C.	34.2	78.5	10.0 - 15.0	29.3
La.	31.6	80.0	14.0	28.3
Va.	27.7	49.2	12.0	18.7
Ala.	21.6	68.4	10.0	26.2
Miss.	6.7	70.2	5.6	35.9

Notes: "Eligibles" means persons 21 years of age and over. Cols. 1 and 2 from Southern Regional Council's study, in New York *Times,* Aug. 23, 1964. Col. 3 from Associated Press dispatch, Washington *Post,* Oct. 1, 1964. Col. 4 from U.S. Census Abstract, 1964 (for 1960), p. 382, table 513. For the eleven Southern States as a whole, Negro eligibles are 19.8% of all eligibles.

I have no doubt that *within these States* Negro registration is even more spotty, as between urban and rural areas, Black Belt and white counties, and particular localities where some special local factor is operative. This would follow earlier-established patterns (v. below, pp. 103-106). As Negro voting is spotty, so must be other aspects of segregation and Negro participation in full citizenship. Indeed, a very recent (1964) report on "North Carolina and the Negro," published by a committee of North Carolina mayors, shows this clearly, even in a State that has gone far in inter-racial adjustment. On the one hand, Negro activism and white cooperation has brought about significant or at least symptomatic change in the pattern of racial relationships in such matters as access to places of public resort, job opportunities, public employment, etc., in Asheville, Durham, Greensboro, and Winston-Salem, for example, and this before the Civil Rights Act of 1964. On the other hand, this very frank and revealing document makes no bones about reporting little or no change in many other places, nor does it conceal the occurrence of disorderly demonstrations, counter-demonstrations, and police repression.

So much for Negro suffrage. What about white politics?

This aspect of my book I cannot hope to deal with on the scale of the preceding pages. It is a matter of eleven States, more than twenty-two differing State parties (Democratic, Republican, and splinter), scores of municipal situations, thirty-four years of unanalysed elections local, State, and national – and the varying backgrounds, social and economic, that go with all this.

I must confine myself to such indications as may be derived from the quadrennial presidential campaigns. Basically there is only one question: with a significant Negro vote, what will happen if a full-fledged two-party system now develops in the South? Asked here of "the South," perhaps it could with greater usefulness be asked of Alabama, of Bibb County, of Charleston, or of the *n*th Assembly District. But for the time being it is only the question that is important; there are as yet no answers.

In 1948, the Democratic national convention committed the Party to "eradicate all discrimination," including discrimination in voting privileges. At election time, in eleven Southern States the Democratic popular vote dropped, in relation to the 1944 election, by eleven percentage points as a minimum (North Carolina and Tennessee) and 83 percentage points as a maximum (Mississippi). In between were percentage-point decreases of 81 (Alabama), 71 (South Carolina), 48 (Louisiana), 20 (Florida and Georgia), 18 (Arkansas), 14 (Texas), and 13 (Virginia). Alabama and Mississippi dropped, respectively, from 1944 Democratic percentages of 82 and 93 to 1 and 10; North Carolina and Tennessee from 67 and 61 to 56 and 50. The Democratic losses were almost entirely to a new and ephemeral Southern party, the Democratic States Rights Party, which called the Democratic civil rights plank "this infamous and iniquitous program."

The Democratic Party in the South did not continue at this low level in the three succeeding elections, when it was once more pitted solely against Republicanism. But the percentage of Democratic to all votes in these eleven States ranged from 44 to 70 in 1952, from 41 to 67 in 1956, and from 46 to 64 in 1960. These percentage ranges must be compared to 67–98 in 1932, 69–99 in 1936, 67–96 in 1940, and 61–93 in 1944. It seems that 1948 may have been some sort of turning point. If so, it is of course not irreversible, and the 1964 election may – before these words reach the reader – tell us more about the future of the Democratic Party in the South and of the South's "solidity."

In the national elections of 1952, 1956, and 1960, in which the Southern branch of the party regained some ground but continued to run behind its past performances, the Democratic platforms again pledged efforts to eradicate discrimination (the Republican Party's were much less forthright). The relatively poor showing of the Democratic Party in these years could plausibly be attributed to the charismatic appeal of Eisenhower in 1952 and 1956, and in 1960 to Kennedy's Catholicism. But it is tempting to think that the school desegregation decision of 1954, the Civil Rights Acts of 1957 and 1960, the passage of the anti-poll-tax amendment through Congress in 1962, the spurt in Negro voters' registrations, and the Negro demonstrations inspired by this chain of events may have been perceived in the South as warning beacons. We may well ask whether either the Eisenhower magic or even

Kennedy's Catholicism would have so reduced the Southern Democratic vote without this chain of events. And even though they came during Republican administrations, neither the Civil Rights Acts nor the passage of the amendment would have been possible without *Northern* Democratic support in Congress. Nor, subsequently, would the passage of the 1964 Civil Rights Act have been. How much will these events have chilled Democratic ardor in the South in 1964? How much will their possible consequences chill it in the future?

It is frustrating to be committing these lines to print a month before the 1964 elections. If the 1964 returns continue to show a dip in the Southern Democratic vote, it will be an indication that while that vote was susceptible to the non-Republican attractions of the 1948 Southern splinter Democratic States Rights Party, it has now become susceptible to outright Republicanism. On the other hand – and confusingly – a Southern Democratic upswing in 1964 may reflect the attractiveness of the Texan Johnson more than any reconciliation to Negro suffrage and civil rights.

These questions have special point in view of the fact that the Republican platform and the Republican candidate in 1964 were widely believed to have been less committed to civil rights than the Democratic. The platform promised execution of the Civil Rights Act of 1964, but with the reservation, significant in its context, that elimination of discrimination "is a matter of heart, conscience, and education, as well as of equal rights under the law." The Democratic platform and the Democratic candidate were unequivocal. The platform emphatically re-stated the 1960 pledge "to create an affirmative new atmosphere" in racial matters. Time may show that the two major parties have permanently reversed their historical roles in relation to civil rights. If so, to what extent will it affect their relative standing in the South?

Already the Northern and national parties have reversed their roles in relation to the issue of "States' Rights." The Republican Party has now for some time been the States Rights party, and it is consistent that its 1952 civil rights platform plank should have described civil rights, too, as "the primary responsibility of the States," a sentiment echoed by its 1964 presidential candidate. But States' Rights is a broader question than civil rights. It involves a whole range of problems that have increasingly since the 1930's been debated and dealt with on a national scale: economic and social problems like social insurance, public education, urban and rural rehabilitation, labor relations, and so on, at length. The debates have involved "States' Rights"; but they have also involved "liberalism" and "conservatism." Here again the relatively poor showing of the Democratic Party in the South in 1952, 1956, and 1960 may rest on a special and significant basis: the "liberal" aura that surrounded the Stevenson and Kennedy candidacies in those years. There is an unverified but logically justifiable belief in a "long term trend towards Republicanism on the part of [Southern] businessmen" (the New York *Times,* Sept. 23, 1964). If the Republican Party commits itself henceforth to forthright economic and social conservatism, in line with its States'-Rights stand, will it increasingly win white Southerners away from a liberal or centrist Democracy?

Is it the case, as is widely believed by reporters and commentators, that the Southern Negro, now voting in increasing numbers, has followed his Northern brother into the ranks of the Democratic Party? Could there be any considerable Southern Democratic Party based on a solid Negro vote plus some part of the white electorate?

None of these questions can as yet be answered. On the national scale, and including the South, they imply – as has been commonly said since the 1964 conventions – the possibility of a new national political realignment on ideological grounds. For the South considered alone, they imply the reappearance of an old spectre: "Let the whites divide, what happens? Here is this dangerous and alien influence [the Negro voter] that holds the balance of power. . . . It must be bought by race privileges . . . or through long and monstrous periods of political debauchery." This quotation, from the lips of a distinguished Georgian, dates from the 1880's (v. p. 88 below). It has many parallels.

We shall probably not hear such words again as loudly as before. But the sentiment they express rests on a long tradition, on entrenched interests, and – therefore – on a strong emotion. This sentiment is not dead, as the events of the "summer of violence" in Mississippi have most recently shown. The sentiment may be dying; there is evidence, cited in this very Postscript, that it is.

Thirty-odd years ago, at the end of the last chapter of this book, speaking of Southern liberalism towards Negro suffrage, I wrote: ". . . in the background of Southern sentiment and tradition, it was still easily possible in 1930 for some adverse factor, some racial difficulty, some negrophobe politician, to set 'liberalism' back, to check it, to prevent for a long time its further development." Twice before in the South there has been a significant Negro vote and a significant white cleavage. Turn the pages, reader, and see what happened. Many things are different now, and it need not happen again.

P. L.

Arlington, Va.
October 1964.

PREFACE

The writer of this study has many indebtednesses to acknowledge for help in its prosecution. The greatest, it is hoped, is in some small measure discharged in the dedication. The study was begun at the London School of Economics. Intensive work was commenced on the 1865-1900 period at the Robert Brookings Graduate School in Washington (not to be confused with the present Brookings Institution), under the guidance of Professor William E. Dodd. A Social Science Research Council fellowship made possible the field trip and the questionnaire on which the last chapters are based.

Many persons have given invaluable help on the form of the manuscript: the Faculty of the Brookings School, several Southerners white and Negro, and especially Jean Atherton Flexner, my "best friend and severest critic." The scores of Southerners, many of them busy persons, who sacrificed time to discuss the local situation with the writer, would in some cases feel ill repaid were their names to be published here. Contacts with them were in many cases established through the coöperation of the National Association for the Advancement of Colored People and the Urban League; letters of introduction came also from Dr. Abraham Flexner, and from Mr. Will Alexander of the Interracial Coöperation Commission. The clipping files of Tuskegee Institute, a mine of valuable information in charge of Dr. Monroe Work, were opened to the writer.

Many Southerners who have discussed race questions with the writer have pointed out that there are parallels in Northern history and politics to certain features of Southern life. This is undoubtedly true, but it is not our present concern; it is perhaps worth while to make clear at the outset that this book implies no comparison or contrast between sections of the country, except in specific matters where similarities or the reverse are plainly pointed out.

P. L.

SWARTHMORE COLLEGE.

CONTENTS

APPENDICES

PART I

SLAVERY, EMANCIPATION, AND DISFRANCHISEMENT

INTRODUCTION

The Southern States have, since the beginnings of American history, constituted a distinct region, with a peculiar economic, social, and political complexion. They have been marked by prominent class distinctions: at the bottom of the scale, the Negro; at the top, the white "Bourbons," once planters, later industrialists, financiers, and landlords. In between stood a class of small farmers, owning few or no slaves, pushed back by the plantation system into the less fertile hills. In the remote mountains and in the pine barrens near the coast, a true agricultural proletariat led a miserable existence of poverty, ignorance, and squalor. Between these white groups a lively economic antagonism found expression in the section's political life down to the Civil War. There was in those days no "Solid South." The Negro, a slave, was not a political power.

The Civil War upset this equilibrium. Through Northern interference, the Negro was both emancipated and enfranchised. That fact altered the course of the white party struggle. It practically killed normal bipartisan political activity, although class antagonisms between the whites continued unabated. When devices were set up for checking the Negro vote, the white South felt free to divide along the lines of the traditional cleavage. But the division brought back the Negro vote, and led ultimately to the formation of a solid white front, for the maintenance of white supremacy.

Yet this white supremacy has never for very long felt either solid or secure. At the present time, many changes are producing local situations favorable to Negro voting. A change in the South's attitude towards Negro voting would profoundly alter the political life of the region. Similarly, changes in the social and economic life of the South, such as may now be observed, if they reach the political level, might easily affect the franchise of the Negro.

It is impossible to tell the story of Negro suffrage in the South without bringing into the picture the political divisions among whites. It is equally impossible to trace white political issues and cleavages without reference to the Negro as the common enemy, the red herring across all political trails. The following pages attempt to make clear the interaction between the racial question and the white class and party struggle in the South.

CHAPTER I

THE LAND OF DIXIE
(to 1860)

I. THE PECULIAR INSTITUTION

The distinctive feature of Southern social and political history from the early nineteenth century to the Civil War was slavery and the presence of the Negro. Roughly to the fifties, the South sustained a bipartisan local politics, and the two parties corresponded to the realities of the Southern class division, between the slave-employing plantation-owners of the tidewater and river-bottom "Black Lands," on the one hand, and the small farmer, city artisan, and frontiersman on the other.[1]

This was the period in which — with decreasing certainty, to be sure — the South was free to work out its own social and economic salvation, undisturbed by Northern or national threats to slavery and racial stratification.

When Northern and national forces began to crowd the South, beginning in the thirties, dramatically in the fifties, the South moved towards an effective, if not unanimous, solidarity, culminating in Secession and Civil War — because it saw an attack on racial stratification and the slave economy.

Thus slavery was the basis at once of Southern division and of Southern solidarity.

Slavery gave form to the Southern class struggle. It fastened the plantation on the South as the ideal productive system, for a group of slaves on a large acreage was a more economical productive unit than one or a few slaves on a small farm. It helped, also, to fix staple-crop agriculture on the South, for a one-crop system involved a minimum period of unproductive slave-training, while the actual crops raised — cotton, tobacco, sugar — were "cash crops" which from year to year carried the large investment in land and slaves, and provided imported necessities and luxuries. The pressure of the plantation itself impressed on the planter the desirability of extending his holdings; the one-crop system and the necessarily unscientific slave-cultivation, by exhausting the soil, seemed to teach the same lesson. Hence the tendency of the plantation to increase in size, always pushing the less fortunate small land-owner and renter into poorer and more remote sections, and setting before the new entrepreneur a more and more formidable competition already on the ground, based on a large investment in slaves, land, and equipment. As the system grew, the price of good land rose; so did that of slaves — the latter, also, by reason of the abolition of the legitimate slave trade in 1808.

Thus a wide gulf in opportunity came to be fixed between the rich and fortunate, and the less-advantaged groups of the South. It was important for the political expression of this social fact, that the two groups became geographically distinct. The planters exploited the Black Belts. Here also there were small farmers. This middle group and the agricultural proletariat (the "poor whites") shared the piedmont. In the upper piedmont, the infertile mountain regions, and the sandy pine barrens just back of the Atlantic coast, the poor whites and the frontiersmen eked out their existence.

Several factors inherent in the slavery system hampered the less-advantaged groups of the South in seeking an opportunity outside of plantation agriculture.

In the first place, social prestige, following economic power, gravitated towards the planter class, creating not only a consciously aristocratic frame of mind among the planters, but a respect and desire for land- and slave-ownership among the lower orders; land- and slave-ownership was the criterion of "class." Slavery brought manual labor into disrepute; only such occupations were honorific as management, and the professions, politics, and soldiering — the perquisites of wealth and social prestige.

In the next place, slavery discouraged industry and commerce in the South. Slave labor itself was thought not to be adapted to industry and commerce, especially in a large-scale shop or factory system. Plantation land and slave labor immobilized capital which might otherwise have found its way into industrial and commercial channels. The plantation scattered population, and prevented the growth of cities and towns which in the North were at once labor and financial reservoirs, and initial markets. To the degree to which the individual plantation was self-supporting, through the activities of its slave carpenters, slave shoemakers, etc., the system further discouraged white industry and commerce; in the very towns, skilled and semi-skilled slave artisans, hired out to shop managers, competed at a low living standard with white rivals.

The whole system, therefore, stratified Southern society. At the bottom was the slave, a chattel rather than a person; at the top, the plantation-owner and slave-holder. Ground between these two millstones were the proletarian "poor whites," "hill billies," "red-necks," and "clay-eaters," and a middle class, mostly agricultural, of small farmers and town dwellers, who — as is usual with middle classes — to some degree looked up with veneration and emulative pride to the aristocrats of the system, to some degree bitterly opposed them.

Having thus emphasized the way in which the slave economy gave form and body to Southern class divisions, it is necessary to point out how it also cemented racial solidarity.

It has often been said that slavery created a psychological bond among all whites by emphasizing the dignity of freedom; in this, at least, the dominant race was equal, and sharply contrasted with the black man. Whatever force this intangible consideration may have had, there were also specific dangers present in slavery of which all Southern whites were conscious. The Southern slaves were aliens, and because of their physical characteristics easily recognized as such. They had never been wholly assimilated to the white society in which they functioned, in spite of their adaptation, at a distinctly low level, to many of its features. Many of them were natives of Africa, and others but one or two generations removed from their primitive background. If they were released from subjection, their alienage might easily constitute a threat to the whole social complex of the South, ethical, economic, and political.

The white man's civilization was maintained, in a region nearly forty per cent black, at bottom by force; not by violence, to be sure, but by the superior social strength which subjection always implies. Based on subjection, it was more or less precarious, and invited the coöperation of all free white men to maintain it.

Slavery was a distinctively Southern institution. It therefore had a claim on sectional patriotism to which all classes responded, as all classes, whether benefiting thereby or not, rally over national distinctions and interests.

To the "Bourbon" slave-holder and plantation-owner, besides these general claims of the peculiar institution, the system represented a cash investment, a means of livelihood, and a way of life. The middle classes, to a lesser degree, had the same vested interest in defending slavery. Slavery, though cutting off many opportunities from the lower middle class and from the poor-white mechanic, renter, and squatter, was at any given moment a bulwark against the competition of black freedmen.

II. CLASS AND PARTY

Southern social and economic stratification found an expression in Southern politics. Cole has pointed out a close correlation between the Black Belt, better soil, large plantation areas and Whig party strength in the South, and conversely between the poorer, mountain, frontier regions of small farms and few slaves, and Democratic strength.[2]

The specific issues of Southern local politics, in some cases dating back to Colonial days, were those common to American experience where more and less developed regions looked to the same State governments for protection and advancement. The poorer sections wanted improvements — roads, canals, even, in Virginia, warehouses — which the older sections already had and were not eager to subsidize further out of taxation. The poorer sections wanted the incidence of taxation always so apportioned as to ease their burden, or to increase that of the richer counties for the general welfare. The more radical middle and lower classes wanted banking restrictions eased and State banks created, to provide cheaper credit; the better-informed wealthy, who in addition to sounder economics had their sales and purchases out of the State and abroad to consider, were inclined to be sound-money men. The line of demarcation in all these issues was largely that between the plantation-owners, on the one hand, and the smaller fry. Politicians magnified the connection between these divisions and class lines.

The "Bourbon" and the poorer sections of the States were also divided over suffrage qualifications and legislative apportionment. North Carolina and Virginia, as late as 1856 and 1850, respectively, required the ownership of substantial property of would-be voters. Three more States, into the eighteen-thirties and forties, had small property prerequisites, or some nominal tax-paying requirement. These were obnoxious to the democratically inclined smaller fry, who certainly in the case of Virginia were placed at a disadvantage by them. The landed Black Belt people inclined to an aristocratic suffrage theory.

Similarly, the Black Belts of the various States were at an advantage over the poorer regions because of the prevailing methods of apportionment for the State legislatures. Where total population of legislative districts was the basis of apportionment, the plantation regions had assemblymen not only for their whites, but for their large numbers of non-voting slaves as well. In States employing the "Federal ratio," three-fifths of the slave population was counted into the representation base. Where representation was a compound of population and property values, it was again the wealthier slave and plantation Black Belt counties which benefited.

As the States varied in economic development, special localized issues reënforced these divisions. Thus, the industrial development of Georgia in the eighteen-forties and fifties emphasized the tendency of the middle and upper groups who had funds to invest and protect to align themselves with the conservative, industrial, and commercial Whig party. In Virginia, as early as 1850, separation threatened between the western portion of the State, which stood for commercial and industrial interests, by reason of its diversified agriculture, its trade with the West and the South, its salt and iron mines, its textile factories and its foundries, and the conservative plantation East.

The fervor of the voting masses over such matters as these was intensified by the invidious class distinctions which both parties invoked against their opponents. The Jacksonian Democracy's original strength lay in the "common people," whose virtues it extolled in contrast to "aristocratic cliques" who "indulge the comfortable position that either education, wealth, or social position give them a right, booted and spurred, to ride over the popular will." [3] In the South, such "aristocratic cliques," of Whig allegiance, could mean only "the empire of . . . coondom," [4] that is, the Bourbon slaveholders and plantation-owners. Similarly, the national party of wealth and social position — the Whigs — naturally attracting the upper classes of the South, sneered at its inferiors; in the South, it was said that a gentleman was not apt to be a Democrat, "but if he is, he is in damned bad company." [5]

The effect of the class division on national politics in the South was not quite as clear as in the case of State affairs. The origin of the Whig party as the antithesis of Jacksonian Democracy, and the conservative Whig leadership, attracted the Southern man of property. The stand of the Whig party for a national banking system, especially after the panic of 1837, appealed more to the planter and large-commercial group of the South than did the "wild-cat" State-banking ideas of the Democracy. The same groups to some extent favored national intervention for internal improvements, seeing profits in the development of the South's non-agricultural resources, known to be great. Some of the planters even favored a moderate protective tariff, in the hope of profiting from the growth of industry in the South, or in order to prevent raw material competition from abroad, as cotton, tobacco, and sugar became important in India, the West Indies, or — until 1846 — in Mexican Texas.

All these considerations gave a somewhat nationalistic color to the political theory of the upper classes in the South which found no comfort in Democracy. The lower orders, on the other hand, were States'-Rights in national politics, by reason of their country and frontier background, and therefore opposed to internal improvements through national initiative; radical in their banking and monetary theory as befitted their agrarian status, and anti-tariff. The national Whig party's reluctance to open the public domain to settlement and development was looked upon with favor by many planters, who foresaw a fall in the price of cotton and a rise in the cost of slaves in the rapid expansion of the staple-producing area. Cheap or free homesteads in the West and Southwest, however, seemed to the smaller farmer and the landless groups the easy and logical way out of their *impasse* at home. Thus the two groups clashed over the Texas issue, many of the planters going with the Whig party against war and annexation, the lower orders with the "manifest-destiny" policy of the Democracy.

III. RACE

The attitude of the Southern whites towards the institution of slavery was greatly influenced by the obvious racial and cultural differences between themselves and the Negro slave. These differences were quickly translated into terms of absolute "superiority" and "inferiority." But for this, it is reasonable to suppose, some scheme of emancipation might have appealed effectively to the South, certainly before, perhaps even after, the peculiar institution had fastened itself upon the Southern economy.

In the colonial period, the South entertained in some quarters grave doubts both of the ethics and of the ultimate social and economic advantages of the system.[6] Even after the invention of the cotton gin and the enthronement of "King Cotton," voices were raised in the South against the peculiar institution. That Virginia in 1831 came close to emancipation is well known.

Doubts arose in the minds of the planter class, but more especially among the more articulate non-slave-holding groups.[7] Especially in regions like western Virginia, parts of Georgia, and Kentucky, as they became prosperous from other sources than slave agriculture, were complaints frequent. In the 1831-32 Assembly debates in Virginia, a westerner voiced the classical argument against slavery: "It is ruinous to the whites; retards improvements; roots out our industrious population; banishes the yeomanry from the country; and deprives the spinner, the weaver, the smith, the shoemaker, and the carpenter of employment and support." [8]

After 1830, the advancement of emancipation, even of colonization, arguments in the South declined. This was due in part to the importance the slave economy had by then assumed, but also in very large measure to the growth of radical abolition sentiment in the North. The increasing violence of attacks in the Northern press and among Northern intellectuals consolidated Southern sectional patriotism in defence of its peculiar institution. The South repudiated reasoned arguments laying its economic and social backwardness to slavery, and even more bitterly resented the blanket ascriptions of personal ungodliness which the more fiery abolitionists hurled at all slave-holders, jointly and severally. It denied the cruelty of slavery to the slave in just as broad terms as abolitionists affirmed it. From doubting slavery, from apologetically defending it, the South in the thirty years preceding the Civil War passed on to proclaiming it a beneficent part of the universal order. It was ordained by God, recognized in Scripture, and sanctioned by the law of nations and of the United States. It elevated the slave to the highest pitch he could hope for, it gave a proper dignity to all white men, it even "improved the condition of the female sex." It was more humane, because more responsible, than what a later age was to call "wage slavery." It was the source of Southern prosperity, and thus contributed mightily to the wealth of the nation; it yielded indispensable products for the use of all the civilized world. To emancipate the Negro and remove him from American soil would not only rob mankind of the fruits of his labor, but would impoverish the South and put an impossible burden of compensation on the nation. Confiscation, of course, was unthinkable. The racial arguments were still more unanswerable: the Negro was an inferior being; "but a grown-up child . . . improvident," who, free, "would become an intolerable burden to society." [9] Removed from the sheltering care of his master, he would languish and starve, and — perhaps even worse — relapse, before total extinction, into the unchristian barbarity of his ancestors. Not to colonize the freedman would upset the social order of the South, for the Negro was "unfit for a state of freedom among the whites, in both an economical and moral point of view." [10] By 1835, the last of such Southern States as had permitted a qualified freedmen's suffrage had withdrawn the privilege.

As abolitionism became more and more doctrinaire, drawing on the self-evident truth that all men are created free and equal; as it advocated, more and more, violent onslaughts on slavery; many Southerners little interested personally in the peculiar institution were driven to defend their section against a possible revolutionary thrust from outside, with fearsome consequences for the social order in which they lived. Where the convinced slave-holder stood on this point, and where the "poor white trash" whom even the slaves despised, needs no explanation.

IV. THE IRREPRESSIBLE CONFLICT

Simultaneously with the moral offensive on slavery, a political and economic offensive developed in the North, based on the different needs of an industrial and commercial section as against the agricultural and exporting South. As this drive made itself felt in national politics, it became apparent that in many ways the Whig party suffered from inherent weaknesses in its claims on Southern allegiance.

Both the tariff and the national bank issue smacked of a Hamiltonian centralization of power which, it had early been pointed out in the South, carried with it a threat to slavery. If the Federal government could intervene in industrial matters through protective duties and in financial matters through a central bank, it followed in theory that it could regulate or even extinguish the peculiar institution. The tariff had but a slight appeal to the vast majority of Southerners, and to many — as witness the South Carolina nullification episode — was positively obnoxious. Similarly, over banking theory there could be, and were, differences of opinion; especially as so much of the South's financial need was taken care of through consignments for credit abroad.

The unwillingness of Northern leaders to open the West freely and rapidly to settlement, and especially, after the Texas episode, to permit the unhampered extension of slavery into the territories, was therefore doubly repugnant to the South. Not only did it cut off rich new lands from the slave and plantation system, lands which all but the most advantageously situated planters of the older South coveted; it prevented the formation of new Slave States whose senators and representatives in Congress would protect the South from the onslaughts of industrial and commercial interests. It rendered the South increasingly defenceless against attacks on slavery itself.

Add to these material and political considerations the irritation of the South over its dependence on Northern manufactures, credit, and shipping, and the bitter resentment aroused by the moral attack on slavery and Negro subjection, and the basis is laid for a sectional loyalty in the South transcending established party lines.

As crisis after crisis supervened, the conservative Southerners drifted into the Democratic party, which, in spite of distasteful elements, held out the lure of States' rights. Some, moved by a genuinely national patriotism, tarried for a while in temporary unionist parties; many remained there in spirit even after 1861. Meanwhile, the Southern Democratic party grew more and more sectional, as the abolitionist fears of the poorer groups were fed by Northern extremists and played on by Southern politicians, and as the genuine dangers to the Southern economy were pointed out by Southern statesmen.

In the North, discontent grew among the industrial and commercial classes because of their inability to get government aid for private enterprise, blocked as they were by Democratic strength. The lower classes, especially in the West, moved into parties promising the gift of Federal land to homesteaders, and "free soil" — the barring of slave competition in the territories.

In 1860, the four-year-old Republican party, on a platform of "Free Homes for the Homeless," no slavery in the territories, and tariff legislation, carried the North and West, and elevated Abraham Lincoln to the presidency. This was interpreted by Southern hotheads as a decisive victory for "Black Republicanism," and Secession followed. The seceding States were Virginia, Tennessee, North and South Carolina, Georgia, Alabama, Florida, Louisiana, Mississippi, Arkansas, and Texas. Modern scholarship has cast grave doubt on the extent of secession sentiment among the Southern people.[11] Indeed, a short-lived new party, placing "Constitutional Union" above everything, carried three slave States: Kentucky, Tennessee, and Virginia. The whole of Tennessee was never effectively incorporated into the new Confederacy, and Virginia, in quitting the Union, lost her western counties, now the State of West Virginia. Kentucky, although divided in sentiment, remained "loyal." In the actual Confederate States, the non-slave-holding areas gave the Richmond government much trouble during the course of the war. Nevertheless, although there were malcontents who reflected the normal Southern class divisions, the threat to slavery and to racial stratification was sufficient effectively to unite the South for four years of struggle and suffering, the result of which changed the face of Southern society.

CHAPTER II

THE RECONSTRUCTION PERIOD
(to 1867)

I. A NEW BEGINNING

At the conclusion of the Civil War the threat which the South had long feared was realized: the Negro slaves were emancipated, without the consent of their masters, and under conditions which seemed to promise disaster to the social fabric. At the same time, the hegemony of the plantation-owner and slave-holder was shattered, and the small-farmer and poor-white class, urged on by a changed economic status, found an opportunity for political self-assertion.

After four years of war against heavy military, technical, and financial odds, embittered throughout by internal dissension, the South in 1865 found itself — save in exceptionally favored localities — in utter confusion, social, economic, and political.[1] Disorganization and uncertainty were intensified by the new freedom of the Negro, partially effected by the Emancipation Proclamation in 1863, and consolidated two years later in the Thirteenth Amendment.[2] In none of the States south of Tennessee was the Negro element less than one-quarter of the population; in five it was one-third or more; in three it was one-half or more.[3] Testing his liberties, the Negro made for the towns, stripping the farms of labor, sometimes leaving wife, children, and aged dependents to be cared for by the white man, and increasing the urban vagrancy problem.[4] The freedman added to the irritation of the native whites by exhibiting what was under the circumstances a natural impudence and distrust, even giving some grounds for fears of a black insurrection at Christmas, 1865.

Plainly the whole post-war situation in the South called for organized and official action on the part of sympathetic local agencies of government. But towards the close of the war, the State administrations of the Confederacy were abolished as the Federal armies advanced, and for four to six months something close to anarchy reigned in the South.

Thus was the stage set for a social revolution. Whether or not it was to take place depended upon the manner of political reconstruction, and this was determined by Northern policy.

Political reconstruction came in two stages. The first lasted from the end of the war until 1867. This was Presidential Reconstruction, carried out by the States, under Lincoln's and Johnson's supervision, with few conditions and not seriously interfered with by national agencies until the second stage approached. The second stage was Congressional Reconstruction, lasting from 1867 to 1876, carried on by the Republican politicians of the national legislature and forced on the unwilling South in detail by national agencies and national partisans.

From 1864 to early in 1867, under Presidential Reconstruction, the South was left free to resume fairly normal political activities. President Lincoln in a proclamation of December, 1863, set forth a plan for the rehabilitation of the seceded States.[5] When ten per cent of the voting population of any State "lately in rebellion," as determined by the election laws in force before the war, had taken an oath of allegiance, they might proceed to form a new State government, which, if republican in form, would be recognized and given protection under the Federal constitution.

Five States — Tennessee, North Carolina, Louisiana, Arkansas, and Virginia — took advantage of the offer during Lincoln's lifetime.[6]

Although Lincoln's plan was already encountering the hostility of Congress,[7] nevertheless, Johnson, upon succeeding to the presidency in April, 1865, took up his Reconstruction program, and in May, June, and July issued proclamations for the seven still unreconstructed States, appointing military

governors and providing for "ten-per-cent" constitutional conventions.[8] But the spirit behind the program was no longer quite the same as Lincoln's. Johnson, a Tennessean of poor-white and anti-Secession origins, gave vent to the detestation of his class for the old leaders of the South, the authors of the Confederacy, by excepting from amnesty ten new classes of "rebels" in addition to the four specified by Lincoln. The most notable of the new classes whose political rehabilitation now depended on individual executive clemency was that of persons who supported the Confederacy and whose taxable property was assessed at $20,000 or more.[9] Further, in communications to the several provisional governors, Johnson made it clear that he would recognize no new constitutions which were not based on the abolition of slavery, nullification of the secession ordinances, and repudiation of Confederate State debts.

Ten-per-cent conventions followed in the seven unreconstructed States,[10] and in a few months State administrations had been set up conforming to Johnson's requirements. The last of these had before it eight months of life until the general disruption by Congressional Reconstruction; [11] none was entirely free from military interference, nor were any recognized by Congress.

The constituencies of the first Presidential governments were small, because of the restricted areas of Federal occupation. With the breakdown of the Confederacy, however, the number of adherents to the reconstructed administrations increased, in spite of the greater stringency of the Johnson oath.[12] After 1865, the South was ready to reënter the Union on the Presidential terms, although how much of this readiness was "submission to necessity" and how much "the acceptance of thinking men" is not now to be determined.[13] In the main, bitterness and defiance towards the United States grew only as the threatening cloud of the Radical congressional policies darkened and spread.

II. THE HOUSE DIVIDED

Under Presidential Reconstruction, there being as yet no question of injecting the Negro into Southern political life, the old class and party divisions of before the war reasserted themselves immediately.

Indeed, even during the war, Confederate patriotism had here and there gone into eclipse under complaints about "a rich man's war and a poor man's fight." [14] The effect of such a division on political alignments in the South was most apparent in the Border regions: Kentucky, western Virginia, and Tennessee.[15] Here middle-class and poor-white strength had the longest history, and here Union sentiment was strongest from Secession to 1865.

In Kentucky, each county was a battleground between Unionist and Confederate sentiment.[16] The hills and thinner soil were Unionist, the level land and fertile soil Confederate. In October, 1861, a shadowy "provisional government of Kentucky" was organized under the Confederacy, not without considerable, though scattered, support. But the effective government of the State, supported by Federal troops, was in the hands of the Unionists — the "radicals" who drew their support from the extreme poor-white constituency. Until the first post-war election, in August, 1865, the Union-Radical party controlled even Congressional elections, so that Kentucky was at no time unrepresented at Washington, and came only for a moment under the shadow of Congressional Reconstruction policies.

In Tennessee and Virginia, the class division was geographical. Both States went into the Confederacy, but Secession produced separatist movements in their mountain sections. In the case of Virginia, the Federal government recognized a new State — West Virginia — in December, 1862.[17]

A new State was never formed from Tennessee. But the separation issue was raised there three times. Tennessee was finally restored to the Union in the summer of 1866, through the adoption by plebiscite of amendments, resolutions, and ordinances of a decidedly anti-Bourbon character. These had been drawn up by the Union party of East Tennessee, which had extra-legally assumed the powers of a constitutional convention.[18]

For a brief period — in Kentucky till 1865, in Tennessee till 1869, in West Virginia till 1870 — "Union," "Radical," or "Republican" parties remained in control of the Border State administrations, drawing their strength from the local opposition to the Bourbons and to the Bourbon Confederacy. In startling contrast to the leniency of the Lincoln plan, they immediately began to pass proscriptive legislation against their old enemies. "Treason must be made odious, and traitors must be punished," ran the famous dictum of Andrew Johnson, while provisional governor of Tennessee under the Union; he added — what is not so well known — "*and impoverished*," and continued: "Their great plantations must be seized, and divided into small farms, and sold to honest and industrious men. The day for protecting the lands and Negroes of these authors of the rebellion is past." [19]

West Virginia and Tennessee passed "war trespass" statutes [20] under which loyal citizens might recover damages for losses suffered during hostilities by distraining upon any property held by a "rebel" in the State. These enactments put Confederate sympathizers under severe disabilities in the courts, especially when they were combined with the requirement of drastic loyalty oaths for jurors, for attorneys, and for plaintiffs on demand of the defendant. Test oaths were also prescribed for teachers and ministers. Treason, sedition, and libel statutes caused the removal of many a suspected officeholder or the expatriation of private citizens beyond the borders of the State.[21]

The new rulers of the Border States sought guarantees of their tenure in drastic limitations of the suffrage. Kentucky in 1865 declared disfranchised all persons who in accordance with an earlier statute had been expatriated for giving civil or military aid to the Confederacy.[22] Tennessee, by legislation of 1865 and 1866, put the burden of proof of "loyalty" upon practically every applicant for the franchise except Federal veterans, by requiring him to produce two character witnesses and to swear that he "was rejoiced at" the downfall of the Confederacy. Similarly, West Virginia in 1867 added to the requirement of a severe test oath, dating back to the formation of the State, a regulation under which the applicant had to "make it appear" that he was free of any rebel taint.[23] In addition, in the last two States registration and polling was carried on, in the new dispensation, under the scrutiny of election officials appointed by the governor and removable by him; in Tennessee, moreover, it was within the discretion of the governor to throw out the registration of any county in which he was "satisfied" there had been fraud or intimidation.[24] The governor, therefore — the agent of the Radical party in the State — was in a position to do practically as he pleased when unexpected Conservative majorities turned up, and in Tennessee his pleasure had much occasion to coincide with the advantage of his party.

Thus did the Unionist parties of the lower classes vent their resentment against their former social and economic superiors, the "authors of rebellion" and the scoffers at "poor white trash"; and endeavor to intrench themselves against their erstwhile political overlords.

It cannot be claimed that these three Border State administrations either represented a larger constituency than the administrations they succeeded, nor yet that they constituted in some sense a better polity. They established themselves by *coups d'état* and remained in power under the wing of substantial national protection; nevertheless they represented a real interest among their constituencies. But there were other interests as well, and internal conflicts of ideas in the Radical groups themselves. Their downfall, and the restoration of something like the political *status quo ante*, was inevitable once Federal troops and marshals were withdrawn.

To begin with, the proscriptive measures we have described overshot their mark.[25] The extreme Radical leaders in the Border States could not hope to persuade the large majority of their own followers that friends, neighbors, and ofttimes relations must continue for all time disfranchised, disqualified for office, persecuted and deprived of property, and debarred from their professions. As the war passions died down, applications for amnesty increased and had perforce to be granted by the new governments, even though the Radicalism of their constituencies was thus diluted. Corruption, too, played its part in weakening the hold of these inexperienced administrations. Whether it was through the use of hand-picked sheriff's posses to push a governor's cause at the polls, or the presence of a notoriously disreputable, partisan judge on the State bench, or the settlement of private grudges and feuds by crooked applications of the new treason laws and the help of the Federal provost-marshal, the Radical tactics fairly soon became unbearable to all but the most fanatical and most selfishly interested Radical sympathizers.[26]

A great stumbling-block in the way of continued Radical rule in the Border States was the alliance with the Negro forced upon the "loyal" parties by the fact of their relations with the Republican party North. This alliance was something that the lower-class leaders had not bargained for and did not desire. Travelers in the South were still writing after the war that "The Southern poor whites, conscious as they are of only a slight superiority over the Negro, and knowing that the suffrage and a few minor factitious distinctions are the chief points of their superiority, are jealous over them accordingly . . ." So, "East Tennesseans, though opposed to slavery and secession, do not like niggers. There is at this day more prejudice against color among the middle and poorer classes — the 'Union' men of the South, who owned few or no slaves — than among the planters who owned them by scores and hundreds . . ." [27] Nevertheless, the national government — to whose advantage these "middle and poorer classes" had broken away from the old ruling class — had freed the Negro slaves, and soon proceeded to grant them equal civil and political rights. This was not on the programs of the Border State Radical parties — save for abolition, which both Tennessee and West Virginia agreed to. Kentucky, where slavery had a much more general hold, refused to ratify even the Thirteenth Amendment.[28]

Before the other national measures for the advancement of the freedman could come up, Kentucky had already gone "Conservative" again. Returning ex-Confederates who could not be prevented from voting, a sudden rush of Southern feeling, and the aftermath of resentment against the national war policies where they hit at the State's north-and-south trade, all combined to give the open or secret adherents of the Southern cause a slight advantage in the very first legislative elections after the war. The next year, by a sudden *coup* in convention, the Confederate element consolidated its power, practically swept Radicalism out of the State in 1867, and finished the work in 1868. Now it became the turn of the Radicals to suffer proscription.

Naturally, Kentucky under Conservative rule rejected the Fourteenth and Fifteenth Amendments. The people of the State, resolved the House in passing on the first, "are unalterably opposed to Negro suffrage, whether unlimited or special, general or qualified." Nor did the Kentuckians fail to discover the means of minimizing the Negro vote, once it was granted by Federal law. The "job-lash," gerrymanders, inadequate voting facilities, dilatory tactics and horse-play at the polls, etc., suggested themselves to the white voters — all devices that had to be reinvented in the lower South some years later.[29]

In the other two Border States, the return of the Conservatives, by then identified with the Democratic party, took longer. Meanwhile, both ratified the war amendments, but not before Tennessee had passed a "Black Code" for the regulation of freedmen,[30] and expressed herself against Negro suffrage. The first election laws both of Tennessee and of West Virginia were for white men only.[31] This was as much due to a fear that "the Negro will vote with his late master, whom he does not hate, rather than with the non-slave-holding white, whom he does hate," [32] as to poor-white dislike of the Negro. But in Tennessee the turn of the political tide towards Conservatism caused the Radicals to enact Negro suffrage in 1867, to add to the Radical strength at the polls.[33]

Two years later, in 1869, Tennessee went Democratic, and proscription of ex-Confederates soon ceased. In 1870, West Virginia followed; her proscriptive laws, we may assume, went into immediate abeyance where they were not repealed, and a constitutional convention made an end of them in 1872.[34]

At this stage we must leave the Border States, with their white-county Radicalism crushed by the weight of its own vindictiveness and tainted by alliance with the "black Republicanism" of the North, and turn to the lower South under Presidential Reconstruction.

In the lower South, the period of Presidential Reconstruction was of shorter duration than in the Border States, because these States remained in the Confederacy to the bitter end. Consequently time did not permit the formation of stable parties before Congress interfered. In some of the States, indeed, the first elections under the new constitutions were the only ones held before Congress swept away the whole Presidential structure. Nevertheless, there were, here and there, rumblings which were later to bear fruit in "moderate" Republicanism. "Before the war political divisions were sharply drawn and feeling often bitter," Fleming reminds us, writing of Alabama; "so also in 1865-67 . . . At first there was no 'Solid South'; within the white man's party there were grave differences between old Whig and old Democrat, Radical and Conservative. There were different local problems before the whites of the various sections that for a while prevented the formation of a unanimous white man's party." [35]

The war itself, bearing of course most heavily on the propertyless poor whites and the small farmer, had had disintegrating as well as unifying effects. Thus, towards the end of hostilities, northern white-county Alabama, a heavy sufferer from cavalry raids, accused the southern country of unfeeling profiteering; what is there in the war for the masses? demanded the small farmers of western North Carolina.[36] The Confederate tax in kind, which took away (when it could get it) one-tenth of the farmer's produce, made current the bitter phrase about "a rich man's war and a poor man's fight," especially since land and slaves were not directly taxed. Where the rich availed themselves of their privilege of evading conscription by buying substitutes, the idea of the "poor man's fight" was by so much intensified. The lower classes of course found themselves much worse off than their social superiors in 1865 upon returning to homesteads where no slaves had remained behind to continue tillage and keep equipment in order. Some of them indeed never again reached the level of subsistence of "before the War." [37]

In Arkansas Unionist sentiment revived and became articulate after the fall of Little Rock in 1863. "Under what obligations are you to slavery or to slave-holders?" William Fishback was demanding of the small farmers and poor whites. "For more than a century you have deferred to his rights, although inimical to your own. In deference to his rights you have for more than a hundred years tolerated an institution that was a burden upon our energies and a blight upon our very best interests. In deference to his rights you have seen your children grow up around you in ignorance, deprived of free schools, and discouraged in every effort at education. In deference to his rights you have seen the poor of your country reduced to a social position despised even by the very slaves of his wealthy slave-holding neighbor. All this you have permitted and tolerated in deference to the rights of about one in fifty of your number." When the State government was reëstablished, it continued to exact the Lincoln oath of its voters, and it passed one anti-Bourbon measure: a stay-law on debts owed to persons not taking this oath.[38]

Everywhere in the convention elections, the political qualifications prescribed by the Lincoln and Johnson amnesty proclamations, by keeping out the Confederate leaders, gave some new emphasis to the non-Bourbon opinions. Louisiana was congratulated on the emancipation of the Negro as "nothing more nor less than that of the whites"; for "the legislation of Louisiana, for the last sixty years, was made by slave-holders for the sole and exclusive benefit of slave-holders." [39] The Texas convention revived a long-debated project for the separation of the slave-holding from the non-slave-holding section of the State, passing a permissive ordinance by a two-to-one vote.[40] Northern poor-white Alabama, having attempted to set up a "loyal" government just before Appomattox, fought in the 1865 convention for more delegates to the State legislature, thus reviving the old issue of Black Belt over-representation.[41] South Carolina's new constitution evened up black and white county representation somewhat, but kept to the old basis, of population weighted by tax payment.[42]

All this was, however, the mere shadow of opposition. The Presidential governments in the lower South were on the whole safely Conservative. The motley dissidents — some lower-class, some Union Democrats, some merely personally ambitious — had as yet no nucleus around which they might crystallize, and could form only shifting groups, in the one or two elections that fell between 1864 and 1867, to flirt with Northern Republicanism.[43]

III. INTRANSIGEANCE

The attitude of all classes of Southerners towards the Negro was not changed by the outcome of the war. They were determined to keep him as nearly as possible in the same position he had formerly occupied, economically, socially, and politically. During the course of the war, Alexander Stephens, Vice President of the Confederacy, had challenged the North for a reason for the bloodshed and waste which he saw all about him. "There is but one plausible pretext for it," he told his hearers; "that is to exterminate our Southern institutions. It is to put the African on an equality with the white man." [44] In the South, under God, this could not be.

As Stephens rightly indicated, the whole complex of Southern institutions depended on the economic, social, and political subordination of the Negro. Of this subordination, slavery had been the basis. When slavery was destroyed, the labor system on which the whole Southern community depended was destroyed with it; and more: the vested rights of the slave-holders were attacked, and the position of the poorer whites as laborers and free peasants menaced. However uneconomical the system had been for the community as a whole, however heavy a charge on the large plantation owners, however great a handicap to the poorer whites, its destruction promised advantages only in the long run. The difficulties, the disturbance of equities, involved in bridging the gap was one of the factors which aborted any early desires in the South for emancipation, whether these arose from statesmanlike vision, or from the enlightened self-interest of either slave-owners or the lower orders. No less was it true that the Negro himself was unprepared to step, simply, from slavery to freedom after two hundred years of assimilation and habituation as a slave; the consequences of a sudden change were bound to be disastrous — apart from the injury to vested interests — both to himself and to white society.

Nevertheless, after 1865 the presidentially-reconstructed States were confronted with a Negro legally emancipated from slavery by the Thirteenth Amendment: "Neither slavery nor involuntary servitude, except as punishment for crime . . . shall exist in the United States . . .," adopted in December, 1865. Southerners felt — and, as events showed, felt correctly — that more was involved in the working out of such a change than the destruction of a labor system and the forcible shifting of economic interests and powers. From Negro emancipation it was, they felt, but a short logical step to Negro "social" equality, and to Negro political enfranchisement. These changes did violence not only to vested economic interests, but to a deeply rooted emotional pattern.

It was not strange, in this background, that the South should resist the effectuation of the Thirteenth Amendment, the entering wedge of "African equality." [45] "An act of Congress might affect the law of property, but it could not immediately alter social and psychological traits in any people. Slavery was the proper condition of the blacks, and even though the mechanism was destroyed, the principle on which it rested . . . still remained. This was the point of view of the representative Southerner." [46] This spirit of intransigeance animated the remarks of a delegate to the Louisiana convention of 1864: "I . . . never believed in slavery as a principle . . . But, sir, slavery has come down to us through legitimate channels . . . I consider slavery one of the best evils that exists upon the earth — one of the best, because the Negro is benefited by it, because it keeps them out of houses of prostitution, out of our jails and workhouses." Similar in tone was a resolution offered to the Georgia Presidential convention: "Whereas the people of Georgia have been required . . . to prohibit slavery . . . we deem it proper to make the following statement . . . We regard the institution of slavery as consistent with the dictates of humanity and religion, and in our judgment the Negro race under our system of slavery has attained to a higher condition of civilization, morality, usefulness, and happiness than under any other circumstance . . . and we are convinced that the destruction of slavery at the South, while it is a great injury to the white race, will prove to be a great curse to the black race; yet . . . yielding . . . to the overruling necessities of our condition . . . It is resolved, that this convention accept in good faith" the Thirteenth Amendment.[47]

The South was not unprovided with an instrumentality for bridging in a controlled and intelligent fashion the gap between slavery and a real freedom of Negro labor. The Freedmen's Bureau, however flawed both in structure and in personnel, might have been at least a model for transition legislation had not the residual slave-holding psychology been so strong.* The Bureau's local officers registered and rated un-

* Created in 1865 under the War Department, its existence, as a separate branch of the national government, was extended by later acts until 1869. In the form in which it functioned after the war, it was administered by a com-

employed freedmen, published information concerning the supply of and demand for labor, and supervised the terms of employment contracts. General Howard, the chief Commissioner, reported to Congress that "in a single State no less than fifty thousand of such labor contracts were drawn in duplicate and filed . . ." The Bureau protected freedmen against such masters as still thought it necessary to restrain the movements of their Negro workers, to inflict corporal punishment for derelictions, and to maintain overseers in old-fashioned plantation style; it looked into cases of cheating in the payment of wages, combinations of masters to keep down wages, illegitimate use of vagrancy laws, and apprenticeship frauds. It was a check on the tendency of local courts to find for the master in labor disputes, sometimes advising, even representing, the Negro in the court room, and in many districts — where the local tribunals were deemed prejudiced — establishing its own courts or boards of arbitration which took complete jurisdiction over cases between freedmen and whites.[48]

Obviously, no matter what the attitude of the South, in 1865 some such agency was required to "stand between the whites and the blacks and aid each class in coming to a proper understanding of its privileges and responsibilities." [49] It has

missioner in Washington, assistant commissioners in charge of districts in the South, and agents on the assistant commissioners' staffs. Its official title, Bureau of Refugees, Freedmen, and Abandoned Lands, indicates its duties other than labor adjustment here discussed: to administer abandoned and confiscated plantations, and act as a clearing house for their return to amnestied and pardoned ex-Confederates; and to provide clothing, shelter, medicine, and rations not only to fleeing Negroes but to destitute whites as well. For the most favorable account of its relief activities, v. the Eliot Report. From "official sources" McPherson calculated that in the ten months from June 1865 to April 1866 the Bureau issued nearly six million rations to freedmen and well over two million to white refugees (p. 69, note). In the background of post-war conditions, the necessity for some organization to carry on these activities was as pressing as that for controlling the labor situation. War feelings and the Bureau's racially non-discriminating policy prevented the Southerner from giving due recognition to this fact — indeed, often made him unwilling to avail himself of the Bureau's facilities when in dire need. Undoubtedly, though, Bureau officials were often as unsympathetic in giving relief to "rebels" as they were tactless in carrying out the new labor policy.

seemed to a modern historian "indisputable that the freedman . . . if left completely at the mercy of former masters, would have suffered serious infringement of those rights to which a citizen and a free laborer may justly lay claim." Here and there even a Southern employer realized his indebtedness to the Bureau.[50]

The South was, on the whole, however, bitterly opposed to the Bureau. In this it had much justification, since the Bureau as constituted fell far short of perfection. Its agents, largely army officers, were tactless, sometimes overbearing, in their solicitude for the helpless freedman. Its personnel was entirely Northern, in itself irritating. Later — but not extensively during the early post-war days — Bureau officials used their powers to create a Negro following with which to invade local politics. But the very purpose of the Bureau aroused antagonism. The South could receive sympathetically no agency which "everywhere proclaimed and often repeated . . . that labor is a man's own property," that the Negro "has the right to dispose of it as he may see fit," that "No substitute for slavery like forced apprenticeship or peonage will be tolerated." [51] Already in 1865, eight months before the expiry of the first law creating the Bureau, it was being urged that this indispensable agency "be allowed to pass away. Its presence is anomalous and unnecessary. Its tendency has been, in a great measure, to disorganization and not to repose." [52] Its presence, it was charged, encouraged rudeness, impudence, and defiance on the part of the Negro; its relief work pauperized. "Look around you and see the result," complained Governor Humphreys of Mississippi. "Idleness and vagrancy have been the rule. Our rich and productive fields have been deserted for the filthy garrets and sickly cellars of our towns and cities. From producers [the freedmen] are converted into consumers and as winter approaches their only salvation from starvation and want is Federal rations, plunder, and pillage." The South was not ready to recognize that such conditions were as much a reason for the existence of the Bureau as — at the worst — a result of its presence. An institution, however little "encouragement to idleness" it might be designed to give, however "carefully" it might instruct the freedmen "in respect to their duties," did not fall within the ambit of the prevailing Southern outlook as long as at the same time "the rights of the freedmen were . . . insisted upon and defended." [53] This could not be the method of dealing with the problems of legal emancipation for a society which but yesterday depended on slavery for its wealth in its upper strata, and in its lower, looked to slavery for a meagre protection from Negro competition.

The South's plans for transition legislation looked rather towards continued subordination of the Negro, "freedman" though he might technically be. The South Carolina Presidential convention heard a proposal that "the Legislature shall have power to restrain Negroes and persons of color . . . from engaging in any species of traffic, in any other department of labor than menial service, agriculture, mining, roadmaking, and the production of naval stores, and employments incidental to these; and to make all laws necessary or proper to enforce this restriction. And the Legislature shall have power to make all laws proper or expedient to encourage industry or prevent idleness, vagrancy, or crime, among Negroes or colored persons, and to declare such laws exclusively applicable to that class of persons." [54] While the Southern legislators never got as far as completely "restraining" Negroes in this fashion, they did "encourage industry" in statutes which showed "the combined influence of the old laws for free Negroes, the vagrancy laws of North and South for whites, the customs of slavery times, the British West Indies legislation for ex-slaves, and the regulations of the United States War and Treasury Departments and of the Freedmen's Bureau — all modified and elaborated" [55] by a natural *penchant* for the pre-war situation.

Eight States enacted statutes which have passed into American history as the "Black Codes" — properly so called in spite of the absence of any mention of the Negro in some of them.[56] They required every Negro to be in the service of some white, and to have a lawful residence as well as employment and to carry an official certificate showing both. Vagrancy penalties were ordained for any person who could not support himself and his dependents and still refused to work for "usual and common" wages, or for Negroes found unlawfully assembling. Nonpayment of the poll-tax levied on all able-bodied male Negroes constituted *prima facie* evidence of vagrancy. The definition of vagrant was extended in one case to include stubborn and refractory servants and laborers who loitered away their time or refused without cause to comply with the terms of their contracts. Persons who offended against these regulations might be sentenced to labor on public works, or be bound out to private employers for terms varying from three months to a year, sometimes in proportion to an unpaid fine or in lieu of a prison sentence. In South Carolina a Negro might be bound out for nonpayment of any fine. Virginia specified that the employers of bound-out vagrants might deduct the cost of upkeep from wages, but the peonage implicit in this provision is only a little more obvious than what could easily result from the others.

Apprenticeship laws contributed to the "encouragement of industry" among the freedmen. The courts were to apprentice all minors whose parents were destitute or refused support, or even those who were in danger of "moral contamination," preferably to their former masters. The masters had parental powers of chastisement; they could compel the return of runaways, or invoke the vagrancy laws against them.

Stringent laws enforced the fulfillment of ordinary labor contracts. A defaulting laborer might be carried back to his employer, lose his year's wages, or have the vagrancy laws invoked against him. The law fixed his hours of labor, imposed fines for "disobedience," including, in one State, "impudence," "swearing," and the use of indecent language; required him to be "quiet and orderly" in his quarters and to "extinguish lights and fires and retire to rest at reasonable hours"; denied him the privilege of having visitors or leaving his plantation without permission from his employer — even fixed a penalty for Negroes found off their employers' premises after ten o'clock at night without a permit. Employers were authorized to deduct from wages the expense of losses, breakages, maintenance, and medical attention. Four States provided penalties for persons who persuaded laborers to break their contracts.

Ordinances which made it a misdemeanor for Negroes to sell farm produce without a magistrate's permit, or which created the special criminal category of driving off live stock for unauthorized sale, are now humorous reminders of the ex-slave's proclivity for chicken-stealing and "toting," but they also illustrate the post-war Southerner's unwillingness to deal with the freedman under the ordinary terms of the law. Only in one case were more serious restraints laid on the Negro's choice of economic activity: that of South Carolina, which forbade him to follow any "art, trade, or business of artisan, mechanic, or shopkeeper," or to engage in any occupation save husbandry or contract labor, alone or with a white partner, save upon issuance of a license after proof of proper apprenticeship.

It is not to be thought that the Black Codes represented any animosity against the Negro among the more cultivated of Southerners. "Our conduct [towards the Negro] should be kind, magnanimous, just," said the president of the Georgia convention of 1865. "The black race must feel that the white man is not his enemy . . . Now, if we cultivate this feeling . . . and this feeling is embodied in a wise and well-adapted code of laws . . . *we may indulge a hope that we may organize them into a class of trustworthy laborers.*" [57] The note of subordination is plain; as a later historian has put it, "The . . . lawmakers had sought a plan for immediate necessities, not a plan for the elevation of the black race." [58]

A number of other than labor restrictions went into the statute books at the same time.[59] While the Negro was everywhere given his day in court, and property rights, and even safeguarded in the making of contracts, he was indiscriminately barred from jury service and from taking the witness stand against whites, and for minor infractions sent for trial to special "inferior courts." In Mississippi he was forbidden to hold urban real estate without municipal permission. He could not preach in one State without police permission, in another without the sanction of an established church. Wiser — and in another context entirely inoffensive — were the regulations against the manufacture of liquor by Negroes, its sale by them, or the sale of weapons to them. The beginnings of the separation policy — today flowering in the "Jim Crow" laws — are also to be traced to this period. Three States provided for the segregation of Negroes in public conveyances. Seven forbade intermarriage of the races, and others penalized "fornication" between blacks and whites. Such States as made any provision for Negro education prescribed separate schools.

The South was, in general, opposed to the education of the Negro. Here again the note of continued subordination is unmistakable. A few voices cried in the wilderness that "A due regard for the public weal imperatively requires that the Negroes be educated, taught at least to read and write . . . Steeped in ignorance, they can never be made to understand the responsibilities that rest upon them as freedmen." [60] But legislation went on the lines that "The sole aim should be to educate every white child in the Commonwealth." [61] Poverty must account partly for this stand: "I am in favor of providing ways and means for the education of freedmen . . . but not in favor of positively imposing upon any legislature the unqualified and imperative duty of educating any but the superior race of man — the white race . . . Our pecuniary condition does not allow us to do it." Often this objection took an even more ungracious form: "I say that the levying of a tax upon us to pay for the education of a race we expect to be torn from us, is an indignity. Why are we called upon to educate these Negroes?" "I will never be so dishonest as to

. . . tax a white man for the education of a Negro. No, sir; I will never disgrace myself by such a vote." [62]

The need for economy was, however, only a part of the argument. Dunning says: "The Negroes were disliked and feared almost in exact proportion to their manifestation of intelligence and capacity"; [63] and there were many reasons in the utterances of Southerners to support his generalization. "Education of the Negroes, they thought, would be labor lost, resulting in injury instead of benefit to the working class." [64] The teachers of the Freedmen's Bureau or of private philanthropies "interfered with labor . . . and encouraged, directly or indirectly, insolence to employers." [65] "Schooling," felt the South, "ruins a nigger."

With these sentiments, in effect unanimous, as to the Negro's economic and social status in the new order, it is plain what the South's attitude towards Negro suffrage must have been. During Presidential Reconstruction no move was made in any State south of the Border group to give Negroes the suffrage, although prior to Congressional interference it was within the power of the separate States to define their own electorates. The Presidential constitutions all retained the white male suffrage provisions of before the war.[66] Mississippi and Kentucky rejected even the Thirteenth Amendment lest its enforcing section be construed so as to give Congress power to enfranchise the freedman by statute, while Alabama, Florida, and South Carolina tacked riders to their ratification attempting to guard against such an event.[67]

In the Louisiana convention of 1864, a constitutional provision was proposed empowering the legislature to "pass laws extending the suffrage to such . . . persons . . . as by military service, by taxation to support the government, or by intellectual fitness may be deemed entitled thereto." This was objectionable "because it will let Negroes who have property vote," "because I find the paragraph refers to Negroes." In this body, one of the unregenerate slave-holders offered to amend the emancipation clause with the proviso "that the Legislature shall never pass any amendment authorizing free Negroes to vote . . . under any pretence whatsoever." [68] This did not pass, nor did an ordinance moved in the Florida Presidential convention: "The people of the State of Florida, in general convention assembled, do ordain and declare, that while we recognize the freedom of the colored race, and are desirous of extending to them full protection . . . we declare it the unalterable sentiment of this Convention, that the laws of the State shall be made and executed by the white race." [69] Nevertheless it is significant that such plans should have been entertained in bodies which, in the end, gave them effect.

Again, as in the case of labor legislation, a more progressive alternative had been laid before the South. Both President Lincoln, in a letter to Governor Hahn of Louisiana,[70] and later President Johnson, advising Governor Sharkey of Mississippi, counseled the bestowal of a very limited Negro franchise. Johnson, indeed, pointed out significantly that such a grant "would completely disarm the adversary," the threatening Radical Republicans in Congress.[71] But a whole arsenal of reasons against enfranchisement was already prepared. Most of them started from the assumption of a general Negro franchise, and consequent "Negro domination"; the intelligent freedman was considered but "a drop in the bucket." [72] It was argued that "this is a white man's government," and that in the sight of God and the light of reason a Negro suffrage was impossible.[73]

A few Bourbons were willing to let the freedman vote, sure that they could control him; a very few middle and lower class politicians felt that Negro suffrage might give their own group an advantage. But the white-county people generally took the stand that the Negro would "vote with his late master, whom he does not hate, rather than with the non-slaveholding white, whom he does hate." [74]

So in Alabama it was the representative of a black county who in 1865 introduced into the short-lived Presidential-Reconstruction legislature a bill conferring qualified Negro suffrage. At this time, we are told, some of the native leaders had come around to thinking that thus they might "gain the confidence" of the Negro and "control his vote." "The Black Belt hoped in this way to regain its former political influence. *The new constitution* [1865] *by making the white population the basis of representation, had transferred political supremacy to the white counties. The hilly section of the state was opposed to any form of Negro suffrage . . . The Black Belt people, who had less prejudice against the Negro and who were sure that they could control him and gain in political power, were more favorably inclined . . .*" [75]

The Bourbon A. H. Stephens, Vice President of the late Confederacy, expressed his willingness to see granted a restricted Negro suffrage.[76] General Wade Hampton of South Carolina went much further: ". . . No harm would be done the South by Negro suffrage," he is reported as saying. "The old owners would cast the votes of their people almost as absolutely and securely as their own. If Northern men expected in this way to build up a northern party in the South, they were greatly mistaken. They would only be multiplying the power of the old and natural leaders of Southern politics by giving a vote to every former slave. Heretofore such men had served their masters only in the fields; now they would do no less faithful service at the polls. If the North could stand it, the South could. For himself, he should make no special objection to Negro suffrage as one of the terms of reorganization, and if it came, he did not think the South would have much cause to regret it." [77]

Such complacency about Negro suffrage made the white-county leaders quiver. President Johnson, discussing Negro suffrage with a delegation of South Carolinians, declared that "he did not want the late slave-holder to control the Negro vote against the white men." [78] And provisional Governor Perry of South Carolina pointed out to the constitutional convention of that State in 1865 [79] that Negro suffrage would "give to the man of wealth and large landed possessions in the State a most undue influence in all elections. He would be able to march to the polls, with his two or three hundred 'freedmen' . . . The poor white men would have no influence

. . ." * The "poor white men" therefore closed their ranks against such an extension of the suffrage.

IV. NEMESIS

The conservative governments of the States below the Border group were destined to have but a short life. The ultimate control of Reconstruction rested, after all, with Congress, and Congress, controlled in turn by the Radical Republican party, feared in a mild Reconstruction policy the return of the Democrats to national power. In the Southern States themselves, Republicanism had developed a vested interest through the formation of the Border-State Radical groups, and through the migration of carpetbaggers to the far South as Freedmen's Bureau agents, missionaries, teachers, and speculators. There were thus selfish partisan reasons for undoing Presidential Reconstruction, and these intensified the publicity given to more legitimate motives. Lincoln's and Johnson's plans were branded almost from the beginning as "executive usurpation." [80] The "lately rebellious," it was pointed out, were returning to power not only in the Southern States, but were even laying claim to seats in Congress, thus endangering the fruits of victory.[81] Finally, the intransigeance of the South towards the Negro was played up, both by selfish partisans and by genuine humanitarians like Charles Sumner.[82]

Congress definitely repudiated President Johnson's policies

* Two years later, however, under the threat of impending Congressional Reconstruction, Perry, then in private life, saw in a union of poor-white scalawaggery with the Negro an even greater menace — that of a proletarian revolution, of an attack on property by the poor: "I greatly fear there are many white persons in South Carolina who will vote for a convention, under the hope of its repudiating the indebtedness of the State. This class may influence the Negro vote to unite with them, and then, in return, they can unite with the Negro in parceling out the lands of the State. One step leads to another: Stay-law first — repudiation next; and then follows a division of lands and an equal apportionment of property amongst all persons. And last of all, the honest, hard-working, industrious, and prudent class must support the idle, dissipated, extravagant, and roguish class . . ." (letter to the Columbia *Phoenix*, reprinted in the Charleston *Courier*, 4 May 1867).

in February and March, 1866, passing over his veto a bill extending the life of the Freedmen's Bureau and a Civil Rights Act, and declaring in a concurrent resolution that no Senator or representative from any of the late insurrectionary States should be admitted to Congress until Congress itself had declared such States entitled to representation.[83]

The next step was the passage of the Fourteenth Amendment. This created a Federal citizenship, and guaranteed "the equal protection of the law" to all persons born or naturalized in the United States. Thus it brought the Civil Rights Act into the Constitution, and opened the door for Negro suffrage. It reduced the Congressional representation of any State which abridged the right of suffrage save for crime. It disqualified for Federal *and State* office any person who, having taken an oath of allegiance to the United States, had engaged in insurrection or given aid and comfort to the national enemy, and made amnesty conditional upon a two-thirds vote of Congress.[84]

By February, 1867, the Amendment had been rejected by all the Southern States, including the Border States. Here, as has been pointed out, the unfolding of the Congressional program helped to bring on a reaction in favor of the Conservatives. Now even the moderate Republicans in Congress went over to Radicalism. "The last one of the sinful ten has at last with contempt and scorn flung back into our teeth the magnanimous offer of a generous nation," cried Representative Garfield. "It is now our turn to act." [85]

And so, in February, March, and July, 1867, the first series of Reconstruction Acts was passed.[86] They declared that no legal governments existed in the late Confederacy, and divided it into five military districts, each under a general officer of the United States Army. New conventions were to be held under military auspices. In the elections for delegates all Negroes over twenty-one years of age might vote, but no white who could not take a test oath or who was disqualified for office by the still unratified Fourteenth Amendment. The new constitutions, when accepted by the same electorate, were to retain Negro suffrage, whereupon Congress would restore the lately rebellious States to their place in the Union as soon as they had ratified the Fourteenth Amendment. The new governments were thus expected to add white disqualification for office to the Negro suffrage imposed by the Acts.

The South was aghast. According to an estimate in the Senate, 672,000 Negroes had been enfranchised, as against a total possible white electorate of 925,000.[87] But some hundred thousand of these whites had been disfranchised, and 200,000 disqualified for office.[88] The worst fears of "Negro domination" — unjustified while it had still been a question of qualified Negro suffrage — seemed about to be realized. Two States — Georgia and Mississippi — made a desperate attempt to have the new legislation set aside by the Supreme Court, but failed.[89] The governors of four others proposed a compromise constitutional amendment, granting a qualified Negro suffrage and acquiescing in the reduction of representation in cases of disfranchisement; but it was now too late even for consideration.[90]

Until Congressional Reconstruction reached its lowest ebb of corruption and inefficiency, a few Conservative leaders made efforts to win over the Negroes, and to commit their party to an acquiescence in the new state of affairs lest worse befall.[91] In every State third parties, of "Moderate" or "Independent" Republicans formed almost from the beginning of Congressional Reconstruction, composed of whites who would not return to Bourbon allegiance under Conservatism, of others who hoped to minimize the evils of "Negro domination" by making concessions to Radicalism, and of still others who simply saw a chance for personal political advantage.[92] Some Southerners became "scalawags": out-and-out Radical Republicans, "content to take office at any price to the country," or "good citizens, who had become so embittered by the war that they were willing to accept the aid even of their former slaves in a fight against the Secessionists." [93] All classes in the South would not act wholly together, until they had experienced "Negro domination" at its worst.

But the vast majority of leaders and ordinary citizens, in bitter disillusionment, boycotted the new régimes. The wrath and despair of the South, its unbelieving astonishment over the extreme course of the Republican party, were best expressed in the speeches and writings of Benjamin Hill of Georgia.[94] He apostrophized the Radicals and scalawags: "You say in your record that you have agreed to an equality of the races, when you know, you vile hypocrites, that the very agreement you make included the disfranchisement of the intelligent, virtuous, and educated, and wealthy white men, and that they shall not be allowed to hold office . . . while any Negro or scalawag may. Is that equality? . . . The white people have refused to consent to terms of Negro dominion, of pauperism in power and ignorance in legislating, and I tell you they never will consent to them . . ." "We do not recognize that the Negro has any political rights whatever," it was said in Arkansas; "his existence in the country is only tolerated by white men on the score of humanity." [95] The beginnings of the KuKlux movement date from this period.[96]

The Congressional program was nevertheless pushed ruthlessly to its conclusion, violent deeds and words in the South only increasing popular support in the North.

In vain did ruined and broken Bourbons beg their late slaves to shun the blandishments of "foreign" politicians. "My colored friends, we are Southern men, born upon the same soil, live in the same country, and will sleep in the same graveyard when life's troubles are over," urged an ex-Confederate General — at what cost to his pride one can only guess. ". . . It is alike your duty and interest to cultivate friendly relations with your neighbors and former owners, who are today, and ever have been, your best friends . . . I am deprived of citizenship . . . I am prostrated by the war, but I will assist you all I can . . . [The Radicals] want office; they want spoils; and they want to retain power. It is quite pleasant and profitable to them. It is not because they love you better than other people. I warn you against [them] and all like [them], at home or abroad . . . I thank you for the respectful attention you have given me." [97]

In the Radical behalf, "Union Leagues," officered by carpetbaggers and scalawags, organized the Negroes into blocks of solid Republican voters, sworn with elaborate ritual and secrecy to perpetual loyalty to the party of emancipation. The Freedmen's Bureau agents, from explaining to the Negro his new rights and reassuring him against the threats of the Conservatives, in many cases passed easily over into campaigning for the Radical party, especially where they were themselves candidates for the Congressional conventions or for office.[98] The registrars, who had to subscribe to an even more stringent test oath than ordinary electors, were in many cases Northerners, military men, Bureau agents, even candidates for office.[99] Under the Reconstruction Acts, they had almost unlimited discretion in refusing to accept loyalty oaths and in adding and striking off electors from the lists. Here and there, a zealous military commander gerrymandered black districts into strategic positions.[100]

As a result of these activities and the disgusted abstention of the whites, more Negroes than whites were registered in five States. In all the States the conventions were elected by the Negro vote, the whites either voting against holding a convention, or abstaining in the hope that they might thus prevent the elections from having effect.[101] The conventions were overwhelmingly Radical. In one case Negroes and carpetbaggers alone were almost a majority; in a few, a considerable number of scalawags turned the balance. "The pillars of the Capitol should be hung in mourning today for the murdered sovereignty of North Carolina," wrote a Conservative editor. "There assembles this morning . . . a body . . . which has not been elected according to our laws nor chosen by those to whom those laws have committed the right of suffrage . . ." [102]

What followed was a matter of course. The new State conventions, meeting in 1867, 1868, and 1869, drafted constitutions and passed ordinances conforming to the requirements of the Reconstruction Acts. In Virginia and Mississippi, the Radicals, acting on the principle "It is expected that you will temporarily disfranchise a number of those who participated in the rebellion sufficient to place the State in the hands of those who are loyal to the United States," [103] wrote into their constitutions even more stringent "rebel" disfranchisement and disqualification clauses than Congress required. These instruments were therefore rejected at first, and were not accepted until Congress permitted the separate submission of the offensive articles.[104] In Alabama and Arkansas, so many whites abstained from the plebiscite that Congress had to make ratification depend on the majority of votes cast instead of on the majority of voters registered.[105] Elsewhere the carefully selected electorate ratified the constitutions as presented, at the same time installing Negro-Radical-Republican State administrations. The Fourteenth Amendment was now duly ratified by State after State, and in 1868 seven States were readmitted with a full complement of Radical congressmen. The last three, Virginia, Mississippi, and Texas, followed in 1870.

But Congress was not yet through. It demanded of the first seven States to be readmitted a pledge that they would never disfranchise on account of race, color, or previous condition, and of the last three that they would not discriminate either in suffrage, eligibility to office, or school privileges.[106] To safeguard these pledges, the Fifteenth Amendment was passed in 1869: "The right of citizens . . . to vote shall not be denied or abridged by the United States or by any State on account of race, color, or previous condition of servitude," [107] Four States were obliged to ratify this for readmission.[108] A second series of Reconstruction Acts — the "Force Bills" — made it a Federal offense to interfere with or prevent the registration of voters, and declared that a proffer of registration should entitle to vote if registration had been illegally refused. The use of bribery, threats, force, or economic pressure to prevent any citizen from voting subjected the offender to heavy penalties and damages. Two or more persons who foregathered to obstruct the equal administration of civil-rights or franchise laws constituted a conspiracy, to combat which the President might use the armed forces of the United States and suspend the right of habeas corpus. Congressional elections were placed entirely under Federal control, the United States Circuit Courts being empowered to appoint election supervisors and deputy marshals to protect the polls and the voters.[109] To aid in the enforcement of this rigorous code, Federal troops were left at strategic points throughout the South until 1876.

For eight years in some States, for a shorter period down to two years in others, the Radicals ruled supreme in the South. Thus had the mighty fallen; "Thus our political subjugation has been made complete." [110] In the first South Carolina legislature, "The Speaker is black, the Clerk is black, the doorkeepers are black, the little pages are black, the chairman of Ways and Means is black, and the Chaplain is coal black. At some of the desks sit colored men whose types it would be hard to find outside of the Congo; whose costumes, visages, attitudes, and expression only befit the forecastle of a buccaneer. It must be remembered also that these men, with not more than half a dozen exceptions, have been themselves slaves, and that their ancestors were slaves for generations." [111] Upon these blacks depended the hated power of the carpetbaggers and scalawags, and for these blacks, in return for the opportunity to rule, the Radicals provided offices and a flattering "social equality" in law. Thus a powerful Negro political machine came into being — for a time supplanting the plantation- and slave-owners' machine — which it required a revolution to turn out, but which returned again to plague Bourbons and lower orders in devious ways.

CHAPTER III

THE FORMATION OF THE SOLID SOUTH (1867-1876)

1. COALS OF FIRE

The events occurring under "Negro domination" in the South once more obliterated class and party divisions among the whites, as the Secession crisis had done before. Furthermore, the course of "Negro domination" left behind it a persistent spectre to be conjured up — sometimes on meagre provocation — by political and economic interests bent on preserving some advantageous *status quo*. To understand both the party solidarity of the South and its susceptibility to the Negro bogey, it is essential to realize what happened in the South from 1867 to 1876.

If during its period of autonomy from 1865 to 1867 Southern policies had been unwise and shortsighted, the Northern policies now carried out by Congressional Reconstruction proved no less so. The South had set its face against effectuating constructively the change from the Negro's status as a slave to his new status as a citizen. The North now proposed to make the change by fiat, without any mechanism of transition.

Opposed by the South, officered largely by adventurers, manned and supported increasingly by the inexperienced and untrained Negro, the new régime could but produce inefficiency, corruption, and oppression. It could but solidify the South behind the old leaders who cried "I told you so!" It could but end in revolution, and a dogged determination to keep the Negro in subjection.

Irresponsibility was the salient characteristic of the Congressional State administrations. They were cut off from the influence of the white population of the South, whose leaders were debarred from political activity, and whose vote — not yet consolidated by a revolutionary sentiment — registered merely an ineffective protest.

The governments installed in the South in 1867-1869 depended primarily upon the Federal executive and Federal patronage for their existence. But these administrations also took measures to reduce the political strength of their local opponents, the Democrats and Conservatives. In the new constitutions or in election codes, certain of the States prescribed drastic "loyalty" tests for voters and for office-holders, over and above the Federal requirements.[1] Adroit gerrymanders switched Negro localities into majority positions in Congressional, State-legislature, and municipal districts.[2] Where Democrats controlled too many minor local posts, the State legislatures simply removed them.[3]

Most of the States centralized the appointment of registration and election officials in such a way that the party in control of the governorship "could . . . control the State absolutely," by rejecting would-be voters, erasing names from the registry books, allowing any person to vote who they were "satisfied" had registered, and throwing out ballots in contested elections. The State courts were deprived of jurisdiction in election disputes.[4]

All these measures constituted an invitation to easy fraud. Behind them the Radical governments put the force of State militias, practically restricted to Negroes by a strict "loyalty" oath, and responsible directly to the governor. Marching and countermarching before the polling places — sometimes guarded by Federal troops as well — they made many an election, held under "martial law" by proclamation of a Radical governor, a bitter farce for the Conservatives.[5] The Conservatives were powerless before the stuffing of ballot boxes, the withholding of Democratic returns, the staging of irregularities to give color to the rejection of returns from incorrigibly white counties, the importation of "floaters" from a neighboring State, the intimidation of Negro Democrats.[6]

Fleming gives chapter and verse on the bad character of many Reconstruction notables: Governor Warmoth of Louisiana had an unsavory reputation before his election, and after enjoyed an unexplained fortune. Franklin Moses, speaker of the South Carolina House and afterwards governor, made a business of jobbery in printing and other perquisites. The Negro legislators of Georgia sang of the local "fixer":

> "H. I. Kimball's on de floor,
> 'Tain't gwine ter rain no more." [7]

Lack of legal knowledge did not debar from the bench, nor illiteracy from positions which involved the drawing up and execution of processes. Towards the end of Radical supremacy, Negroes themselves were shocked by Republican corruption and venality.[8]

There is a mass of evidence for administrative extravagance and corruption.[9] The ruin which as a result overtook the finances of the Southern State governments during this régime is too notorious to require more than brief recapitulation.[10] A Republican committee of Congress in 1872 fixed the increase of Southern State debts in a four-year period at an amazing figure. Virginia and North Carolina were confessedly bankrupt in 1875; Alabama in 1874. The amount of indebtedness in some States remains undiscoverable, because no records of bond issues were kept.

Increase in taxation kept pace with the issue of bonds, and led to organized protest on the part of the taxpayers. In Arkansas, the assessor was encouraged to boost taxable values by being allowed three and one-half per cent of collections. One result was the selling out of thousands of small proprietors for nonpayment of taxes; Louisiana newspapers in 1875 were three-quarters filled by notices of tax sales. Another was the "strangulation" of counties which on account of debt and tax arrears lost self-government and to the dismay of their white inhabitants passed bankrupt under the rule of Radical appointees.

The expenditures of the Reconstruction State governments

were in many respects legitimate, in some legitimate but unwise, in others shady, in many patently fraudulent. There were two respects in which Reconstruction legislation particularly displeased the native white population, not only because of the expense entailed, but also because they bore on the race issue.

The first was the application to the sparsely settled South of the New England system of decentralized township and county government.[11] This was a great drain on the public treasury, especially when jobs were multiplied for deserving Radicals. But the results were even more unpleasant to the whites when the new division of authority gave the Negro additional power either by weight of numbers in the black counties, or through ingenious gerrymanders *ad hoc.*

Another extravagance under the circumstances was the establishment of public school systems on advanced Northern models. These were of course especially irritating because, being open freely to white and Negro children, they actually did nothing for the white population which paid for them. Nor had the South foregone its unwillingness to have the freedman educated. In Arkansas, the Conservatives denounced the new school system as a scheme under which the whites were to be mulcted to subsidize "indiscriminate social intercourse" between the children of the two races.[12]

The imminence of "social equality" blanched many cheeks. The Negroes inclined to take full and often tactless advantage of their new position, as in the unsettled period immediately following emancipation. The free intercourse between them and their Radical leaders gave deep offense; Benjamin Hill could find no worse indictment to lay against the Republicans of Georgia than the charge that they were "miscegenating bacchanalians." [13] The Black Codes, where they had not been withdrawn from the statute books under the Presidential régime, under pressure from the North, were now either explicitly repealed or relegated to innocuous desuetude. There was, of course, no desire under the Congressional administrations to enforce the subordination of the Negro towards which they looked. In some States, Civil Rights Acts were passed, similar in tenor to the Federal Act, fixing penalties for discriminations in public conveyances and places of resort.[14]

The Radical régimes thus flouted the white South on three points. They consolidated the new economic position of the Negro — at least in law — refusing to mitigate the effects of emancipation by restricting the Negro's activities. They advanced him in the "social" scale by establishing his civil rights, and gave political content to his advancement by admitting him to the party councils — at least in form — and giving him the badge of high and lesser officers. They put a burden on the tax-paying community by extravagance and malfeasance. This last injury, of course, the South was also not slow to attribute — and with much justice — to the preponderance of the Negro in the electorate.

Unable to check these developments by the ordinary processes of election, the white South, politically weakened by the Reconstruction code, not unnaturally turned to irregular and violent means to regain control, and thus added to the difficulties of the period disorder and bloodshed. Sporadic affrays between whites and self-assertive Negroes were numerous, nor were they always confined to the times and places of elections.[15] The KuKlux Klan and similar organizations came into being throughout the South, and assumed the functions of a guerilla police according to the varying demands of the regions in which they operated.[16] Their methods did not differ; secrecy, terrifying disguises, grandiosely menacing warnings, tar and feathers, whipping, unofficial but none the less effective banishment everywhere were the means they used, chiefly against Negroes, also to some extent against white Radicals.

The objects of the various branches of the movement were not everywhere the same. The political and social divisions among the whites of the up-country encouraged the aspirations of the Negro; here the Klan was most repressive. The differences between the two white classes gave the Klan in poor-white Alabama a very different complexion from its branches in the Black Belt of the State. In the former, the poor whites tried to use their organization to drive Negroes off the rich lands which they themselves coveted; in the latter, the Bourbons used it to keep the Negroes from migrating and to stimulate their efforts and orderliness.[17] Here, a Klan body supplemented the work of the lower courts, corruptly lenient towards Negro rogues and vagabonds; there, maintained "social supremacy" for the whites, punishing Negroes "known to associate with low white women"; everywhere, it endeavored to awe the freedman into the respectful attitude of slavery days. Although it has been claimed that the Klan organizations had no political motives,[18] the ritual of the various secret societies pledged the membership to combat "Negro domination" and Negro participation in politics.[19] In several States it appeared at critical moments during the election campaigns which eventually wrested "supremacy" from the Radicals.

II. A WHITE MAN'S PARTY

Starting with a divided opinion as to how Congressional Reconstruction should be met, by 1870 the white citizenship of the South was well on the way to reunion under the pressure of the developments we have just sketched. Opposition to Negro politics, deepened by the misgovernment suffered under the Negro-supported régime, crystallized into effective political activity supported by force. By 1876, Conservative "White Men's" parties were in control of every Southern State.

Unlike the situation in the Border States, where the struggle against Radicalism was more strictly one between opposing white parties, in the lower South one side of the political battle line was manned almost wholly by Negroes under foreign Radical leadership, and the other by whites who were at first themselves divided among Conservatives, moderate Republicans, and scalawags.

In every Southern State, immediately upon the intervention of Congress local groups calling themselves Conservative parties were formed to oppose the Radical policies laid down in Washington, and to dispute political power with the Negroes and carpetbaggers. These groups acted in national politics with the Democracy, into which they were gradually absorbed. At first, under the influence of moderates like Stuart of Virginia, Conservatism was disposed to seek Negro adherents, but it soon drew the "color line," to fight the battle for "white supremacy." This policy was foreshadowed in local party meetings as early as the autumn of 1867.[20]

Practically unanimous Negro solidarity under Radical leadership helped commit Conservatism to an all-white policy. "Every day," noted Alexander Stephens in 1868, "it becomes more painfully evident that the estrangement between the races is widening — on the part of the Negroes from the effects of such instruction as teaches them to distrust and oppose the whites, and on the part of the latter from an abhorrence of the Negro leaders and an instinctive aversion to be ruled and legislated for by ignorance and semi-barbarism." [21] It must be borne in mind that the affiliation which the Conservatives offered the Negroes, where such an offer was made, amounted to saying: accept our leadership or be damned, and — as a thoughtful Southerner himself admitted — "after the opposition which the mass of the whites had exhibited in 1867 and 1868 to enfranchising the blacks," to say nothing of the economic and social legislation of the Presidential Reconstruction period, the Negroes "had some cause to distrust" Conservatism.[22] As a result a Republican convention in Virginia in 1867 shut out all the white delegates save fifty carpetbaggers and scalawags. This Morton calls the turning point in the political history of the Virginia Negro.[23] "Negro suffrage had come to mean carpetbaggism and radicalism" in Virginia and throughout the lower South, and on this combination Conservatism turned its back.

But the solidarity of the simon-pure Democracy of the South was not in itself enough to bring about the "redemption." As the hopeless bankruptcy of the Negro-Radical régime became more and more evident, Conservatism received welcome recruits from the ranks of the moderate Republican parties. These gradually lost their separate identity through mergers with Conservatism after 1870.[24]

Schisms also rent the Radical parties themselves almost from the beginning. Often they arose over the division of political spoils, as in Florida, Arkansas, and Louisiana,[25] and were so bitter as to bring about attempts to impeach Radical governors on the part of disaffected rings.[26] They weakened the Radical hold on the State machines, and here and there brought additional voters into the Conservative ranks.

Among the scalawags — native Southerners gone Republican — there were many honest enemies of Bourbon rule who were at first willing to swallow Radicalism whole in their desire to change the complexion of Southern politics. These were the nearest counterpart in the lower South to the Border State poor-white partisans. Like their Border State fellows, as Radical misgovernment increased, they could less and less bear with their new party and with the Negro who supported it and gave it some of its most unpleasant impetus. They too felt themselves compelled to join a "white man's party," and this meant for them a return to Conservative allegiance. Even carpetbaggers of the better sort, despairing of turning an honest penny, joined the natives or left the country.

In the early seventies, therefore, only the less reputable elements among the whites were left to Radicalism. The process of defection continued until 1876, when the Republican party was split in every Southern State it still controlled.

The Federal government was also beginning to loose its grip on the regions "lately in rebellion." Individual and group amnesties helped swell the Conservative vote. In 1871, the "ironclad" oath was repealed, readmitting many Southern leaders to eligibility for office. Finally, in 1872, a national amnesty act restored to political rights all but some six hundred ex-Confederate officials.

From this time on, the existence of the Negro-Radical governments depended entirely on the presence of Federal troops.

III. THE REDEMPTION

The redemption of the South was not wholly the result of the legitimate political shifts we have thus far sketched. The period 1869-71 was the heyday of the KuKlux Klan's activities. The Klan "greatly aided in the recovery of the States" which went Conservative in those three eventful years. "It also assisted the whites in the other States to regain control of the white counties." These successes were achieved by the use of intimidation, force, social and business ostracism, purchase of votes, drawing the color line, discharge from employment, forced resignations from office, the "shotgun plan," and "Rifle Clubs." [27] In 1871, a Congressional committee investigated KuKlux activities, unearthing several volumes of major and minor atrocities, and brought about the passing of an act to enforce the Fifteenth Amendment. Radical governors pressed President Grant to use the powers it gave him to suspend habeas corpus, proclaim martial law, and send Federal troops into their jurisdictions.[28]

The emergence of revolutionary tactics showed clearly how deeply the South resented the participation of the Negro in politics. Misgovernment was, indeed, an issue, but elsewhere misgovernment did not produce the violent reaction we shall now describe. The force of arms, economic and social pressure, the rejection of orderly methods of election, were not invoked against the Tweed Ring in New York, or the Gas Trust in Philadelphia. Nor do the burdens imposed on the South by Radical extravagance wholly account for the passion of the "Redemption." For the burden of bond issues and increased taxation for improvements bore heavily on the inhabitants of Northern and Western States in the same period; yet even where repudiation was demanded as a remedy, settlements were effected without recourse to revolution.[29]

With the aid of some measure of force and fraud, North Carolina, Virginia, and Georgia went Conservative in 1870 and 1871; in 1873 and 1874, assisted by the newly liberalized national amnesty policy, three more States — Texas, Arkansas, and Alabama — passed under white control.[30] After a revolutionary interlude in the remaining States, the Hayes-Tilden deadlock over the presidency gave the opportunity for a compromise. In the States with disputed elections, the electoral-college votes were counted Republican, and in return President Hayes in 1877 withdrew the remaining Federal troops from the South. This sealed the doom of the Radical governments.

The use of revolutionary tactics reached its zenith in three of the States last restored: Mississippi, South Carolina, and Louisiana.[31] Since the Conservative forces took over some of the methods and devices which the carpetbag governments had used to put themselves in power, it is worth considering their tactics at some length, for — used twice in one generation — they fastened themselves upon the South like a bad habit, and reappeared again in Southern politics of a later period.

After disorderly elections in 1876, South Carolina and Louisiana were left each with dual governments, one Radical and one Conservative, on the verge of actual civil war. Mississippi's campaign of 1875-76 resulted in a decisive Conservative victory, but only at the cost of a period of disorder and guerrilla warfare which became proverbial as "the Mississippi plan." [32] A Negro militia was one of the chief immediate issues. In October, 1875, after Governor Ames had taken the additional precaution of ordering one hundred copies of *Infantry Tactics*, a leading Conservative newspaper declared that the time had come for the "protective" companies of private white militia to step forward. Both sides imported arms, both paraded in force up and down the State, both fired artillery salutes which terrified all Negroes within hearing. There was a series of large-scale riots which compelled an unofficial Federal investigation; as a result, Governor Ames was induced to promise the disbanding of the Negro militia, and much further bloodshed was thus avoided. Nevertheless, disorder and killings continued until close to the day of election, 3 November. The polling itself was "quiet," but there were "occurrences highly discreditable to the whites" which influenced the results in five counties: the training of cannon on a polling place, a parade of imported Conservative cavalrymen from Alabama around voting booths, the guarding of fords across a river from the Black Belt to the ballot box "to prevent the Negroes from seizing arms" on the eve of the election. Intimidation was practised also by the Radicals.

These were not the only campaign methods employed. Agreements were published in a number of counties in which local employers pledged themselves not to give work to Republicans, to discharge the leaders of Republican clubs, to refuse them the rent of houses and land, and to publish a blacklist of political objectionables — "Republican" being by this time practically synonymous with "Negro."

The Democracy carried the State by 30,000 ballots. In each of three strongly Republican counties there were four, twelve, and seven Republican votes, respectively, the last out of a known Negro-Radical majority of 2000. Another county with the same normal majority went Democratic by 1515. Governor Ames resigned under threat of impeachment, other objectionable officials followed suit, and the new government immediately instituted a program of economy. Within ten months the State Republican party was officially dissolved.

In Louisiana, events were much the same. The revolution started with the State campaign of 1874. The Conservatives were organized in "White Leagues" and had ordered arms; these the Radical governor Kellogg tried to seize, and in a pitched battle in New Orleans, forty persons were killed and one hundred wounded. The Radical government immediately collapsed, but was reëstablished — for New Orleans only — by Federal troops. Although the election first showed a Democratic victory, the governor's returning board manufactured a Republican legislature. Warfare continued up to and throughout the 1876 campaign. In the latter election, Federal office-holders were openly used as Radical tools to supervise the polls. The Democracy claimed an 8000 popular majority, but the returning board certified a Republican majority of 1000. Two governments established themselves and all but declared war on each other in New Orleans. But when the Federal troops were withdrawn by President Hayes, the Radical organization disappeared.[33]

In South Carolina there were the usual semi-military and unofficial organizations of Conservative whites, here called "Rifle Clubs." [34] "The red-shirt rifle club procession was a feature of every campaign meeting — the number of mounted men in uniform varying, according to the white population of the county, from 500 to 5000. The use of mounted men had the effect of exaggerating in the estimate of onlookers the number of men actually present. The city fellow who saw a red-shirt procession for the first time might honestly misrepresent its numbers. A thousand men on horseback, riding in easy order, every man yelling as long as his throat could stand the effort — the marshals meantime riding up and down the column, carrying orders or 'closing up' the men — the route to the speaking ground lined with men . . . women, and children, waving flags or hats or handkerchiefs to the riders and doing their part to increase the volume of lusty yells and defiant hurrahs — such a body of men might well be taken for one double their number in fact."

Campaigning went on on the economic front as well: "R. S. Tharin will be open on alternate days of the week to register Democratic workmen and to take orders for employers"; "The Workingman's Democratic Association conducts a labor exchange for local Democratic merchants, wharf-owners, and tradesmen generally." [35]

South Carolina did not escape without violence and bloodshed. Edgefield County was in a state of continual turmoil; Governor Chamberlain, then President Grant, ordered the dispersal of the rifle clubs, supporting the injunction with troops. According to a local historian, they instantly and obediently disappeared.[36]

It took until April, 1877, to confirm the Conservative victory, after five months of fraudulent canvassing, extraordinary court proceedings, and threats of pitched battle between rival legislatures.[37] Chamberlain resigned, Wade Hampton was inaugurated, and the local historian cannot resist the temptation of describing his apotheosis: "Just as the Governor released the Bible, the 'Hampton Saluting Club' (successor to the Columbia Flying Artillery, 'dispersed' [sic] by President Grant's proclamation) fired a national salute, and the assembled multitude sent up a volume of cheers long and loud."

IV. SELF-DETERMINATION

After 1877, the native white population, under its own political leaders, was in a position to effect what reforms it desired in the South. The consolidation of white supremacy from this time on was greatly facilitated by conditions at Washington. The Amnesty Act of 1872 had expedited the work of "redemption" and — at the same time — the rehabilitation of the national Democratic party. From 1875 to 1879, neither party controlled both houses of Congress and the presidency, and there was a consequent deadlock over questions of Southern policy. Meanwhile, the effectiveness of the "bloody shirt" issue began to wane, and a series of new national problems claimed attention: tariff, currency, civil service reform, agricultural depression. National scandals also diverted the attention of Congress and of the people from the South. President Cleveland, after 1884, cut away the last important prop of the Southern Republican organization by bestowing Federal offices in the revenue and postal services on Democrats. In the Congress which sat from 1869 to 1871, there had been twenty Republican senators and forty-four representatives from the South. To the Congress which sat from 1889 to 1891, the South sent no Republican senators, and only three Republican representatives.[38]

One by one, Congress removed the restrictions which had been placed on the political freedom of the South.[39] After 1878, the use of the army at elections was forbidden. Last attempts were made in 1888 and 1890 to enact new Force Bills for the Federal supervision of elections. Both failed ignominiously. In 1894, the appropriations for special Federal marshals and supervisors of elections were cut off, never to be renewed. In 1898, the last disabilities laid on the disloyal and the rebellious were removed in a final Amnesty Act.

Meanwhile, the Federal courts had been handing down decisions which weakened and finally destroyed the effectiveness of the suffrage amendment and of the Federal Civil Rights Act.[40]

The legal position established by the Supreme Court is, briefly, as follows: No positive grant of the suffrage is implied either in the Fifteenth Amendment or in the Enforcing Acts passed under it. A denial of the right to vote by the States must, to make a case for the Federal courts, be on grounds of race, color, or previous condition of servitude, and such discrimination must be alleged in any indictment under the Amendment or what remains of the Enforcing Act.

It has been further established that the constitutional prohibition runs only against States, and individual offenders against franchise rights, on whatever grounds, must be sued in State courts. A commentator adds that when the rights of Negroes are curtailed by discriminatory State action, probably "the Federal Court can only declare that the State statute is unconstitutional," but can afford no remedy.[41] Finally, disfranchisement has been held not to be a tort, and the Federal courts have refused to entertain actions for damages arising out of a denial of the franchise.

These decisions were not reached without several reversals. As early as 1875, however, when the appeal from U. S. *vs.* Cruikshank came up, the Supreme Court handed down a decision which left the South to settle its problem as best it could, without judicial interference.

The problem which the South was now left free to tackle was twofold. Southerners set themselves the task of disfranchising the Negro, as the simplest method of restoring honest and efficient local governments. There was a second task, which they did not themselves visualize so clearly. How were conflicting interests among white groups to be adjusted, while at the same time preserving intact the "White Man's Party"? Internal struggles, as a matter of fact, did put a severe strain upon — even temporarily disrupted — party solidarity, and this disruption in turn brought the Negro back into Southern political life.

CHAPTER IV

THE AGRARIAN BREACH
(1876-1896)

1. JIM CROW

From 1876 to the first years of the new century, two parallel developments engaged the attention of the South. The Negro suffrage problem was met first by a series of statutory disfranchising devices, enacted during the seventies, eighties, and nineties. At the same time, class divisions, corresponding fundamentally to those of the slavery and plantation period, began to undermine white solidarity, and from 1890 to 1896, the White Man's Party was actually disrupted. Statutory disfranchisement proved insufficient to keep the Negro from the polls when both white groups solicited his support. As a result, "Negro domination" once more became an issue, and the white South once more closed its ranks, this time to take drastic steps towards Negro disfranchisement and to write them into the State constitutions.

In the period we are here to consider, efforts at social subordination went hand in hand with political repression. The racial separation laws that made a brief appearance during Presidential Reconstruction were again inscribed on Southern statute books.[1] Perhaps the earliest were the prohibitions of interracial marriage, beginning with Tennessee in 1870, and Virginia and North Carolina in 1873. From these dates on, they spread to every Southern State, and were embodied in at least three constitutions. The "Jim. Crow" law proper — prescribing racial separation in railroads and street-cars — also first appeared in Tennessee, where a permissive statute passed in 1875. The rest of the South again rapidly fell into line in the eighties and nineties, from time to time making permissive action mandatory, and adding depots, wharves, and waiting rooms to the list of public places in which separate accommodations were to be provided.

At the same time, legal action was taken to secure what white public opinion was already enforcing: the ineligibility of Negroes to be served in white hotels, barber shops, restaurants, any but restricted parts of theaters, and other places of public resort. Through laws of this sort, or simply by the action, not always silent, not always peaceful, of the sovereign white opinion, there fell to the lot of the Negro the poorer accommodations in public places, the worse districts for residence, and the more menial occupations in the economic sphere. The Negro's contacts with white manners and white tradition were restricted in the church, in fraternal orders, in unions where such existed, in libraries, and in educational institutions. His protection in the courts [2] against exploitation by landlords, creditors, and employers, and against personal violence, was not the matter of course that was at least the ideal for his white fellows.*

As these prescriptions followed, to a degree, the indications of the Black Codes, so provision for Negro education harked back to the sentiments entertained against the Freedmen's Bureau schools.† Schools were slowly established, but the

* These conditions had their repercussion on the security of white life and liberty in the South. "... The very institutions which our discriminations were at first invented to protect are soon, by the increasing bias of those very discriminations, emasculated of their proper power," says Murphy (32), going on to expatiate on the difficulty of law enforcement in a community accustomed to lynching, to unequal meting out of justice at the bar, etc. Whites as well as Negroes were lynched in the South, white tenants and sharecroppers as well as Negro fell helpless into the toils of the "anaconda mortgage."

† Even as late as 1920, Southern expenditures for Negro public schools were niggardly in comparison with the amounts given to white education. The per capita outlay in the three States most backward in this respect was in Georgia for white schools, $16.31, for Negro $2.83; in Louisiana, $25.37 and $3.49; in South Carolina, $19.33 and $2.06. In no Southern State were the appropriations for Negro schools proportioned to the colored population. Here the most backward States were South Carolina, with a population 51.4 per cent Negro to which in 1923-24 went 11 per cent of the educational appropriation; Alabama, with a population 38.4 per cent Negro, getting 9 per cent of the appropriation; and Louisiana, 38.9 per cent Negro, giving 10 per

races were of course segregated, Virginia and Kentucky leading off in 1869, the other States all following by 1885.[3] The result was naturally to leave the emancipated race with the worse accommodations.[4]

Bearing these social developments, collateral to our theme, in mind, let us now return to the political history of the South in the years from 1876 to the turn of the century.

II. "THE PEACEFUL MAJESTY OF INTELLIGENCE"

Immediately after 1876, the redeemed South bent its energies to minimize the Negro vote. It could not at once sweep the black man out of the political arena. It had still to devise adequate machinery, and in this process it was checked by Northern sentiment and by the early decisions of the Supreme Court, which for a time showed some tendency to enforce strictly the Fifteenth Amendment and the Federal election law of 1870. Almost from the beginning, too, Negro voting power was made use of in factional fights and local elections.[5] From time to time, therefore, Negroes continued to appear as voters and as members of legislative bodies. Thus, in the Mississippi Black Belt, for example, the Democracy had a "fusion" arrangement whereby certain minor posts went regularly to Negro Republicans; [6] and a Florida editor took it as a matter of course that two "tonguey but thoughtful" Negroes should sit in the constitutional convention of 1885.[7]

But the main current ran the other way: towards Negro disfranchisement. For this purpose the South had learned much from its Radical overlords, it had devised more during the Redemption, and its political inventiveness was by no means exhausted.

Intimidation, violence, and fraud, naturally, did not stop abruptly after 1876. "What a refreshingly frank piece of news that was from Jackson, Mississippi, concerning the municipal

cent of its appropriation to Negro schools. With such conditions existing in the nineteen-twenties, it may be imagined that matters were still less satisfactory in the previous half-century.

elections . . . and published by [our Democratic contemporary]," wrote a Republican editor in Tennessee in 1890. " 'Thus far no Negroes have made application to vote, and so long as such is the case, no trouble is likely to occur.' What a pleasant assurance! . . . And further on it is stated: 'There were a great many strangers in town, many of them coming here purposely to assist the Democrats. It is believed that their presence had the desired effect of preventing trouble.' What lamb-like innocence! Peace-loving Democrats stood about the polls 'to see that there was a peaceable election,' and they meant to have it or fight." [8]

Such measures, however, showed a tendency to decrease, especially since anything of the nature of rioting continued to cause bad feeling in the North. The Southern genius invented other apt extra-legal devices: [9] Polling places were set up at points remote from Negro communities. Ferries between black districts and political headquarters went "out of repair" at election time. The white voters challenged each other and Negroes promiscuously, indulged in amusing horseplay, and quarreled violently, holding the attention of their black fellow-citizens until just enough time remained for the casting of Democratic ballots. Without notice to the Negroes, the location of polling places might change, or the Negroes be told of a change which was then not carried out. The stuffing of ballot boxes and the manipulation of the count developed into fine arts. Since the uniform official ballot was not in use during the first years of the post-redemption period, it was a simple matter for some faithful servant of the Democracy to prepare a dozen or a score of tissue ballots to cast with his regular ticket. When the count was made, the law required a blindfolded man, or an election official, to withdraw the excess of ballots over registrants, and it was generally the Democratic votes which remained for canvass.

Bribery was of course an obvious tool for capturing what Negro votes remained. Our Virginia authority enables us to add a very pretty device to the more obvious ones already enumerated: "Several colored candidates would appear in the field. The whites would studiously avoid the appearance of uniting on one candidate and at the same time agree among themselves to vote in a body for only one man. In some instances the whites went so far as to put forward colored candidates to divide the colored vote." [10]

Even when the voting process was changed by law, ostensibly to check corruption and fraud, it "caused many Virginians to become ashamed." The change seemed almost to have the purpose of directing and facilitating questionable practices. "It is an open secret that, under these laws, many frauds have been perpetrated by the election officials." [11]

To such means we must suppose it was that Henry W. Grady referred in addressing the Boston Merchants Association in 1889: "It is on this, sir, that we rely in the South. Not the cowardly menace of mask or shotgun; but the peaceful majesty of intelligence and responsibility, massed and unified for the protection of its homes and the preservation of its liberties." [12]

Grady could, however, have pointed to duly promulgated statutory devices which accomplished a great deal for the "preservation of (white) liberty." For some twenty years these were the enacted expression of sentiment against Negro political privilege in the South.

Two of the most important were a heritage from Radical rule: the gerrymander, and highly centralized election codes. To them, the Democratic legislatures added the centralization of local government, poll-tax requirements, elaborate and confusing registration schemes, and devious complications of the balloting process.

Virginia, early redeemed and late forced to forthright disfranchisement, had a long period in which to develop regulations of all these types, and her history from 1871 to 1894 shows specimens of almost every variety. Reapportionment began in 1871, was employed again in 1874, in 1876, in 1878, in 1883, and in 1891.[13] The legislature of 1883 altered the congressional districts; the same session amended city charters in order to reduce the representation given large Negro communities in the city councils. In 1874, the legislature abolished the New England township system which the carpetbaggers had installed, thus taking the control of local government in the Black Belt out of the Negroes' hands.[14]

Next, petty larceny was added to the constitutional suffrage disqualifications. "This was the first time that discrimination had been made against the Negroes through legislation striking at their peculiar characteristics." The payment of a poll tax was made prerequisite to voting, a provision "aimed chiefly at the Negro." [15]

A complete new election code was enacted in 1894.[16] Registration certificates, secured long in advance of the election, had to be shown at the polling place; a change of residence or a change in the boundaries of one's precincts involved getting a new voucher. The Negro, migratory and unused to preserving documents, felt these requirements more keenly than his white neighbor, as was intended. For the actual voting, a modified form of Australian ballot was prescribed, on which the names of candidates were arranged, not by party, but by office. If other voters were waiting, time in the polling booth was limited to two and a half minutes. These requirements were called "educational." They offered obvious opportunities for keeping the Negro from the ballot, or of invalidating his vote on technicalities.

The effects of this code were to lessen bribery and effectively check the use of bogus ballots. But many illiterate voters "were practically disfranchised . . . in spite of the fact that they could receive official assistance if necessary. Many Negroes hesitated in getting a Democratic election judge to assist them in marking their ballots; others were timid or ashamed to acknowledge their ignorance; and many that attempted to vote could not correctly mark their ballots in the allotted time. In some voting precincts, from a third to a half of the ballots had to be thrown out because they were incorrectly marked. The governor of the State actually proposed in 1898 that emblems be used on the ballots to distinguish the candidates of the two parties in order to enable illiterate voters to vote as they desired. Fortunately [sic], the General Assembly did not consider this proposition." [17]

South Carolina went farthest in complicating the actual voting process. Under the election law of 1882, a special ballot and a special ballot box were required in every voting place for each office to be filled. They were properly labeled, and the election managers might read the titles on request, but no one could speak to the voter, nor insert his ballot for him; if it went into the wrong box, it was not counted.[18]

The remaining Southern States used some or all of these devices.[19]

If it is still believed in any quarter that this body of State legislation was not intended to have any bearing on the Negro as such, it still must be conceded that it was admirably adapted to bringing about black disfranchisement. "It will be noticed that the complexities of these laws are enough to confuse a mind better trained than that of the average Negro. To him, they are, for the most part, beyond comprehension. It is said that as soon as the ignorant voters began to understand the arrangement of the boxes [under the South Carolina plan], the boxes were shuffled, and many votes were lost before the order was again unraveled. It will be seen, also, that the registration books are closed on the first of July [again the example from South Carolina], while the voter has to present his registration certificate on voting day. Now, a Negro is not used to preserving papers; it frequently happens, therefore, that the certificates are lost or worn out, and they can be renewed only under certain limitations." [20] Like Virginia's petty larceny clause, "striking at the Negro's peculiar characteristics," the registration laws had some bearing, too, on the Negro's tendency, natural in a poor and landless class, to move about.

At any rate, that eloquent Southern gentleman on whom we have already drawn to enliven these pages, Henry W. Grady, felt able to write in 1890: "The Negro as a political force has dropped out of serious consideration." [21]

Now, election figures are notoriously hard to get at, and

especially since no separate count has ever been kept of the Negro vote (with a few exceptions in the sixties) it must not appear that we have attained any exact knowledge of the degree to which disfranchisement in the South was carried out in the years from 1876 to 1890. But after weighing the emotional force of the reasons, good and bad, which moved the Southerner to distrust the Negro politically; after, too, examining the elaborate structure of voting qualifications and prerequisites, obviously aimed at a political animal at least closely resembling the Negro, we are prepared for a startling decrease in the number of Negro votes, such as Dunning found in three States, between 1876 and 1884.[22] He saw a reduction of one-half in South Carolina, of one-third in Louisiana, and one-quarter in Mississippi, and estimated that by 1900 the Negro vote in the South as a whole had practically disappeared.

III. THUNDER ON THE LEFT

The process of disfranchising the Negro by statutory devices began to meet with opposition in white circles as time went on. Depending, in the letter, on tax and literacy prerequisites, it aroused the fears of the less literate and poorer rural white counties. The concern of these sections over their right to vote was strengthened, as the years after 1876 passed, by the emergence of grave issues which divided the agrarian middle class and proletariat from their Bourbon leaders in the Democratic councils, making the ballot an important weapon for them.

The economic and social antagonism between the plantation lowlands and the piedmont and hill sections of the South extended back as far almost as American history itself. So far as white solidarity existed during the Reconstruction period, "It was the necessary creation of the reconstruction policy of the Federal Administration, by which . . . discordant elements were welded into one mass, in a common, all-controlling struggle for white supremacy . . . The Democratic Party

. . . was . . . a fabric in one sense unnatural . . . composed of incongruous and unsympathetic elements." [23] These elements were by the eighties ready to crystallize out into separate and mutually destructive masses. The immediate reasons were two: agricultural depression, and a change in the character of the Bourbon leadership.

From 1870 until the close of the century the farmer throughout the whole country struggled through a period of bitter depression.[24] The Granger movement, the Farmers' Alliance, Greenbackism, and the People's Party successively claimed his allegiance against the oppressor; all rested on the same grievances. The agricultural frontier had been pushed far to the West and agricultural production immensely increased under the combined influence of demobilization, the closing of the war industries, increased immigration, the homestead laws, improved farm machinery, the expansion of the railways. The result was a marked downward trend of agricultural prices. What touched the South particularly, the average price of cotton at the farm remained consistently below the general wholesale index figure after 1875, both falling throughout the period, till cotton touched $.06 in 1898. Meanwhile, the gold dollar appreciated 200 per cent between 1865 and 1895, with a sharp peak in the late seventies, coinciding with the Greenback movement, and another in the early nineties, the heyday of Populism.

Under these circumstances, the farmer's wrath turned on the financial powers that had foreclosed during the crash of 1873, and that kept up interest rates in spite of the fall in price of farm products. It turned on the railroads, whose rate favors were all for the large corporations and for the towns and cities, who abused his early confidence by watering the stock he had bought in them, who held millions of fertile acres for a speculative rise. It turned on the corporations whose tariff demands, too easily granted by a complaisant government, raised the cost of his manufactured purchases. It turned on the government itself for the taxes which fell so heavily on the easily assessed property and improvements of the farm, and for "Wall Street's" sound money policy which "crucified mankind upon a cross of gold."

In the South, the discontented farmer had only one going political concern — the Democratic party — to work through. On account of the recent experience with "Negro domination," all classes in the South were now committed to this party, as the means of maintaining "white supremacy." The Democratic party of the South was, however, controlled by conservative interests.[25]

Party leadership was no longer solely vested in the once slave-holding plantation-owner. Into his place there had stepped figures not altogether new, indeed, in the South, but of a new significance in the era of industrialism and business enterprise. Some of the old aristocracy adapted themselves to the new methods in agriculture and retained both estates and influence, although by the eighties "social prestige no longer depended upon the ownership of land" as in the days before the war.[26] Others drifted into the honorific professions, especially the law, and so kept in touch both with politics and business. Still others, although shorn of economic power, retained political influence through family and personal prestige; these picturesque survivors of "befo' de Wah" were often useful to the new political leaders, as window dressing of guaranteed Confederate quality.

The new men in Democratic councils were of two groups: the industrialist, and the financier and "merchant farmer." The first embraced those progressive individuals who were heeding the warning of Benjamin Hill, uttered in 1871: "We have refused to mine our metals and give employment to our water-powers . . . This process cannot continue. Our coal and iron will not always sleep in the shallow earth because we think it unbecoming the social position of an educated gentleman to wake them up and lift them out . . . Nor will the educated laborers of other states and countries always, or even much longer, send here, and freight away, at great expense and labor, our raw materials for foreign shops to manufacture." [27] The industrialist had a hold on the voters not a little strengthened by the "curious sort of prestige, as of public affairs" [28] which quite naturally attached to the venturesome and on the whole unprecedented business of developing Southern resources.

The South began to develop native bankers and merchant farmers. Through the "anaconda mortgage," these men secured control over a considerable portion of land, and during the agricultural depression used this power remorselessly to reduce independent farmers to the status of share croppers and tenants, or to replace them with cheap Negro labor.[29]

Such "new Bourbons" as these gathered around the Confederate hero Wade Hampton for the Redemption of South Carolina in 1876, and ran the State from that time till 1890.[30] In Georgia, a triumvirate composed of a plantation-owner and two promoters of railroads and industrial enterprises shared in rotation the offices of governor and United States Senator throughout the seventies and early eighties. None of these men "was personally representative of the small or middle-class farmers . . ." Thus, "The new Bourbon régime in Georgia was essentially a business man's régime. To a greater or less extent this was doubtless true of other Southern States." [31]

Such a régime was naturally the target of the agricultural radical, the perennial debtor, and, in a period which was full of disaster for him, his protest brought on a political revolution.

He demanded for the South the "Granger laws" which were being enacted in the Middle West in the seventies and eighties; the regulation of railroad rates; State aid for agriculture in the form particularly of State Boards of Agriculture and agricultural colleges; the lightening of his tax burdens and heavier imposts on corporate activities; the scaling down of State indebtedness whose interest charges went into his tax bills.[32] He looked, too, for a national party which, more than the Democracy, would push his interests at Washington.

With these issues in the air, the agrarian-radical group was not anxious to entrust its right to vote to the new election laws of the period. The rebelliously inclined felt that while these laws might further put down "niggerism" and Republicanism, their poll-tax clauses, their eight-ballot-box arrangements, their nonpartisan ballot specifications would of themselves hit the poor and the illiterate rural voter; and further that administrative provisions for throwing out misplaced and surplus ballots, for "helping" the illiterate voter, for a time-limit on the voters' stay in the polling booth *could be made* to hit the poor and illiterate voter. In so far as these measures struck at the Negro, they pleased both white groups; but their possible incidence on white voters could please only the Bourbons.

It seems possible that the vicissitudes of the Tennessee poll-tax requirement are to be traced to lower-class suspicion and opposition: enacted in 1870, it was suspended in 1871, and repealed in 1873.[33] For the same reason, Florida ignored the franchise provisions of her constitution of 1868, which called for the application of a literacy test after 1880.[34] When in 1885 it was proposed to enact a poll-tax requirement, for local protection against the Negro, it was immediately pointed out that the Black Belt needed no protection against Negro county government, since the County Commissioners were appointed by the safely white and Democratic central administration.[35]

The famous eight-ballot-box election law, accompanied by a stringent registration code, was debated in the South Carolina legislature throughout the session of 1881-82, when agrarian discontent was at a high pitch. The final vote was several times postponed amid much wrangling. The report of a special "harmonizing" committee revealed plainly between the lines that the objectors to it were not only Republican and Negro. A Democratic legislator, endangering himself, doubtless, with his party leaders, opposed entrusting a single supervisor with the power to determine the legal qualifications of voters: "The bill was doubtless intended for a wise purpose, but it might be made the engine of oppression." [36]

These examples might be multiplied indefinitely. When a stringent registration and election law was passed in Virginia in 1883, it was the target of agrarian-radical shafts.[37] In 1900 "it was generally admitted by men of all parties" in Virginia "that the Negroes were being defrauded at the polls and that those who had charge of the party machinery in local elections *often treated the whites who differed with them in the same fashion.*" [38] The Alabama dissidents opposed the Sayre election bill of 1893.[39] The Louisiana agrarians even joined the remnants of local Republicanism in 1892, charging that "the State electoral machinery was in the hands of the democratic politicians, that the republicans alone could not secure a fair count of the vote . . ." [40]

The discontented farmer of the white counties had still other grievances against the regular Democratic politicians of the Black Belt. His influence, he felt, was already too much handicapped by overrepresentation of the Black Belt, and by the tenacity with which the Bourbons clung to office.

Representation, both in the State legislatures and in the party conventions, was based on population. Thus it overweighted, as in the days before the war, the influence of the Bourbon Black Belt, where Negroes, who had no share in the "white man's government" save at the behest of ward politicians, were nevertheless counted into the representation base. The black counties were of course well satisfied. In South Carolina, "Pitchfork Ben" Tillman, the agrarian leader, fulminated against the legislature for failing to carry out the required decennial reapportionment.[41]

The preponderance of Bourbons, old and new, in office also infuriated the rank and file. "Do they want every office?" demanded an often disappointed up-country leader. "Is there not some way to satisfy their greed for office? Parties are not made for the advancement of individuals and families. The door must be left open to all . . . The autocratic and aristocratic leaders will be driven to the wall whenever the issue is made up between them and the mass of the people." [42]

But the issue was still not to be joined for some time. Threats of revolt within Democratic lines were met with appeals from the Bourbon leadership to stand firm against the danger of a Negro balance of power.

It had been a real danger as well as a real fear of a Negro balance of power which in 1868 inspired Benjamin Hill's impassioned appeal for white solidarity: "I charge you this day, as you honor your children and your household, and would preserve your good name for your posterity, never suffer a single native renegade who votes for the vassalage of these States, and the disgrace of your children and your race, to darken your doors, or to speak to any member of your family." [43]

By the eighties, there was no longer the menace of "Black Republicanism." Irregularity among Democrats now called down similar Olympian thunders. "Storms of abuse have pursued me without pity or cessation," wrote Tom Watson, leader of the agrarian rebels in Georgia. "Slander has nailed me to her cross, and bitter hatred has broken me on her wheel." [44] The Bourbons warned that any defection from the white man's party would inevitably bring in the Negro, with his undoubted legal right to vote, either to redress the political balance, or — what was worse — to seize the loosened reins of white domination. In a letter dated 1882, Hill adjured a Georgia agrarian leader against "re-opening the race issue" by "encouraging local division among the Democrats of the South on any and all questions that are available for the purpose" and by "blatant pretences of reform, and still more blatant outcries against that mythical monster — the Bourbon Democracy of the South." [45]

"Many wise men hold that the white vote of the South should divide, the color line be beaten down, and the Southern states ranged on economic or moral questions as interest or belief demands," said Henry Grady. "I am compelled to dissent from this view. The worst thing that could happen, in my opinion, is that the white people of the South should stand in opposing factions, with the vast mass of ignorant or purchasable Negro votes between." [46]

As the farmers' plight grew worse, however, and nationwide agrarian organizations spread into the South, the revolt overrode such arguments as these.

IV. THE EMBATTLED FARMER

The first of the new organizations was the National Grange, or the Patrons of Husbandry, which flourished from 1868 to 1874. Nonpartisan to begin with, it was further kept within bounds in the South because of the then still present danger of Negro-Radical rule. Nevertheless, it was symptomatic of discontent, for it was eagerly taken up by the Southern farmer, who was well organized in 1874. After 1875, the strength of the Grange waned, in the North as well as the South, sapped by unwise coöperative enterprises and by the hostility of its business enemies.[47]

The Southern Farmers' Alliance made its first appearance after 1873. It grew with amazing rapidity.[48] Under various names, organizations appeared in State after State, from year to year carrying through interstate and regional mergers, until in 1889 the two most important coalitions in the South united as the National Farmers' Alliance and Industrial Union. This body a year later claimed three million members. Meanwhile, the Farmers' Alliance of the Northwest had also made itself an important factor in its own territory.

This organization took up the political weapon. In some Southern States it ran independent candidates, in some it affiliated itself with the Greenback party, in others it worked through the remains of Republicanism, in several it captured the regular Democracy. Finally, at conventions held in Cincinnati and Omaha in 1891 and 1892, the enthusiasm of the Southern agricultural radical was won for the People's Party.[49]

Even before the climactic struggles which now ensued, bitter political fights between the white factions had disturbed the peace of Southern States. During the course of such battles, the temptation was often irresistible to use Negro voters against the opposition, and, during the eighties and nineties, renewed attempts were made on the part of both groups to tighten the statutory restrictions, already described, which kept the Negro from the polls. It is difficult to determine whether this legislation originated wholly in the dislike of all groups for "political niggerism," or in a desire to lessen the hazards and expense of the internecine white struggle. But since during these years the Bourbon elements remained in control of the States, it is not difficult to see why the bolters, the agrarian independents, were moved now and again to oppose the restrictive legislation which might handicap them rather than the party in control of the electoral machinery, both in putting forth their own full strength at the polls and in offsetting Bourbon Negro votes with agrarian-radical Negro votes.

From the middle eighties onwards, both parties charged each other with every species of fraud.[50] The devices of Reconstruction and the Redemption were refurbished: massing at the polls to keep the opposition voters from the ballot box,[51] breaking up meetings by strong-arm methods,[52] repeating, throwing out ballots on technicalities,[53] even the threat of arms, if not actual warfare.

The year 1890 was the high-water mark of the agrarian movement in the South. It gained a sweeping victory in Georgia. It secured complete control of the Democratic organization of South Carolina, electing Benjamin Tillman governor, gaining an overwhelming majority in both houses of the State legislature, winning one national senatorship, and seating a majority of the State's delegation to the House. In Tennessee, the president of the State Alliance was elected governor. It was an off-year for State elections in Virginia, North Carolina, Mississippi, Louisiana, and Kentucky, but five out of ten congressmen sent up from Virginia were pledged to the Alliance platform, eight out of nine from North Carolina, two out of seven from Mississippi, four out of eleven from Kentucky. In the South as a whole, about forty national representatives and several senators were committed to the Alliance. The farmers of Florida and Texas dictated the platforms of the winning parties.[54]

But in the heat of these battles, and especially in the Populist contests of 1892 and 1896, the direst prophecies of the regular Democracy came true: the statutory restrictions designed to keep out the Negro proved inadequate in the face of the white division. The South saw a great increase in corruption and intimidation, both of whites and blacks, and a recrudescence of overt violence in many cases comparable to the stormy days of early Reconstruction and the Redemption. The Negro vote was used by both sides, but it is thought that the regular Democrats, by reason of their Reconstruction experience and their control of the State administrations, were more successful at the game.[55]

The Louisiana Democrats in February, 1892, received forty cases of Winchester rifles and thirteen boxes of cartridges, explaining, "We are providing ourselves with these simply to protect ourselves against any scheme, armed or otherwise, to deny us a 'free ballot and a fair count' in the coming election . . . [We have heard] that . . . the machinery of the existing State administration was to be used" against the regular ticket.[56] In Georgia, the Bourbons carried the day. "Many of the planters and owners of turpentine stills took their 'hands' to the polls and voted them in gangs. In some of the towns and cities, all-night revelries were held for the darkies on the night before the election. Barbecue was served, with beer and whisky by the barrel. Next morning the dusky revelers were marched to the polls by beat of drum, carefully guarded lest some desert in search of another reward. In some cities bands of them were said to have been taken from one polling place to another and voted under different names . . . The evidence further indicates that the 'job-lash' was used by at least one of the Augusta mills to force employees, white and black, to vote 'regular' . . . The Democrats were not the only sinners, to be sure; but they were more resourceful, and hence more successful." [57] These scenes of 1892 were repeated in the succeeding campaigns.

Another account told of the Louisiana elections of 1896. Here the agrarian party figured as the aggressors. "The campaign was marked by much disorder and some bloodshed, the most serious outbreaks occurring in the parish of St. Landry, a strong populist center. Many of these grew out of registration troubles. It is alleged that after the sheriff failed to appear on account of threats to his life, republicans and populists took possession of the town of Washington, on April 3d, and 'went through the form of registering the Negroes.' Counter action was taken by organized bands of white men, presumably democrats, who, under the name of 'Regulators,' undertook to maintain white supremacy by whipping and killing Negroes in an effort to intimidate them. . . . The situation became so serious that state troops had to be sent to maintain order in the parish.

"The state election, which took place April 21st, was one of the most disorderly ever held in Louisiana. Charges of fraud, intimidation at the polls, and ballot-box stuffing were too numerous to mention. Twice the militia had to be called out to down riots. The democrats won as usual, but with greatly reduced majorities." [58]

CHAPTER V

DISFRANCHISEMENT
(1890-1908)

I. PEACE

There were now additional reasons for dealing drastically with Negro suffrage. As long as the Negro could vote, it was argued, the whites could not hope to prevent corruption, and dared not divide along lines of natural political cleavages. The better class of politicians and citizens in both groups were altogether disgusted with the fraud that seemed necessarily involved in the franchise situation as it stood. The regular politicians were perfectly willing to cut out the expense and trouble of gathering in Negro voters if by a sort of disarmament treaty they could get their opponents to do likewise. The independents wanted administrative discretion in the application of the election laws strictly circumscribed so that these laws could not be diverted from their proper use — against the Negro — and turned on them.

Negro disfranchisement thus again became a leading issue from 1890 onward. Sometimes the demand came from the white counties, seeking protection against the use of the Negro by Black Belt politicians,[1] sometimes, where "the more responsible of the democrats" took alarm, from the Bourbon party.[2] In Georgia and in South Carolina definite deals over Negro disfranchisement, engineered by the agrarian leaders Tom Watson and Benjamin Tillman, swung the farmers' vote back to Democratic regularity.[3] Everywhere, after the agrarian movement as a national political force had collapsed in 1896, disfranchisement helped to reunite the South. "Political niggerism" was an issue on which the vast majority of Southerners thought alike.

There were, however, two difficulties in the way of disfranchisement: The Fifteenth Amendment still ran against overtly racial discriminations, and yet any scheme aimed at the Negro but cast in general terms must be so framed as not to exclude white citizens. We have already seen how unfavorably the poorer white electorate tended to regard the statutory election codes of the seventies, eighties, and early nineties. The new movement was indeed in part designed to safeguard more rigidly the suffrage rights of dissident whites. In the debates over new suffrage restrictions, this necessity was often pointed out, and not a few veterans of the agrarian revolt showed how double-edged a weapon disfranchisement might prove to be.

In this perplexity, God, "who," according to Senator J. Z. George of Mississippi, "raises up a servant for every great emergency," inspired one McGehee to invent several of the key devices under which it became possible for the South to disfranchise the Negro without contravening the Federal constitution, or, on their surface, cutting out any white voters.[4]

These were adopted by the Mississippi constitutional convention of 1890. Seven States followed Mississippi's lead between 1895 and 1910, improving, in some cases, on the early model. The others continued to rely on statutory methods.[5]

The requirements of the eight States with disfranchising constitutions were on the whole similar.[6] They perpetuated, in the first place, certain devices of the statutory election codes: A poll tax or other taxes must be paid by the applicant for registration. Registration was to take place months in advance of polling time, and a receipt for taxes paid must be shown to either registration or election officials, or to both. It was left to the officials, actually though not necessarily in law, to ask for these receipts, so that the Negro voter, unused to preserving documents, could often be disfranchised through sheer carelessness on his part.

Among the new features introduced was the property qualification. This ran to two or three hundred dollars. One or more alternative qualifications might be offered by the would-be voter. Crude literacy — reading and writing — was one. Another was a sort of civic "understanding," tested by the ability to interpret the State or Federal constitution to the satisfaction of the election officer. "Good character" might also qualify, when supported by sworn testimonials, or by evidence of steady employment during a specified preceding period, or by an affidavit giving the names of employers for a period varying from three to five years. The property and literacy qualifications cut out large numbers of Negroes automatically; the alternatives could easily be manipulated by the officers in charge.

In addition, residence requirements were greatly extended throughout the Southern States, and the list of crimes involving disfranchisement diversified until it included petty larceny, wife-beating, and similar offenses peculiar to the Negro's low economic and social status.[7] To safeguard whites of low intelligence or small property, the so-called "grandfather clauses" were devised. For a period of years after the adoption of the respective constitutions, permanent registration without tax or other prerequisites was secured either to persons who had the vote prior to 1861 and their descendants; or to persons who had served in the Federal or Confederate Armies or in the State militias and to their descendants. This exemption from tests obviously ran only for whites.*

From only one State — Louisiana — are reliable figures available to show what the new constitutions did. They are sufficiently impressive. For the 1896 national election, the last before the disfranchising code, there were registered in the State 130,344 Negroes; Negro registrants were in the majority in 26 parishes. For the 1900 national election, two years after the adoption of the new constitution, there were registered only 5320 Negroes, and no parishes showed a majority of Negro registrants. While Negro registration fell off by 125,000 — 96 per cent — white registration decreased by only 30,000.[8]

* These "grandfather clauses" have now all expired according to their own terms. The Supreme Court, too, has held them unconstitutional under the Fifteenth Amendment; Guinn *v.* U. S., 238 U. S. 347 (1914).

II. THE WHITE MAN'S BURDEN

The new Southern constitutions embodied a theory of qualified suffrage based on the tested fitness of the voter. The theory was most broadly stated in the Virginia Convention of 1901-02: "... No person should enjoy the privilege of suffrage unless he, in some way, gives (in the language of the Bill of Rights) sufficient evidence of his permanent common interest in and attachment to the community ..." In the actual constitution, here as in other Southern States, "sufficient evidence" meant "conspicuous and deserving public service" (the exemption of war veterans from all tests, e.g.), "participation in the public burden" (poll-tax and property-holding qualifications), or "substantial contribution, not in the form of property, to the industry, development, and welfare of the State" (literacy, "character," and "understanding" tests).[9]

The proponent of the qualified suffrage theory stands in a defensible position. "We say, and we justly say, that it is not by mere numbers, but by property and intelligence that the nation should be governed," argued Macaulay during the English suffrage debates of 1831. To this day, Massachusetts and New York, among Northern States, require literacy of their voters.

The incapacity of the Negro race for "self-government and the intelligent exercise of the power of voting" [10] was put forth from Reconstruction well into the twentieth century. "What has the Negro race accomplished ... indeed, during the whole period of their existence on earth?" demanded an Arkansas Conservative.[11] "Where is its language? ... its literature? ... its arts, its sciences? Where are its commercial interests, its ships, its flag? It has none. I repeat, it has none!"* This view has always been strongly buttressed by arguments showing the Negro's lack of intelligence and moral stamina.

* This speaker was prepared to make some concessions to Africa: "I will admit that there have been many ... great Africans ... Hannibal was, indeed, an African; but ... his hair was straight; he had high cheek bones; he was not black. Neither was he a white man, but something of a walnut color."

The Negro, nevertheless, from the seventies to the opening years of the century made considerable forward strides in the culture of the white population around him. In this, of course, he was doing nothing different from what he had already done in the pre-war period, when the very contacts of slavery, as the masters themselves pointed out, were a force for assimilation.[12] Negro illiteracy decreased between 1870 and 1890 from 79.9 per cent to 57.1 per cent, and by 1900 to 44.5 per cent.[13] Secondary, collegiate, and technical institutions came into being, supported by Negroes as well as by white philanthropy, sending out an increasing number of Negro holders of the undergraduate degree.[14] A few Negroes in the ordinary universities in the North were meanwhile demonstrating their capacity to profit by the best collegiate instruction available. The Negro professional group grew from next to nothing at the close of the war to 34,000 in 1890 and 47,000 in 1900.[15]

Such advances as these were creating in the United States a Negro community modeled, as far as poverty, lack of educational opportunity, and subordination allowed, upon the surrounding white culture, and centering in 1890 about 1,800,000 homes. Of these homes, almost 265,000 were owned by their Negro occupants — a figure which rose by 1900 to some 397,000.[16]

It had become, therefore, less and less possible, between 1870 to 1900, to make blanket statements that "the intelligent freedman is but a drop in the bucket," [17] that the Negro had no stake in the community, that he was shiftless and incapable of advancement.[18]

Nevertheless, the framers of the new Southern suffrage codes were committed to complete Negro disfranchisement.*

* Their frankness in debate, it was feared, might endanger the new constitutions when adopted, should their suffrage clauses come up in a Federal court under the Fifteenth Amendment. It was therefore "suggested that by abolishing the stenographic report the members can discuss the question . . . without leaving a record of their remarks . . . Several attempts have been made to abolish the stenographic reports, but they have uniformly failed" (Birmingham *Age-Herald*, 15 July 1901). These fears were common; they

All sorts of suffrage clauses were proposed from the floor of the 1901 Alabama convention, but "Many . . . are wasted on the desert air. Some of the delegates pay no attention to them . . . What they want is a scheme pure and simple which will let every white man vote and prevent any Negro from voting." A poll-tax requirement would not suffice for the purpose, because the records showed that large numbers of Negroes paid their taxes, sometimes more readily than white citizens. Even the grandfather clause, especially designed to let the illiterate and propertyless white slip by, was dangerous, because "there are in Alabama as in all the States, large numbers of Negroes, who perhaps would be unable to establish legitimacy of birth, but could nevertheless easily establish the identity of white fathers or grandfathers" and thus win a vote.[19] Negro literacy was discussed as a "threat" in the Virginia convention of 1901-02; a delegate adding that "there is no educational test founded upon the simple rudiments of mechanical learning that can keep [the Negro] from the ballot box. One half of all the Negro electorate in this State can read and write at the present day . . . and two-thirds of all those under twenty-one years of age can read and write . . ." [20] Senator Vardaman of Mississippi was "opposed to Negro voting; it matters not what his advertised mental and moral qualifications may be. I am just as much opposed to Booker Washington as a voter, with all his Anglo-Saxon reënforcements, as I am to the cocoanut-headed, chocolate-colored, typical little coon, Andy Dotson, who blacks my shoes every morning. Neither is fit to perform the

reveal a consciousness on the part of the delegates that the Amendment was being violated at least in spirit. V. Natchez *Democrat*, 22 July, 23 August 1890; Raleigh *News and Observer*, 22 January 1899; e.g. Hence movements for the repeal of the Amendment; e.g., resolution of the Mississippi legislature calling upon Congress, Natchez *Democrat*, 1 October 1890. On the other hand, when a Georgia legislator opposed disfranchising measures on constitutional grounds, as a matter of conscience, an Atlanta editor asked: "Why let a small obstacle like an oath to support the Federal constitution stand in the way? Shall 'conscience make cowards' of the legislature? Surely the public conscience is entitled to some consideration" (Atlanta *Constitution*, 27 July 1907).

supreme function of citizenship." [21] The only real safeguard against the effects of regular appropriations and Northern charitable contributions for Negro schooling, said Senator Tillman to the South Carolina legislature,[22] was the repeal of the Fifteenth Amendment.*

The clearest admission of the intent of the new disfranchising devices came from Virginia. Here it was plainly stated that the *administration* of the new election code was to bar Negro voters who might meet the letter of the law. "The committee is not blind to the fact that this is not an ideal test . . . But it would not be frank in me, Mr. Chairman, if I did not say that I do not expect [it] to be administered with any degree of friendship by the white man to the suffrage of the black man. I expect the examination with which the black man will be confronted, to be inspired with the same spirit that inspires every man in this convention . . . I would not expect for the white man a rigid examination. The people of Virginia do not stand impartially between the suffrage of the white man and the suffrage of the black man. If they did, the uppermost thoughts in the hearts of every man within the sound of my voice would not be to find a way of disfranchising the black man and enfranchising the white man. We do not come here prompted by an impartial purpose in reference to Negro suffrage . . . Again, I expect this clause to be efficient, because it will act 'in terrorem' on the Negro race. They believe that they will have a hostile examination put upon them by the white man . . . and they will not apply for registration." Later, it was asked whether the elimination of

* Dislike of the educated Negro on other than political grounds still further impairs the ingenuousness of arguments for disfranchisement based on ignorance. Mr. Watson of the Virginia Convention of 1901-02 opposed educational tests because he felt they did injustice as between faithful old servants and the new educated Negroes: "Now, sir, the old-time Negro is assassinated by this suffrage plan. But this new issue—your reader, your writer, your loafer, your voter, your ginger-cake school graduate, with a diploma of side-whiskers and beaver hat, pocket pistols, brass knucks, and bicycle—he, sir, is the distinguished citizen whom our statesmen would crown at once with the highest dignities of an ancient and respectable Commonwealth" (Debates, vol. ii, 3070).

the Negro would not be accomplished by "fraud and discrimination" under the plan finally adopted. The author, later U. S. Senator Carter Glass, replied: "By fraud, no; by discrimination, yes. But it will be discrimination within the letter of the law . . . Discrimination! Why, that is precisely what we propose; that, exactly, is what this convention was elected for — to discriminate to the very extremity of permissible action under the limitations of the Federal Constitution, with a view to the elimination of every Negro voter who can be gotten rid of, legally, without materially impairing the numerical strength of the white electorate . . . It is a fine discrimination, indeed, that we have practiced in the fabrication of this plan." [23]

This "fine discrimination" was of course also apparent from the care taken to provide all possible loopholes for white voters, illiterate and propertyless though they might be. In behalf of the mountaineers of western Virginia, who were not only poor and illiterate but in many cases Republican as well, a delegate admonished the disfranchising convention:

> "Let not ambition mock their useful toil,
> Their homely virtues or destiny obscure;
> Or grandeur hear with a disdainful smile
> The short and simple annals of the poor." [24]

The Democratic party in Alabama, Virginia, North Carolina, and Georgia went on record with pledges to disfranchise no whites save for crime.[25] Both Louisiana and Mississippi claimed the honor of having invented the "grandfather clause" and the series of alternative tests through which racial discrimination was to be accomplished; both congratulated themselves on having discovered an "*elastic* test — that is, a test which could be interpreted by registration or election officers to exclude most of the Negroes and to include most of the whites." [26]

It was evident, therefore, that the attitude of the South had not effectively changed since Reconstruction, when four

Southern States rejected, or tacked riders to their ratification of the Thirteenth and Fourteenth Amendments, in order to guard against Negro suffrage; when Louisiana and Mississippi rejected the advice of friendly presidents to confer a limited Negro suffrage; when the Congressional Reconstruction code called down storms of sweeping abuse for its Negro suffrage provisions.

III. THE POST-PRANDIAL NON-SEQUITUR

A distinctive line of reasoning against Negro suffrage started from the Southerner's fear of "social equality" — what, after H. G. Wells, may be called the post-prandial non-sequitur. Mr. Wells wrote of a Southerner who told how an ostensibly white man married a white girl and begot coal-black offspring: "This story of the lamentable results of intermarriage was used, not as an argument against intermarriage, but as an argument against the extension of quite rudimentary civilities to men of colour. 'If you eat with them, you've got to marry them,' he said, an entirely fabulous post-prandial responsibility." [27] Similarly, if you let them vote, you've got to let them marry your daughters.

Such coupling of political and social privileges into a single nightmare started very early in the struggle over Negro suffrage. Political equality will lead to social equality; and the two together are "the stepping-stone to miscegenation." "In enfranchising the Negro, you make him your political and social equal. It is to invite him into your house, and make him the companion of your social hours. In my opinion, if he should be enfranchised, he would be taken into the parlors of all that vote for him — to marry their daughters, and, if necessary, hug their wives." [28] This was the burden during Reconstruction. During the Redemption period, the KuKlux Klan and its sister organizations made this matter one of their chief concerns. One ritual set forth: "It becomes our solemn duty . . . to maintain . . . the supremacy of the Caucasian race, and restrain the . . . African race to that position of social and political inferiority for which God has ordained it . . . As an essential condition of success, this Order proscribes absolutely all social equality between the races. If we were to admit persons of African race on the same level with ourselves, a state of personal relations would follow which would unavoidably lead to political equality . . ." [29] With the agrarian revolt, Henry W. Grady was moved to warn the South that "by dividing" politically, it was "destroy[ing] the defences of its social integrity"; "This alien influence [the Negro] that holds the balance of power . . . must be bought by race privileges as such." [30]

In the disfranchising conventions of the nineties and thereafter, the "post-prandial non-sequitur" seems not to have appeared. The sentiment on which it was based, though, still existed, and was inscribed on Southern statute books through the various Jim Crow laws. And it was still a damning charge against any white politician to say that he "fraternized" with Negroes. [31]

IV. LEAD US NOT INTO TEMPTATION

The dread best and most continuously substantiated by the history of Negro suffrage was that of accompanying corruption. The inevitability of enfranchisement by the Arkansas convention of 1868 called forth the prophecy that political debauchery would follow to "shame Catiline or Danton." [32] This was a favorite note with Henry W. Grady, sounded particularly, be it noted, in the late eighties, when the agrarian revolt was splitting the solid white Democratic vote. "If the [Negro] vote was not compacted," he declared, "it would invite the debauching bid of factions, and drift surely to that which was the most corrupt and cunning . . . Perhaps in time the bulk of [the] race may adjust itself. But, through what long and monstrous periods of political debauchery this status would be reached, no tongue can tell." Again, "Let the whites divide, what happens? Here is this dangerous and alien influence that holds the balance of power. It cannot be won by argument, for it is without information, understanding, or traditions . . . It must be bought by race privileges granted as such, or by money paid outright . . ." [33] In the Virginia convention of 1901, a delegate still spoke prospectively of the danger of corruption: When the whites divide, said Mr. Gordon, "you will have the white men of your State bidding for the Negro vote against each other." [34]

It is hardly necessary here to attempt to demonstrate that Southern elections since the beginning of Reconstruction were notably corrupt, and that this corruption grew out of the presence of the Negro. The fact has been quite generally admitted by Southern politicians and publicists, and made, indeed, what is perhaps the most convincing, least *a priori*, argument in the Southern brief. Grady himself, having shown how "every approach to the ballot box" must be "debauched" by the presence of the Negro, continued: "It is against such campaigns as these — *the folly and the danger and the bitterness of which every Southern community has drunk deeply* — that the white people of the South are banded together." [35] Especially for the period of white independency, culminating in the restrictive constitutions, were such admissions general. "The system under which we are now living is crushing the intelligence of the State." [36] "I believe that the greatest evil flowing from Negro suffrage has been that it has polluted the sources of governmental power, that the poison . . . if allowed to go, would have made a mass of reeking corruption of the social and political order of this State." [37]

Similar expressions were common in all the deliberative bodies of the disfranchising period. A member of the Georgia legislature "hoped never to see again the scenes witnessed [in 1892], when Negroes were herded like sheep, and their votes bought and sold." [38] An Alabama convention delegate recounted how "Both Republicans and Democrats had to buy [Negroes] and it made it quite expensive [laughter]. He himself had never bought a vote, but he had chipped in to the campaign fund [laughter]. Negro voters had gone to ten dollars a piece, and, Mr. President, it makes it awful on our people [laughter] . . . The Republicans . . . are as anxious to get rid of the Negroes as we are . . . [applause]." [39]

Perhaps disfranchisement, even by force and fraud, was called for during Reconstruction, when the unlettered freedman, the "janizary of party tyranny," [40] was corrupted by the alien Republican carpetbaggers, and the white South cut off from ordinary political redress by Congressional proscriptions. But, during the 1890-1910 period, why was not corruption struck at in some more direct fashion than by aiming at the complete disfranchisement of the Negro?

The more drastic purge was repeatedly alleged to be absolutely necessary for the purification of politics, e.g. in Virginia. When qualifications for voting less severe than those finally adopted were proposed to the convention of 1901-02, the reply was: "Our objection . . . to the plan proposed by the minority is that it is not efficient . . . that it is based on an erroneous conception of what the problem really is . . . it . . . relegates us again to the very condition which the fond hopes of our people believe we can relieve them from . . . because the problem is not the political supremacy of the black man . . . that question . . . has been settled . . . forever . . . We do not fear his numbers. We fear his presence . . . As long as he is with us in any numbers, our curse is still upon us . . . He will still be a destroyer of our political standards, because there will always be a large faction among the white people of Virginia that will continue to justify anything that will keep the black man out and put the white man in political control . . ." [41]

This, to the South, was the lesson of the agrarian revolt. The only alternative to corruption and fraud was a complete white solidarity, or total Negro disfranchisement. White solidarity it had been impossible to maintain, nor did it seem desirable after the events of the eighties and nineties. "With the Negro out of politics," said Representative Bankhead, explaining Alabama's 1901 constitution to Congress, "I believe the time would come when Alabama would be divided between two great parties . . . and that elections would be decided by the candidate and the issues . . . This cannot be as long as the Negro question remains unsettled." [42] As long as there were Negro voters, their influence would be sought by whites, sometimes corruptly. Corruptly and fraudulently, too, other whites would seek to counter this influence. Corruption and fraud would then infect the casting and the counting of white votes. This corruption and fraud — it seemed to the South — had to be reached by means of complete Negro disfranchisement, not by political education and carefully safeguarded election laws, "because the white people . . . will continue to justify anything that will keep the black man out."

V. THE WHITE MAN IN THE WOODPILE

With such strong convictions on the Negro's inferiority as a citizen, and on the "social" menace and the threat to clean politics involved in Negro suffrage, the disfranchising States should have passed their restrictive constitutions with dispatch, and almost without discussion. As a matter of fact, the convention and legislative debates on disfranchisement, and the plebiscite campaigns when the new constitutions were put to the vote, were as heated as any the troubled South had witnessed since the Civil War.

The late agrarian rebels evidently not only remembered the corrupt use of the earlier statutory disfranchising measures against themselves, but apprehended more and worse from the infinitely more complicated and constitutionally fixed schemes which were now proposed. It has been pointed out that the franchise qualifications were especially designed to exclude Negroes and to admit whites; but responsibility for exercising the proper discrimination rested necessarily in the hands of the local administrative officials. The great centralization of electoral machinery in the South, extending even to the appointment of the registration and election officials in whose hands this discretion lay, gave additional color to the apprehensions of the politically irregular. This centralization was partly a heritage from the days of Radicalism, when the Republican administrations created centrally appointed registration and election officials, and gave sweeping powers of review to Boards of Control generally composed of the three highest State officers. Having seen how well these devices served the Republicans in prolonging their grip on the Southern polity, the returning Conservatives retained them, in order to continue the good fight against "Negro domination." But what was to prevent the Bourbon wing of the Democracy from using them against the agrarian faction? Obviously, whatever group was in power under one of these highly centralized election codes was at a great advantage — if it cared to be unscrupulous — in a fight to retain office.

Since the new constitutional tests centered in literacy, taxpaying, and property-owning prerequisites, they carried a definite threat of disfranchisement for the poor and illiterate rural and mountain counties. On the other hand, there was no guarantee, except the promises of politicians, that the richer Black Belt would give up its Negro mercenaries.

In this background, it may easily be understood why the irregular elements at the time of the disfranchising conventions and legislatures should again and again insist that the eight-ballot-box law, the ballot without party designations, the poll-tax certificate requirement, centralization, and the other statutory devices, together with the newly developed "white primary," sufficiently guaranteed the South against "Negro domination." Even under the old regulations, it was argued, white voters offensive to the State machine could be — and were — disfranchised. What would happen under the vague "good character" and "understanding" tests? [43]

A week before the Mississippi disfranchising convention met, a newspaper of independent politics said: "Altogether this body will meet under phenomenal circumstances . . . There have been no burdens, grievances, or hardships under which the people have suffered, for the removal of which the convention has been ordered to assemble; there have been pointed out no specific changes to be made by any general voice of the people . . ." When the "understanding" clause was proposed to the convention, this editor bitterly opposed it under the rubric "That Abomination," and cited other papers in support of his statement that the people opposed it. On the floor of the convention it was once stricken out, and many times considered and reconsidered. [44]

In Georgia, a member of the legislature wrote: "It is by no means certain . . . that there is now any real popular demand for [a disfranchising] scheme. There is a demand for pure elections . . . As a separate issue [disfranchisement] has not yet been passed on by the people . . ." [45]

As to the necessity for further disfranchisement, " . . . At present white domination in local offices is as complete as the superior race chooses to make it." [46] Or "the primary system is sufficient to exclude all undesirable citizens and is sufficient to include all who are necessary. It allows each county or district to work according to its peculiar needs . . ." [47] Indeed, "We already had the Negro practically eliminated from politics by the white primary." [48] Elsewhere a simple poll tax was advocated as a sufficient deterrent to the Negro.[49] Practically everywhere, when some devious educational or "character" test was proposed, preferences were expressed for the comparatively simple schemes of the statutory disfranchising codes.[50]

"Fraudulent" intent was charged to members of the franchise committee from the floor of the Mississippi convention.[51] Sometimes the legislators were addressed more mildly, as in Georgia: "Gentlemen, you are not legislating for today or tomorrow, but for the years to come, and you are fixing it so that you may strike at my children and yours in the future. You had better go slow. You are aiming at the Negro, but you may strike a white man." A good-character clause is "a gap which will give politicians a wide field to wield an influence for their own selfish ends." [52]

Perhaps the most heated debates occurred in the Alabama convention of 1901. A "sensational speech" on the floor called the grant of discretionary powers of examination to the Boards of Registry "a device by which the wily politicians in control of it would take care of their own interests." The minority of the suffrage committee objected to the clause requiring proof of good character, as giving too much power to the registrars. A series of editorials expressed or plainly implied a fear of misuse of discretion in registration by whatever party happened to be in control of the administration.[53] An "honored citizen" declared in an interview: "The registrars may do whatever they please . . . the methods of appeal being costly and therefore impracticable . . . The scheme will not only perpetuate fraud, but will lend [it] legal protection . . . A most objectionable provision for unpunishable fraud is found in the exemption of all men over 45 . . . from the poll tax. After a Negro is thirty, no man can guess within fifteen years of his age. Therefore a great majority of the Negroes in the Black Belt will each be over 45 . . . for since the registrars are to be the sole judges . . . they may at will put all the Negroes on the poll lists . . . There being . . . no purging of the lists, the names of registered Negroes 'over 45' would remain permanently unchanged, for in the Blackbelt, you know, a Negro never dies as far as voting is concerned . . . These voters the bosses of the registrar could use on election day as they pleased to suit any purpose . . ." [54]

Equally scathing were the strictures of a member of the Georgia House: "The gentleman from Laurens [sponsor of the disfranchisement proposal] declared that 'it was an artfully drawn bill.' He is right. It is the most artfully drawn bill I have ever read. It is so artfully drawn that it conceals its real meaning. He also said that the registrars could put to any voter any questions they wanted to. They can ask a Negro a question he can answer if he is going to vote right and puzzle a white man if he is not going to vote right . . ." [55]

In North Carolina, when the new constitutional amendments were submitted to plebiscite, newspapers carried lurid stories:

THREATENED WITH
ARSON AND MURDER
Horrible Menace Against the
Whites at Whitsett
OVERHEARD BY SEVERAL
Slaughter of Men, Women, and
Children if Amendment
Carries

". . . This conversation was overheard by [four] responsible and trustworthy gentlemen . . ."

NEGROES THREATEN
TO APPLY THE TORCH
Carry Amendment and They Will
Burn Franklintown

". . . The report spread this evening . . . Such things only make votes for the amendment by the score [sic] . . ."

A SHAMEFUL SCENE
Negro Cursed and Abused
an Old Man
Result of Incendiary Advice by Bad
White Men, Many Such
Scenes Will Follow if
Amendment Fails

These stories were calculated to arouse white determination that the amendment should not fail.

In the legislature, at the final passage of the bill, Representative Winston, in "one of the most eloquent appeals that has ever been heard in the Capitol of North Carolina," proclaimed: "In the French Convention, old Barbereux arose and said, 'Send to Marseilles for six hundred men who know how to die.' They sent . . . and the revolution had begun . . . In the name of the fair women [loud and continued applause] who sat at home cowering with fear while you and I were away earning the morsel of bread, I appeal to you [Applause].

Rise to the heights of this occasion. You represent men who dare to do and die. Be not less brave then they! [Applause] . . ." [56]

The capstone was placed on this structure of tragi-comic mutual suspicion in Mississippi and Virginia, where, defying usage, law, and the promises of the Democratic party, the new constitutions were not submitted to plebiscite, lest they be defeated, but were put into effect by proclamation.[57]

The agrarian revolt, that great disturber of Southern political equanimity, also brought the issue of apportionment to the fore. In 1894, a Virginia newspaper complained: ". . . By the present methods the white people in the Negro belt receive as much representation as double their number receive in the white counties. What do the people in the white counties think of this?" [58] Exactly the same controversy arose in Alabama. "When the ignorant Negro vote is eliminated," said a leading independent newspaper during the sessions of the 1901-02 convention, "a white voter in southern Alabama will . . . far exceed a white voter in Jefferson, where the population is largely white . . . Representation should be based on votes cast . . ." A "prominent citizen" wrote: ". . . There are 232,224 white voters in Alabama. The thirteen black counties have 25,092 of these and the white counties 207,202; yet these Black Belt counties have a majority of our representatives in the two houses [of Congress] and more than half of the State officials and employees, and about one-third of the members of the Legislature and State conventions . . . So long as the Black Belt had the Negroes to deal with our people were content . . . but when the Negro is disfranchised, why should one white man in Dallas equal five in Jefferson?" [59]

In the end, the desire to get rid of the Negro voter triumphed, drowning out the Cassandra-like warnings of those irregular politicians who opposed the new constitutions. Race feeling had always run high among the poorer whites. After the war, hatred based on social and economic rivalry increased, rather than diminished. "The poorest whites felt that the Negro was not only their social but also their economic enemy, and, the protection of the owner removed, the blacks suffered more from these people than ever before. The Negro in school, the Negro in politics, the Negro on the best lands — all this was not liked by the poorest white people, whose opportunities were not as good as those of the blacks." [60] Thus we find that the politicians most virulent in their attacks on the Negro after the eighties were poor-white leaders: Tillman, Vardaman, Cole Blease, Jeff Davis of Arkansas, e.g. They helped to put over the new constitutions, risking — or not seeing — a hoist from their own petard.

PART II

FROM THE DISFRANCHISING CONSTITUTIONS TO 1930

INTRODUCTION

We have now traversed the history of the South through the period of agrarian revolt and constitutional revision. This survey has had a double focus: on the popular tradition of a "Solid South," which it has been our endeavor to dispel; and on the place of the Negro as a voter in the South.

The South has never been solid, save, perhaps, at three crises. The first was Secession, culmination of a period of attack upon its slave economy. Reconstruction, the second, brought unity at its climax of "Negro domination." Harmony dawned once more in the murky political morning after the agrarian revolt, when again the Negro, this time as a balance of power, played the rôle of bogey.

We have reviewed at length the issues which have in the past made Southern politics a genuine battle ground. Apart from the usual alignments common to all societies — rich against poor, town against country, class against mass — we have noted the peculiar divisions arising out of slavery and the presence of the Negro. The political rights of the Negro himself we have seen to be a fluctuating quantity, varying with changes in the white body politic.

We have now to ask of the period from 1908 to 1930: was the South "solid"? and for how long? Was Negro suffrage a thing of the past? and what of its future?

The answers to these questions are not simple, despite journalistic and propagandist certitudes. We are dealing here with a contemporary problem, and are faced, therefore, with a two-fold difficulty. Our materials lie all about us, and — paradoxically — are for that reason inaccessible and raw. They have not been sifted, and their import, because of the gravity of the issues involved, is clouded by partisanship. Further, the more or less schematic treatment appropriate to the historian of events long past must almost inevitably appear somewhat hasty when applied to events close to us. We may simplify the past to guide the future, but it is rash to offend the present by obliterating the least of its subtleties.*

It may be platitudinous but it is not the less important to add that social change during the period now under discussion became kaleidoscopic. For a study of American politics and racial relationships, this means that account must be taken not only of such unexpected irruptions as the War to make the world safe for democracy. The stereotype is used advisedly, for it aggravated the race consciousness which the war must have created in any case, over such matters as promotion, the salute, camp social facilities, the wearing of officers' insignia after discharge, etc.[1] There were steady, cumulating changes as well. To suggest a few is sufficient to indicate the uncertainties both of Southern politics and of race relationships: the industrialization and urbanization of the South; Negro migration; changes in living standards; modern philanthropy, very markedly directed towards Negro welfare; the development of propaganda technique, available alike to Interracial Coöperation Commissions and KuKlux Klan, for example.

Now specifically as to Negro suffrage: When the charge was brought against the South by liberal elements that its Negro population was illegally or unethically disfranchised, a spokesman for the South, often of high official position, could always be found to reply that the Negro was as free to vote in Mississippi as in Illinois, that if he did not vote, it was because he did not choose to.[2] Between these two extreme views lies a mean well summarized by a Negro leader: that nowhere in the South of 1930 did Negroes vote in representative numbers.

Even this moderate statement, however, fails to sound a

* John Galsworthy, presenting two lawyers discussing a delicate case, writes: "Very young Nicholas, knowing all the facts, had seemed quite unable to see what line could possibly be taken. Sir James, on the other hand, appeared to know only just enough."—"The Silver Spoon," p. 226.

sufficient note of caution about generalizing on the status of Negro suffrage in the South in the three decades following the enactment of the "disfranchising constitutions."

Four factors contributed to the presence and increase of Negro political activity in the South. Of greatest importance was the "open" election, an election, that is, held outside of the white primary system, whether for officers or — as a referendum on bond issues, amendments, etc. — for measures. The other three it would be difficult to rank comparatively. A favorable white sentiment, or a lack of race feeling in the surrounding white population, stood high. Skilful and active Negro leadership, and economic strength, coupled with high cultural standards (schooling, taste in the amenities of life, serious social organizations, e.g.) also had their effect.

The list of adverse factors is a little longer, and for that reason alone should perhaps dispel any undue optimism generated by the preceding formulations. Most important was a complete white primary system, extending to all offices, and sometimes coupled with a total absence of Republican opposition. A strongly opposed white sentiment was equally effective, and was indeed the bulwark of the white primary. Negroes themselves were inclined to emphasize their own lack of leadership and their political indifference. Negro poverty was a factor operating directly through the poll-tax voting requirement, and indirectly through weakness under economic pressure. Lastly, there remained in some members of the Negro group, by force of circumstances, a residuum of the irresponsible slave psychology: "Politics is the white folks' business."

It will readily be recognized that the favorable conditions we have enumerated — nonpartisan elections, white liberality or indifference, and leadership, economic strength, and cultural achievement among the Negroes — were more likely to obtain in cities than in the country. And, partly because of urbanization itself, partly because of greater wealth and activity, they were more prevalent in the Old South, from Virginia to Georgia, than in the Far South. These two sections were also set off from each other, to the advantage of the Negro voter, by the distribution of Negro population, which — being less in the States of the Old South — somewhat mitigated the fear of "Negro domination." The still smaller proportion of Negroes to total population in the Border States and Texas operated in the same direction.

It was therefore true on the whole that the Border States — West Virginia, Kentucky, Tennessee, and Arkansas — and Texas placed few direct obstacles in the way of the Negro voter at general elections. Conversely, the States of the Far South — Alabama, Mississippi, and Louisiana — had an almost wholly negligible number of Negro voters. Elsewhere — and in appropriate measure in these two sections — the Negro vote was larger in the city than in the country, for a variety of reasons; and for somewhat the same reasons it may be ventured that university or college centers, Negro or white, showed a trend towards a larger Negro vote, even where they were only small towns.

But even these generalizations are imperfect. In any given place, several conflicting factors, as well as temporary and irrational conditions, must be reckoned with.

Thus, Tennessee is a Border State. Yet, Fayette County was reported as having only some fifty colored voters in 1930 out of a Negro population of 21,095; Haywood, none out of 17,227. In Shelby County, on the other hand, the Negro vote was something to be reckoned with, in primary as well as general elections. All three of these counties, in the order named, stood at the head of the State in proportion of Negro population. But the first two were rural counties of the river-plantation type, with a population 73 per cent and 66 per cent Negro, while Shelby was dominated by the city of Memphis, and had a population only 42 per cent Negro.[3]

Birmingham and Atlanta are both large and active cities of the Far South; in Birmingham, Negro registration was difficult and amounted to very little, while in Atlanta it was large and had made itself felt. Richmond and Charleston are both old and socially conservative cities; but Negro registration was easier in Richmond than in Charleston. Hampton, Virginia, and Orangeburg, South Carolina, are both the seats of Negro institutions of higher learning, but while this made Negro suffrage easier in the conservative State, it made it harder in the comparatively liberal Old Dominion. A Negro druggist wrote of his experiences within the State of Georgia: "At Cordele, Crisp County, I was not permitted to register . . . I went to Americus . . . and in 1920 tried to register but failed, although I stayed there five years and paid poll tax each year. I moved to Columbus in 1925 and in 1926, after paying taxes, I registered without difficulty." [4]

The same illogical diversities which prevailed at the polls and registrars' offices could be found in other circumstances. Thus, it was in 1929 possible for a Negro to secure Pullman accommodations without resort to subterfuge from Durham, N. C., to Jacksonville, Fla., but not from Jacksonville to Durham. In Winston-Salem, N. C., it was difficult for a Negro to get Pullman accommodations, but if he took a short bus ride to Greensboro, in the same State, he could board his Pullman there without unpleasantness. So for street improvements, lighting, and sewerage in Negro sections, and school facilities; the traveler in the South found them adequate, and sometimes more, in unexpected places, or primitive or entirely lacking where he had every reason to look for them.

With such a confusing history behind us as we have already traversed, and before us a welter of living facts, it may be well to state, roughly, our findings in advance. The South of 1930 was not "solid," although its political machinery operated under a single trade mark. As to Negro voters, there were many fewer than an Abolitionist might hope, but rather more than even Southerners suspected.

CHAPTER VI

DISFRANCHISEMENT AT WORK

1. PRELIMINARY CONSIDERATIONS

No complete demonstration has ever been attempted of the assumption that the Negro vote in the South was, up to 1930, negligible. The task is well-nigh impossible. In the first place, election returns in this country did not show the race or color of voters. Registration lists hardly offered a more practical field of investigation. They were not kept by color in all States. Save in Louisiana, where there were fairly accurate centralized statistics, registration lists were available only at county seats, of which there were hundreds in some States, or — what was much worse from the investigator's point of view — by wards or precincts, of which there were thousands. Even these figures did not tell the story. For in most of the Southern States, registration was an act separate from the payment of poll taxes, although both were a prerequisite to voting; and it would therefore be necessary to compare the registration lists with the tax-paid lists, name for name and precinct by precinct.

Yet this assumption — that in the first three decades of the century the Negro vote in the South was so small as to be negligible — is a fair one. Only in the glare of unpleasant publicity did some official spokesman for the South deny it — and not always then.[1] No intelligent Southerner denied it in private conversation. The very figures which we shall use to exhibit Negro voting strength, such as it was, bear it out. The more widespread net of a questionnaire yielded the same sort of figures. Both coincide with the observations of investigators in the field, be it W. E. B. DuBois of the National Association for the Advancement of Colored People, Frank R.

Kent, the experienced political observer of the *Baltimore Sun*, or the present writer.[2]

The question arises whether the paucity of Negro voters in the South represented active *dis*franchisement by some white agency, or political indifference on the part of the Negroes. The politician-apologist for the South, admitting as he must that the Negro voter was a rarity, usually added to his denial of disfranchisement the statement that Negroes did not vote because they had lost interest in politics. It must be conceded at once that there was a large element of literal truth in such assertions. Not only did reputable white leaders in the South, men active in interracial movements and Negro welfare work, say that the Negro was unconcerned over his political condition, that he took little interest in politics, even that he did not register and vote where he easily could. This was the burden of complaint of thinking Negroes themselves, and was encountered by the writer almost as often as complaints of disfranchisement.

"I believe more colored people could vote if they would pay their poll tax, register, etc.," wrote a teacher in Baton Rouge. "Many do not attempt to test the possibility of their entrance into politics." "As a group," added a Norfolk physician, "we are sleeping." "Am expecting quietly to organize a [political] club," said a druggist in Greenville, S. C., "but cannot get any followers, so at present just haven't bothered." [3]

On the other hand, there were the registrars who said frankly: "We register just as few niggers as we can"; "We can't have too many of them voting." [4] There were the communities in which registrars told Negro applicants that they would lose their jobs if they registered colored people. There were the registration offices in which Negroes were very brusquely treated in the presence of other whites, although dealt with in a businesslike way if they happened in alone.[5]

In all truth, the question is begged when put simply, "Were Negroes disfranchised, or were they just indifferent?" Both factors may have been at work — and were; and, further, in the Southern background, the origin of Negro political apathy is a matter worth careful scrutiny.

Why was the Negro vote in the South so small? In accounting for either apathy or discrimination, the Negro's social and economic position must be borne in mind.

To begin with, it will be readily conceded that the Negro in the South occupied the position of an inferior class not only in white psychology, but in cold fact. His chief occupations were agriculture, mostly as a tenant farmer, laborer, and very small owner; personal service; and unskilled labor. In all the South, there were in 1920 only about 50,000 Negro professional men and women, school-teachers and ministers forming at least 50% of this total. The agricultural and personal-service groups accounted for 64.7% of the working population among Southern Negroes. His illiteracy was 28% as compared with 7% among Southern whites. He was poor; for example, Negroes in the South owned 24.6% of their homes, as compared with 50% of white homes owned by their occupants.[6]

As to the Negro's status in mass psychology, it is necessary only to mention lynching, Jim Crow accommodations on public carriers and in places of public resort, residential segregation, and his comparatively small share in the expenditure of public funds, whether for education, for which the figures are available, or for such basic improvements as sewerage, water, street lighting, and paving, where the evidence was apparent to the most casual traveler in the South.*

II. THE UNWANTED VOTER

Under the social and economic circumstances we have sketched, the Negro was of course sensitive to any unfavorable

* It is not the intention of the writer to suggest that the Southern white man of 1930 glowered upon sight of a Negro. Nor is there any desire to minimize the intentions or accomplishments of the many white Southerners who devoted themselves to Negro welfare. Public expenditures for Negro welfare, too, increased during the period under discussion. Similarly, in calling attention to the handicaps under which Negroes in the South still labored in 1930, it is not intended to disparage the great forward strides made by the race up to

attitude among whites towards his political activity. That such an unfavorable attitude existed needs little demonstration. As late as 1908, the argument for thoroughgoing disfranchisement of Negroes under State constitutions was being urged elaborately and heatedly. Between 1890 and 1908 it had resulted in eight States in the passage of new constitutions or of constitutional amendments frankly designed to bar the Negro from the polls.

Evidence of the same sort continued to be provided long after. Senator Blease of South Carolina was among the franker politician-spokesmen of the South. Admitting the purpose of the 1895 constitution of his State, in a speech in Congress, he added: "I think Mr. Coolidge received 1100 votes in my State. I do not know where he got them. I was astonished to know they were cast and shocked to know they were counted." [7] This statement, of course, was made with calculated bravado; yet it was meant at least to impress Blease's country constituents. "I shall urge the enfranchisement of all white women in accordance with the Anthony amendment," declared the governor-elect of Georgia in 1920, "and the disfranchisement of all black women on the same plan that the Negro men are now disfranchised in Georgia." [8]

Similarly effective in showing the Negro his political place according to white opinion, was the use of Negro support as a damning charge against a candidate.* Such charges were made, for example, against the "courthouse ring" in a Montgomery municipal election in 1927. "I never registered a darkey in the city," replied the outraged candidate; "I never want one to vote for me." [9]

that time. Nevertheless, the Negro was still at a disadvantage both as to the tangible amenities of life, and the intangible assets of racial good-will.

* Such appeals to negrophobia were losing their effectiveness in many Southern cities. Made in Raleigh, an editorial in a white newspaper deplored them; made in Durham, the same editor insisted that no complaint could be made if a Negro citizen and taxpayer voted; that the vote enabled Negroes to make demands for their own welfare; and that if Negroes were just being marched up to the polls, they were being misused, probably against their own best interests. Even this, the editor added, was a matter for which Negroes themselves were responsible. (Durham *Herald*, 28 April 1927, 3 May 1929.)

Even the suspicion of friendliness towards Negroes, involving no "use" of their votes, could be turned against a candidate. This was most amusingly demonstrated in Birmingham. In 1925, the two chief contenders for the city's highest office were J. M. Jones and W. J. Adams. The campaign was warmly fought, and towards election day, Adams headquarters charged the Jones people with "spreading various malicious and ridiculous reports over the city in an undercover appeal to prejudice." Among them was the charge that Adams if elected would appoint fifty Negro policemen. Adams was defeated. Four years later the same two men contested for the same office. This time the Adams people got in first with "nigger-lover" charges. Jones, it was claimed, had during his term of office actually appointed four Negro policemen. He was "forcing social equality" by establishing one-man street-cars, on which both races must use the same door. But alas! Adams was defeated again. He was a Roman Catholic.[10]

Better known is the "Morton story" of the 1928 presidential campaign, directed against Alfred E. Smith. Pictures were circulated of a New York City civil service commissioner, a Negro, dictating to a white woman stenographer, with printed matter to explain that this sort of racial relationship would spread even into the Federal service if the representative of Tammany were sent to the White House.[11] Some Southern papers showed fear of Smith as a negrophile, others felt obliged to nail as canards the rumors of his friendliness to colored people.[12]

The "lily white" movement in the Southern Republican party was another indication of the South's opposition to Negro suffrage. The term seems to have been coined in Texas in 1888, after riots between white and Negro Republicans struggling for the control of a convention. It was applied to bodies of white Republicans in Southern States determined to purge their party of Negro leadership, Negro control, and a Negro share in the spoils of victory. Its argument was that the white South should divide between the major parties, that the time had come for many reasons for Southerners to be converted to Republicanism, but that the Southern white men would not join a Republican party which trafficked with Negroes. Lily white groups functioned in every Southern State except West Virginia and Kentucky, and up to 1930 had been strong enough, on and off, to give considerable trouble to Negro "regulars." Their object was, ostensibly, to attract white men into the party, and to accomplish this, they felt obliged to discourage Negro voters, depose Negro committeemen and convention delegates, and thus — as they themselves put it — "clean up" the party.[13]

The most striking evidence of the Negro's place in politics according to the Southern view was the so-called "white primary." This was simply a declaration by the Democratic party authorities in each State that only white men were eligible to membership and permitted to help, in the primary elections, in the nomination of the party candidates. White men of known Republican sympathies were generally admitted to the Democratic primaries, but no degree of Democracy would admit a Negro save in exceptional circumstances.[14] Since nomination by the Democratic party was equivalent to election in all State-wide contests in the South, and for nearly all lesser offices, debarment from the nominating process was in effect disfranchisement.[15]

The white primary system of the nineteen-twenties and -thirties was not a new thing. Its history may be traced back to the "color line" of Reconstruction days, which the white "Conservative" parties drew as the then newly enfranchised Negroes were swallowed up by Radical Republicanism. From this time down to the agrarian revolt, the "white man's parties" of the South, first called "Conservative," then simply Democratic, never admitted Negroes to their councils.

The primary election as it is known today first made its appearance in the South outside the law.[16] The discontent which on the one hand brought about the agrarian revolt, on the other compelled a counter-reformation within the Democratic parties whereby control over platforms and nominations was given to the rank and file through preëlections held under party rules. In these preëlections, Negroes were generally barred by tacit rule, although it cannot be established that they were not here and there used in close contests.

This system had by 1907 in Georgia reached such a point of efficiency that an opponent of the constitutional-disfranchisement scheme was able to say: "We already had the Negro practically eliminated from politics by the white primary." [17]

By this time, the legally regulated primary had begun to take its place on Southern statute books. The nominating process became a part of the established procedure of elections, more or less regulated by the State, sometimes paid for by the State, sometimes even officered by the State. Such regulations as the party made under authority given it by the State became more formal. In 1930, it was possible to point to eight States in which the Democratic party by a definite State-wide rule barred Negroes from a share in the nominating process.[18] These were Alabama, Arkansas, Georgia, Louisiana, Mississippi, South Carolina, Texas, and Virginia. In three more — Florida, North Carolina, and Tennessee — there was no State-wide rule; but the rules of county and city Democratic committees took its place, with a few important exceptions in the two States last named.[19] West Virginia, which has figured in our earlier discussions as a Southern State, had no such rule. Texas attempted in 1923 to bar Negroes from the Democratic primary by law, but was checked by the Supreme Court of the United States.[20] Her party rule, however, remained in effect.

The background of Texas' attempt to bar Negroes specifically from Democratic primaries is an interesting commentary on the way in which racial feeling is injected into all sorts of political controversies in the South, regardless of their origin or actual import. The statute in question may be found in the General Laws of Texas, 2nd Extra Session of 1923, p. 74. When it was voided by the U. S. Supreme Court, a wave of dismay passed through the South, accentuated by the appearance of suits brought by Negroes in several States for the voiding of superficially similar laws. It was widely felt among whites that the white primary, bulwark of white supremacy, was gravely imperiled. Yet the law did not originate in a Negro situation, but was the result of a minor squabble among white politicians in Texas.

The facts were as follows: In 1918, one McAskill and one Tobin were aspirants in the Democratic primary of Bexar County for the district attorneyship. Up to that time, Bexar County had been one among several to admit Negroes to Democratic primaries, in spite of the party's central-committee rule barring them. Both McAskill and Tobin had previously had the support of Negroes in local primaries, and both this time counted on Negro support for victory because of past favors each had shown Negroes. The Negro primary electorate, however, was this time swung for Tobin, and Tobin was elected. Thereupon McAskill, not as an attack on Negro domination, but as a means of weakening his rival's county organization, began campaigning for the statutory bar which was eventually enacted. He played upon the feelings of legislators from negrophobe counties which had in the past been glad to comply with the party rule barring Negroes. The plea was made that all Negroes were of course Republican, and were merely being corruptly herded into the Bexar County Democratic primaries. Gradually, sufficient sentiment was aroused to secure the passage of the act in question. After it was voided, and the State returned to the normal arrangement of barring Negroes under a party rule, several counties in Texas returned to the practice of admitting Negroes to the white primaries, at least occasionally.

This, then, was the atmosphere of white disfavor in which the economically and socially handicapped Negro was obliged to carry on whatever political activities he could compass. It was compounded of the memories of all the struggles and debates which had culminated, not so many years before, in the disfranchising constitutions; and of the everyday perception, not only of general discriminations with their invidious connotations, but of the fact that publicly at least no one wanted him in politics.

An atmosphere so charged, naturally, sometimes flashed lightning.

The white primary absolutely barred Negroes from sharing in the nominating process of the Democratic party, save in Kentucky and West Virginia.[21] In the Solid South, this at once restricted the Negro to nonpartisan and special elections of one sort or another, and to presidential elections, in which his Republican vote was a gesture.

Even in these cases, however, there were obstacles to be surmounted.[22] The poll tax, universal, save recently in North Carolina, was the first hurdle he encountered. Varying in amount between one and two dollars, payment was required long in advance of the election, in some States for three years previous to voting, in some for the whole period of liability, from the age of twenty-one to the age of forty or sixty. The Negro registrant or voter was always asked for his tax receipt, the white man seldom. The white voter in districts where votes were valuable to the "machine" might even be visited by the tax collector or registration officer and urged to qualify by paying. Such an occurrence in the Negro quarter would be highly exceptional.

The next step was actual registration. This was a complicated procedure, which began with the entry of the voter's name, age, address, residence, and sometimes half-a-dozen other personal details in the registrar's file. Here again a Negro could be put off.

The Virginia law, for example, demanded that all the required information be written down by the applicant "without aid, suggestion, or memorandum." In Richmond, this statutory injunction was embodied in an application form about the size of a check, on one side of which was printed the voter's oath. The other side was blank. After filling in his name and signing the oath on the printed side, the applicant was expected to turn the paper over as if to indorse it, and write on the back, "without aid, suggestion, or memorandum," all the required facts demanded by law. Asked by the writer whether there were not a good many ordinary respectable citizens who were unable to comply literally with the law, the official in charge answered, "Oh, if I see that they are decent and respectable citizens, I can give them a little hint."

Even in Roanoke, where, in the discretion of the registrar, the application blank was printed with indications as to the information required, it was not easy to fill out; and it was easy to find fault with when filled.* In Hampton, headed applications were given to whites, blank sheets to Negroes.

REGISTRATION FORM FROM NEW ORLEANS

COPY OF

Educational

Form of Application For Registration

Ward No. ......
Prct. No. ......
Cert. No. ......

Residence No. ....St. I am a citizen of the State of Louisiana.
My name is Mr., Mrs., Miss. ....
I was born in the State (or country) of...................................
Parish (or county) of ....on the .... day
of ....in the year.......................I am
now ....years...........months and ....days of age.
I have resided in the State since...................... in this Parish
since ....and in Precinct No....................in Ward
No. ....of this Parish continuously since.................and
I am not disfranchised by any provision of the Constitution of this State.
The name of the householder at my present residence is....................
My occupation is ....My color is.............
My sex is ....I am affiliated with the.................Party
Signature here ....
Sworn to and subscribed before me ....192.... ....
REGISTERS OF VOTERS.

Granting that the applicant's tax payments were in order, and that he made verbal or written replies to the formal questions not merely correct, but also "satisfactory" to the

* V. the illustration of the New Orleans form. The catch often used there was the "Years . . . Months . . . *Days*" line under the heading "Age."

REGISTRATION FORM FROM MONTGOMERY

OATH OF APPLICANT FOR REGISTRATION

I do solemnly swear (or affirm): 1. I know of no reason why I am not entitled to register and become a qualified elector; 2. I am generally known by the name under which I desire to vote, which is ....; 3. My occupation is ....; 4. I am (single or married) ....; 5. My sex is............; 6. My race is.....................; 7. The name of my husband or wife is ....who was born in ....and whose residence now is ....;
8. My residence is ....
(if in city or town give street number); 9. During the last five years I have resided at ....
.....................and during the said time have been known by the name of ....; 10. I have been a bona fide resident of the State of Alabama for the past two years and of ....County for the past twelve months and of ....
Precinct No. ...., District No. ....,
for the past three months; 11. I am engaged in the following business or employment ....; 12. My employer for the past five years has been ....
and his business address is ....;
13. I was born at ....on the ....day of......................, 1........;
14. That ....
and ....have personal knowledge of my residence in Precinct No. ....,
District No. ...., for the past three months.

....

Sworn to and subscribed before me this ....day of............................, 192......

...................., Chairman }
.... } Registrars.
.... }

registrar, he might now be subjected to an examination in constitutional law and American history. This examination was made under the "understanding" clauses, and the questions that were asked would often have done credit to a board of college examiners.

"I appeared before the commissioners of registration in 1924," wrote a Negro school official from New Orleans. "Had I been requesting registration to practice law, the examination could have been but little harder." "Many ignorant white democrats are employed at the registration offices here," added a physician from the same place. "Whenever a Negro comes to this office, they are asked to interpret the constitution of the United States, and these illiterates are to determine if their answers are correct. In all instances they are wrong." [23] Mrs. Cora Trotter, the first Negro woman to attempt registration in Birmingham, was given a piece of paper and told to write what she knew of the constitution of the United States. The registrar decided that it was not enough, and refused to enroll her.[24] William Pickens, of the staff of the National Association for the Advancement of Colored People, was told at Talladega, Ala., where he was a college teacher in 1905, that "I could not register unless I just wrote off a number of sections of the Constitution." [25]

In some sense the most flagrant cases of unfair examinations come from Virginia. For in Hampton at least, examinations of this sort were still being conducted in 1929-30, in spite of the fact that the 1902 "understanding" clause had expired in 1903. Registrars could no longer ask such questions as "When did the United States buy Alaska, from whom, and at what price," "Give the boundaries of the smallest republic in the world," etc., although these questions were always dubious evidences of an "understanding of the duties of citizenship" such as the law had required.

There remained in the constitution, however, a clause requiring the applicant to "answer *on oath* any and all questions affecting his qualifications." [26] Under this clause, Negroes applying for enrollment in Hampton were still asked general legal and political questions, such as "Who is an elector?", "Who is disqualified from voting?", and "Can a minor hold office in Virginia?" — the catch in this last being that notaries public need only be eighteen years of age. These questions were asked of, and used to disqualify, members of the staff of Hampton Institute. That they were wholly illegal in the context of the required oath, was the entirely plausible contention of a local Negro leader, who brought a case before the highest court of the State to settle the matter.[27]

If these tests were ever applied to white applicants, the fact did not come to our notice, although — as has been said — they were intrenched in the statute books for such use should the politicians behind the registrars want them.[28] On the other hand, the complaints were many which recount how white voters were passed without examination, while Negroes were patiently questioned until finally "stumped."

Besides these calculated elaborations of the actual registration laws, there were many other ways of making registration difficult for a group as socially handicapped as the Negro. In many places Negro applicants were simply refused,[29] or some vague excuse given, such as that "there is no provision in the law for registering Negroes," or quite openly, that the "quota" of Negro votes had been filled. In many places, "It is an understood policy . . . that Negroes not be allowed to register in sufficient numbers to matter in any sort of election." [30]

Delay was a favorite device. "Was referred to county seat, when there it was told us 'too late' "; "Was given an application blank and told to fill it out and return next day . . . when I returned only one member of the board was present . . . he could not register me unless the other two were present . . . the next day . . . the third member was sick, and would not be able to attend on the board any more that session." Meanwhile, "They were continually registering white people . . . They had all the certificates signed with each member's name, and when a white person came the member present would fill out and hand him his certificate."

This process of delay was sometimes carried forward from

registration to actual voting.[31] This was especially true in a State like Florida, where poll-tax payment automatically carried registration with it, and no "understanding" or "character" clause was in force. The Negro who appeared at the polls with his registration certificate might find that his name did not appear on the voters' list, that his initials or address on the certificate did not tally with those on the list, or that his name had inadvertently been put on the white list. He could be bluffed out of voting over alleged technicalities of this sort, with no recourse save to an unfriendly court, at his own expense.[32] Where the election law permitted separate party "tickets" instead of requiring a general Australian ballot, the Negro Republican was told that there were no Republican tickets available; it took a courageous citizen to demand that the enemy party's ballot be produced for him, the unwanted voter.

"Friendly intimidation" kept a North Carolina teacher from the registration office: "Threats of what would befall my group if I should register. Statements made that such scenes as marked the Wilmington riots would be reënacted in this locality — that my request to register had been reported at three places and I was being closely watched by hostile observers." Or: "Told me . . . 'If you vote you will never return home alive' . . . I was a very conspicuous character, as I was the only Negro in the county that made any attempt to register." "Colored people 'just don't' vote here . . . for the sake of peace and harmony between the races." "I was asked why I wanted to register. My reply was 'In order to become a registered citizen.' 'Well, you have always been looked on as a good character. But from now on you shall be looked on as a dangerous character.' "

In view of the lack of interest Negro citizens were charged with, it is particularly relevant to read that "few of our people vote in my town owing to fear of hostilities; yet I do not recall if there had been any serious maltreatment. *The atmosphere is somewhat filled with offense at the sight of a group of ours voting.*" [33]

Many Negroes remained away from registration offices and polling places to avoid humiliation. "Upon entering the office of the registrar the first question is, 'What do you want, nigger?' " "There are cases of embarrassment that causes one to be somewhat reluctant about registering" (from a woman). "I haven't registered because of humiliations we have to suffer." "To go to the polls would mean a gross insult."

Even the conditions under which a Negro knew he could vote, were often such as to discourage him from taking advantage of them. Where a physician felt that "It is hard for educated Negroes to get registered . . . It is much easier for sôme 'Uncle Tom' ignorant Negro," * he was apt, in bitterness, to give up the attempt.[34] Many highly trained and cultured Negroes simply would not ask for the use in their behalf of white influence sufficient to secure their registration without question, although they could have had a message to the registrar for the asking. Others, requested to register because of their standing in the community, would refuse. They were unwilling to have a merely personal exception made for them, to serve as a window-dressing of "liberality," or to risk making enemies among whites whom they needed for support in some other enterprise.

III. LOCAL VARIATIONS

The use of these devices, and the sentiment which underlay them, varied from place to place. In West Virginia, there seemed to be very little to prevent a Negro from being as active in politics as he wished; several had been elected to the State Legislature between 1914 and 1930.[35] In Kentucky, the general elections were open to Negroes, and no complaints of primary disfranchisement were made. In Tennessee, the general elections were open in all but two or three river-bottom counties; the primaries, however, were white save in Memphis, Nashville, and perhaps some other cities. Arkansas

* "Uncle Tom Negro" is slang among colored people for the old-fashioned, deferential type among the race.

stepped out of the "Border State" classification with her State-wide white primary rule; and it was claimed that her Negroes were kept from voting by intimidation, or by the kind of "political indifference" we have been discussing in rural districts, especially in the Black Belt of the State. Texas falls between a State like West Virginia and Arkansas: a State-wide white primary rule, much Negro "indifference," but, on the other hand, considerable local Negro power in certain cities.

The real South of the suffrage problem, therefore, extended from Virginia through Louisiana. Here disfranchisement and non-voting among Negroes were, with exceptions, more prevalent in the country than in the cities, more prevalent in the Black Belt of each State than in the counties of fairly equal population, more prevalent from South Carolina southward, as the proportion of Negroes increased.

The reasons for this general state of affairs were obvious. The Black Belts and the southernmost States of the South were most easily impressed with the "Negro domination" and "balance of power" arguments. The country districts, isolated and unprogressive, were least touched by recent developments like the interracial movement; had lost the more active and open-minded element of their white population to the cities; and had the least evidences of Negro advance in the shape of professional men, teachers, and successful business men. Negro leaders capable of openly or subtly aggressive protests also left the country.

As to the difference between Virginia and North Carolina on the one hand, and the States to the south on the other, several explanations are possible. Virginia, since about 1900, had been continually in the hands of the descendants of the Bourbon Democrats; that is to say, of the group traditionally less bitter, more paternalistically benevolent towards the Negro. North Carolina, whose Democracy during the same period acknowledged more kinship with the "red-shirt" plebeian traditions of her agrarian revolt, had nevertheless profited from the liberalism of Governor Aycock (1900-

1904),[36] and by reason of her phenomenal industrialization had been laid open to the influences of urbanization, and perhaps of immigration from the North. Both States were more urbanized, more industrial, and wealthier than their neighbors to the South. The influence of cities on Negro suffrage we shall discuss in our next chapter; with wealth came the possibility of more educational and economic advantages for their Negro population, and consequently an opportunity for Negro leadership. At the same time, education and a better economic opportunity perhaps softened the outlook of the white population, reduced the bitterness of economic competition, and developed a white leadership prepared to consider a change of interracial *mores.*

To the south of these two States, the reverse of all these conditions seemed to prevail. Political leadership among the whites remained with the plebeian element since the agrarian revolt, with few exceptions; and such figures forged to the front as Heflin of Alabama, Blease of South Carolina, and George of Georgia, who were the most outspoken negrophobes in the United States Senate. The governors in 1930 of Mississippi and Louisiana, Bilbo and Long, were proud to acknowledge their kinship with and dependence on the hillbilly and cracker type. Whatever the personal feelings of such characters, their political affiliations prevented them from initiating or even countenancing much advance in welfare legislation such as might have developed strength and leadership among Negroes. Except for Alabama and Georgia, this group of States had few cities, little industry (discouraged by a "trust-busting" attitude [37]), and little developed wealth. Under all these circumstances, they did not offer the opportunities of Virginia and North Carolina for conscious or unconscious overhauling of the social contract and body politic.

Thus it was that even the cities of these States were the scene of non-voting among Negroes, whether from Negro apathy or white antagonism.*

Local conditions constantly cut across the lines of these

* V. Table I, p. 123

generalizations, sometimes reënforcing, sometimes correcting, the regional tendency. Lynchburg, Virginia, close to the liberal Roanoke, with a nonpartisan municipal government, in a section of the State not heavily populated by Negroes, with a certain degree of white Republican strength, witnessed very little Negro political activity. This was perhaps accounted for by the quietness of the town, and by changes in its tobacco industry which had thrown many Negroes out of work, to the extent of markedly diminishing its Negro population.[38] The Negro Y. M. C. A. secretary claimed that it was very hard to keep any sort of Negro activity or organization afloat; it was, in short, a poor and leaderless backwater, perhaps for both races.

TABLE I

NEGRO REGISTRATION IN CERTAIN SOUTHERN CITIES

Upper South			Lower South		
City	*Population*	*Negroes Registered*	*City*	*Population*	*Negroes Registered*
Ptsmth.	54,387	761	Mobile	60,777	150
Louisville	234,891	free	N. Orl.	387,219	1,723
Raleigh	24,418	1,500	Jackson	22,817	50-100
N. Nws.	35,596	1,000-2,000	Columbia	37,524	100-200

The cities are: Upper South — Portsmouth, Va.; Louisville, Ky.; Raleigh, N. C.; and Newport News, Va. Lower South: Mobile, Ala.; New Orleans, La.; Jackson, Miss.; Columbia, S. C.

The population figure is the Census total for 1920; the registration figures are from Appendix II, Table III.

Again, although we have said that political activity among Negroes increased with the distance from the Black Belt, this process reversed itself when the almost wholly white mountain counties were reached. For this there are several reasons. The mountain counties are the home of the "poor whites" whose anti-Negro bitterness we have discussed at length. Such educational influences as schools and newspapers had penetrated these fastnesses least of any region in the South. They were cityless, and leaderless save for local chieftains and such Negro-baiters as the late Senators Tillman and Vardaman. Therefore the absence of large numbers of Negroes did not have its logical effect of political toleration. Nor did the close division between Democrats and Republicans in such regions as the Ninth Congressional District of Virginia have the expected result of competition for Negro votes. In some such counties there were no Negroes, in others too few to bother about when the white vote was easily corruptible, and in all the two parties watched each other very closely for a chance to raise the "Negro balance of power" issue. On the Negro side, there was great and almost unrelieved poverty, and a total absence of any of the conditions in which leadership or organization might flourish.

Hampton, Virginia, offers a special local case. It is the seat of the well-known Institute which gives technical, and, in lesser degree, college training to Negroes. As will be seen, the presence of such an institution elsewhere improved interracial relations. Here, however, it had long been extremely difficult for Negroes, even propertied and educated members of the Institute staff, to secure registration. A score of cases, based on the ridiculous questions asked under the "understanding" clause, were carried to the local court by Negro attorneys after the 1902 constitution. The Negroes themselves believed the reason to be partly jealousy of the Institute, partly fear of its influence, partly merely the personalities of the successive registrars. Hampton Institute is wealthy, well equipped, and well kept; many white institutions in the South might envy it. Its faculty is mixed, the white members coming mostly from the North; to the disgust of the local whites, these "Yankees" do not hesitate to "fraternize" with their Negro colleagues and students.

IV. THE QUESTION OF "APATHY"

We are now in a position to discuss the question of Negro apathy in a more realistic manner.

To judge by statements, both written and verbal, the Negro's attitude towards politics was comparable to that of many whites the country over. Some Negroes, that is, were simply cynical about the effectiveness of the ballot; some of them — especially those painfully establishing themselves in business or in the professions — begrudged the time required; many were deterred, like their equally poor white neighbors, by the annual levy of the poll tax on their slender finances.

There were also reasons for political apathy peculiar to the Negro. Thus, the poll-tax requirement was prohibitive to many more Negroes than whites, because of the Negroes' greater poverty and economic uncertainty. Some Negroes of the old country type perhaps felt quite genuinely that "Politics is the white folks' business." Others — and this occasionally came up in interviews and questionnaire forms — were committed to the somewhat quietistic philosophy of Booker Washington: devoting themselves to self-improvement, they expected suffrage and other barriers to be let down when the race had established itself more firmly in the ways of the white man.

All this we may accept as genuine apathy. Yet, while there was of course no reason to think of the Southern Negro as being markedly politically-minded, many Negroes, in all stations of life, were deeply conscious and quietly resentful of their lack of political power. This was not only because of the mark of inferiority which disfranchisement put upon them. They also realized their powerlessness to obtain for themselves those services which elected officials will generally grant only to a group which wields the ballot. Wherever local conditions created a Negro electorate, as will be seen, there was apt to be bargaining between Negro leaders and white politicians over Negro schools, parks, paving, better police treatment, etc., all matters in which the colored group was at a disadvantage in the period under discussion. But even favorable local conditions at best offered only an occasional chance for effective political action. This discouraged efforts to surmount even the normal obstacles.

Even should a few hundred Negroes succeed in passing

every barrier to registration and the ballot box, what good would it do them? "The value of the power to vote here is utterly worthless," ran the comment of one of our questionnaire subjects, "as the number of Negroes who vote is almost negligible." One is almost inclined to say that here lay the chief reason for the Negro's "apathy." It was the exceptional place which allowed Negroes to register freely. In many places, a shifting "quota" of colored voters was permitted, with the understanding that there should never be a large enough number to make any difference whatsoever. Often a Southerner, white or black, commented on the "liberality" of his own community; when asked what would happen should the number of Negro voters perceptibly increase, the answer was always the same. "Then we would have trouble." In a large number of comparatively "liberal" places, the informal requirements for Negroes were extremely high: only recommended Negroes bearing white credentials, or a few colored leaders — preachers, principals, physicians — were admitted. With so few voting, there could be no Negro power even in elections not governed by a white primary, no Negro political or civic organization, no Negro leadership.

But most elections in the South, as we have said, were decided as soon as the white Democratic primary had named its candidates. Again, what did it profit a Negro to cast his ballot on election day for the primary nominees whose victory was certain, nominees who moreover had no responsibility save to the white primary electorate? The Negro could on occasion vote for a Republican. Notably this was true every four years, at presidential elections. But his vote here was merely a gesture. In few States south of the Border group were there any local Republican candidates. Where there were, their election was extremely uncertain. In some cases, for a Negro to vote for a Republican for local office was even greater racial treason than to cast a meaningless Democratic ballot. Thus, to vote for a Republican governor in Florida or Texas meant supporting a lily white, a man committed publicly at least to "purge" the party of its Negro element, a man whose faction engaged every four years in a struggle to unseat Negro delegates to the Republican national convention, and in off years fought the Negro leader in Federal patronage matters.

Why, then, asked Negroes throughout the South, — why run the whole gamut of registration annoyances, delays, and expense?

There was still good reason, as many of the professional men and other thoughtful Negroes realized, for taking an interest in politics, since the colored people were so greatly in need of services, such as education and sanitation, which only the State could render. It was important, they said further, because the day might yet come when a divided South would call on the Negro voter. A large Negro registration might even bring about independency among candidates, leading, perhaps, to the formation of new parties. And, finally, if the white primary was ever broken down by appeals to the Fourteenth and Fifteenth Amendments, the registered Negro would be able to take his place in Democratic factional politics. On a lower plane was the feeling among Negro Republican committeemen, that a large following at the polls would enable them to hold their places against lily-white factions.

These were, however, slim arguments with which to urge the Negro citizen towards the registration office, in view of the trouble that awaited him there. It is at this point that the necessity for Negro leadership was stressed: leadership which would not only organize the Negro's civic interest and get him to keep up his registration, but leadership which would make possible understandings, "deals," with white leaders whereby Negro suffrage might be made easier, and Negro votes traded, after the American fashion, for Negro benefits.

V. NEGRO LEADERSHIP

Such leadership among Southern Negroes was not entirely lacking, but Negroes themselves felt that it was inadequate.*

* Again it must be understood that there is no desire here to minimize the accomplishment of Negro leaders. The work of some of the local figures

In discussing this inadequacy of leadership, as in the case of Negro "apathy," it is a little hard to draw the line between factors inherent in the Negro's general situation and those traceable to white political antagonism. The leaderlessness of the Negro arose, to some extent, from the economic and social handicaps of the group, too poor to organize, untrained in coöperation, and scattered to so large a degree as farmers and farm laborers. The well-schooled generation was in 1930 only a recent factor, and its cream, the college graduates, could number only about 25,000 at the most.[39]

There was thus a great gap between the potential leaders and the great majority to be led. The great majority was compelled by circumstances to be conservative, and was apt to be suspicious, as well as sometimes jealous, of "radical" leadership. Thus, a teacher in a Texas college wrote from what he described as a "typical country town of the Old South": "I am an outsider . . . Any outsider who tries to arouse [the colored people] would make himself undesirable to both races . . . What I could say would be discounted by old residents . . . Success would depend on organization of staunch supporters . . . Too many are of the type to pat you on the back and encourage you to go on, while at the same time they go around to 'Marse John' and tell him 'That nigger from de Norf is trying to make trouble between us poo' niggers and you good white folks." Or, from Florida: "The race people here 'enjoy' a state of intellectual lethargy. It is hazardous for him who tries to wake them. The danger lurks in the race." "There's no interest among property owners and old citizens, hence the young ambitious mind is at loss."

At the same time, the "young ambitious minds" were often too busy establishing their dental practice, their law business,

is described in the next chapter, section II. Such national figures as Dr. DuBois of the National Association for the Advancement of Colored People, and Dr. Moton, principal of Tuskegee Institute, are too well known to require comment. Dr. DuBois has confined himself to voicing, on the whole, the general political demands of the Negro; and Dr. Moton, like other figures in the educational and social-welfare field, has eschewed politics, save in his discussion of "What the Negro Thinks" (1928).

etc., to bother with politics. Many, too, left the South for Harlem, Chicago, or Washington.

As for the two groups of Negro leaders who might have been most effective — the preachers and the skilled politicians of the Republican committees — neither, for special reasons, led the Negro communities towards civic and political organization. The preacher, probably the greatest influence among the mass of Negroes, was conservative by profession. He ministered that Christian religion of resignation and passive hopefulness so well adapted to an oppressed class. "When I get to *Heav'n*, gonna put on my shoes," says the spiritual. Meanwhile, "Nobody knows de trouble I see."

The Negro politician was generally accused of wanting to keep the Negro vote down, in order to prevent the rise of rival aspirants to power and expense accounts. How true this was, cannot be determined; it was not often brought up during the writer's investigation in the field. The Negro politician had no special incentive to drum up registrants because his job was secured through the national Republican organization, no matter how few were the Republican votes in his district. If he became too active, he might find himself faced by a lily white movement, and have trouble with his white customers in the Federal patronage business. He might well have been more anxious to increase the voting strength behind him if he had felt it to be of any use; even if only an occasional victory provided more spoils to go around the organization.*

The conservatism of preachers and the abstention of the professional classes from politics also reflected directly the

* It is the strong feeling of the writer that criticisms of the Negro Republican committeemen, etc., in the South misconceive such personages' situation when they are directed against their alleged inactivity in getting out the vote. In the circumstances which we have been describing, what vote were Negro politicians to get out? Where were the funds to come from? Why should they bother to get out the vote, unless they were *unusually* public-spirited men? As a matter of fact, the writer knows to his own satisfaction at least that several Negro politicians—Davis of Georgia, MacDonald of Texas, to a lesser degree Cohen of Louisiana—did urge upon Negroes the necessity of registration, and marshalled Negro voters for the common welfare in various elections.

surrounding white antagonism in many cases. For example, "We established a school here thirty-five years ago," wrote a teacher from Alabama. "To have tried to vote then would not only have deprived [the colored people of the neighborhood] of educational advantages, but would have jeopardized our lives . . . we'd feel none too safe to try to vote now . . . Tolerance of our school would be turned into vicious accusations that we were teaching 'niggers' politics, or 'Social Equality,' the great bugbear of these ignorant and vicious Southern whites." Negro colleges were dependent either upon State subsidies or private benefactions for funds, and could not function in a hostile atmosphere generated by the political activity of members of their staffs. Negro churches depended on white contributions for building funds and charitable work. Negro physicians were obliged to be careful to protect their hospital connections; lawyers, their standing in court; even business men, their credit with white middlemen and banks. That many such natural leaders, with a strong position among their own race and white contacts to boot, should lean over backwards in political caution was but the result of an appreciation on their part of the importance of their special work to the race as a whole.*

With quiet bitterness, the president of a State normal school for Negroes admitted to the writer his inability to fight the battles of his race along the entire front, pointing to a row of fine new buildings as the result of "minding his business." His attitude, he added, cost him the support of radical Negroes; were he to be more aggressive, endangering the toleration of his own important enterprise, he would alienate the conservative Negroes. In the last analysis, the normal school was a going concern, but the attainment of the franchise — and other rights — was a gamble.[40]

* The same caution necessarily prevailed among many white friends of the colored race in the South; much as they may have wished for a change in the political position of the Negro, they dared not risk their influence with other whites by advocating Negro suffrage, lest their hands be tied when it came to school appropriations, the mitigation of penalties for minor offences, or plain charity.

All these factors in the disfranchisement situation were, as may easily be recognized, cumulative and viciously circular. The smaller the vote, the less incentive to vote, and the greater the tendency among whites to disregard Negro demands and needs. This disregard discouraged attempts to vote. The smallness of the vote diminished opportunities for leadership, yet leadership was essential if suffrage was to be extended and bargains struck over Negro needs.

Could this circle ever be broken? This is the next point in our examination.

CHAPTER VII

THE NEGRO AS A VOTER

I. THE URBAN NEGRO

It cannot be too strongly emphasized, at the beginning of a discussion of the Negro as a voter, that during the period we are here considering he voted nowhere in really large numbers, at least south of the Border States. Even where his vote was comparatively unrestricted, it was ineffective because of the greater or less effectiveness of the adverse factors we have just analyzed. If white supremacy could here and there suffer an unexpectedly large body of Negro voters to function, it still resisted anything approaching a steady Negro balance of power. It is fair to say that some Negroes voted, because far more did not. Still these exceptional cases merit close attention as straws in the wind.

As has been indicated, most of the Negroes who did vote, voted in the cities. It was in the cities that Negro suffrage was most discussed, whether privately, or publicly through the medium of newspapers, interracial bodies, and Negro welfare organizations. It was in the cities, as will be seen, that elections occurred in which Negro votes were more or less openly solicited; it was in cities that stories arose, sometimes verifiable, sometimes not, of an occasional Negro balance of power.

This correlation between urban conditions and a — comparatively — large Negro vote is the closest approach to a generalization that our investigation offered. It is therefore worth careful scrutiny; the more so as the South was yearly becoming more urbanized, and as cities are always a focal point of change.

The Negro urban vote was due in part to certain structural

and functional features of municipal government: the form of city government, the frequency of municipal elections, an unwonted bipartisanship in city politics, the city-dweller's concern with referenda on tax and bond matters, etc., where no personal issue or question of "supremacy" is involved. Underlying these phenomena of municipal politics were certain cultural aspects of city life, common to all sections of the country, but of special significance for the South's special problem. These cultural aspects it will be well to consider first.

A Southern Negro who wished to register and vote could do so under two conditions: if his white neighbors were willing, or if they were indifferent. If they were willing, this represented, in the Southern background, a changed (if not a liberalized) attitude. Change (we will eschew the term "liberality") and indifference are both urban phenomena.

To the cities and large towns of the South came, in the largest number, the Southern graduates of colleges, the Southern professional men, the men of affairs with business and social contacts in the world beyond Mason and Dixon's line. The city newspapers attracted the most experienced and best trained editors. The city churches called to their pulpits the more cultured and humane ministers. The cities were the natural refuges of the *révoltés*, the *déracinés*, the sophisticated. The cities were the natural headquarters of welfare organizations: interracial commissions, bi-racial Community Chests, Y. M. C. A.'s, and church councils. Atlanta had a bi-racial church council which met regularly for the discussion of racial problems. Vicksburg was the home of a woman who gave funds for "Y" buildings of almost equal convenience for white and black; in the administration, at least, of the organization's affairs, the races came in contact. Richmond campaigned among black and white for Community funds to be distributed among white and black. It was in some of the cities of the South that colored citizens were beginning to be addressed as "Mr." and "Mrs." City newspapers like the *Columbus* (Georgia) *Enquirer-Sun* thundered against lynching and discrimination. City ticket offices sold Pullman accommodations to Negroes.

It was in the cities, therefore, that one was more apt to find an acceptance of Negro voters at least among a substantial minority of the white citizens, and often one or two individuals who looked towards an even greater political equality than existed. It was in city newspapers that editorials invited Negroes to vote on this or that local matter, discussed the letting down of white primary bars, deplored the intrusion of racial arguments into political campaigns.

With this changed, this receptive attitude towards the Negro voter went a certain urban indifference, similarly a common feature of city life. There is not so much active concern among city dwellers with the affairs of their fellow-citizens as is usual (and deplorable) in the small town and rural community. Atlanta, Memphis, Charlotte, and their peers were too big and too busy to permit their residents close acquaintance with and supervision over each other's affairs. The would-be Negro voter, therefore, enjoyed a certain anonymity in the exercise of his political rights. When he went to one of ten, a score, or fifty registration offices and polling places, he was not under the eyes of the whole community on which he depended for his livelihood and protection. Nobody cared about it, perhaps because nobody knew about it.

Where it was thus easier for a Negro citizen to register and vote as one depersonalized city-dweller among thousands, it was also easier for his white friends to help him. In a Louisiana parish, the registrar told a Negro that she dared not register him for fear of losing her job.[1] In Roanoke, Virginia, however, such Negroes as applied were freely registered if qualified, and the colored list was purged by the registrar with the help of an old and respectable Negro business man of the city.[2] Under cover of the protective anonymity of city life, too, a quiet bid could be made for Negro votes where conditions did not warrant open dealing, a bloc of Negro votes could be quietly assembled at a remote polling place in the Negro quarter, and the Negro citizenship thus be given the immense stimulus (usually entirely lacking) of knowing that its vote was wanted, was needed, and would have some effect. Finally, the question arises — merely as a question — whether the corruption that flourishes in American city politics may not have increased the number of voters, both white and black, who cast their ballot for a consideration.

So much for the effect of urban conditions upon white attitudes. It must also be plain that a Negro city community had certain advantages which strengthened its political position. Just as the abler, better-trained, and more active white citizens of the South drifted to the cities, so it was with the Negro citizens.[3] Any large, and some small, Southern cities contained a Negro fraternal building, in which might be found the offices and leading spirits of Elks, Masons, Pythians, etc.; all active centers of welfare work and discussion, and often closely linked with the Negro Republican committee. In the same building or separately was the professional quarter of the Negro community: physicians', dentists', lawyers' offices; the regional headquarters of one or more of the substantial Negro insurance companies; several real estate firms; a branch of the Urban League or the National Association for the Advancement of Colored People. The city community was endowed with a better school system than the broken-down shack which often served a rural community, and this system was operated by a correspondingly better-trained staff of teachers and principals. In some cases it was the focus of the civic interest fostered by a Parent-Teachers Association. Negro academies, colleges, and universities were generally located in cities. There might be in such a city a private or even a public hospital for Negroes, or a Negro ward in the white hospital, drawing into the community Negro physicians, surgeons, dentists, nurses, social workers, etc. One — sometimes two or three — Negro newspapers gave voice to the aspirations and dissatisfactions of the local colored group. One or more Negro theaters, a street of shops, a segment of the colored quarter owned by individuals or by a colored real estate dealer, perhaps a bank — all these gave undeniable evidence of substance and culture among the colored group.[4]

In such a community lived many Negroes to whom it was hard to refuse the ballot. This is not to say that a great many qualified Negroes of the professional group were not so refused. Nor does it take account of the large number of Negroes who, discouraged by their general political situation, never attempted to register even under favorable conditions. But, where other factors were equal, racial relationships, including suffrage attitudes, were noticeably softened in the presence of a considerable group of educated and well-to-do Negroes. Unless a member of such a group was an open critic of the existing order, or the center of some racial agitation, his white neighbors were often, albeit in a condescending manner, proud of him.[5]

A further source of strength to the urban Negro group was the possibility of organization. As has been indicated, the city Negro community was rare which did not support several fraternal bodies. Some of these, if you will, were absurd, feeble, even dishonest; but many also were active, vocal, and businesslike, and buttressed by a national organization and treasury. In a number of cities there were branches of the National Association for the Advancement of Colored People, quick to seize upon wrongs to the colored race; in others, the steadier Urban League, engaged in social work, research, and conference. The cities were the headquarters of the Negro or "black-and-tan" Republican committees, to which some unwilling attention must quietly be paid by the white community if only because of their influence upon Federal patronage. In a surprisingly large number of Southern cities, the years following the enactment of the disfranchising constitutions witnessed the growth of Civic Leagues and Forums for the discussion of public questions affecting the race, of Non-Partisan Leagues which coached Negroes to pass registration examinations, and fought cases of disfranchisement through the local courts and sometimes — as in Virginia — to the highest tribunal of the State.

The contacts among colored citizens fostered by such bodies, as well as by ordinary intercourse in a large and substantial community, could all help to secure more rights and privileges than was possible in villages and country districts. For such a community could fight, and while it was of course never strong enough to win by moral or physical force, it could sometimes secure concessions in order to avoid unpleasant publicity and litigation.[6] Such a community was also — in rarer cases — useful, if placated, in some local factional fight among politicians, some tax referendum, some bond issue election.

Out of an urban background such as has been here described — a background which was to be found in some or all of its details in Atlanta, in Raleigh, in Newport News, in Memphis, in Houston, e.g. — arose leadership. In view alone of the self-confessed political apathy of the Negro group, leadership in the struggle for political recognition was an essential condition of progress. More than this, however: in several cities which acknowledged the Negro as a factor in politics, one of the underlying reasons was skillful, tactful pressure upon influential white citizens on the part of Negro leaders.

The cities, therefore — not all of them, but they more than the little town and the country — provided for Negro suffrage a background of white apathy and Negro anonymity. The cities drew in a varied group of whites ready, perhaps anxious, for change. The cities were the seat of Negro culture, prosperity, and organization. The cities and their varied activities developed Negro leadership. Where white and Negro forces pulled in the same direction, there change was most clearly to be seen. A wealthy Negro real estate operator and his white banker, a Negro bishop and his friend in the city's liberal white church, a capable and obviously respectable Negro high-school principal and the white superintendent whom he had helped in a school bond election, a tactful old Negro of influence among his people and the liberal white editor whom he used to shave — such combinations accounted for many curious cases of "liberality" in Southern cities.

A few of these we shall now examine. The reader will bear in mind that conditions such as we have described operated effectively in a minority of Southern cities, that in no city were all of them effective, and that peculiar local factors added their force to certain situations.

II. URBAN CONDITIONS AND LEADERSHIP

Memphis, Tennessee, exhibited several of the urban phenomena we have described, and is interesting because of its importance in State (and therefore also national) politics. With a colored population in 1930 of 96,550 out of 253,143, it has voted as many as 3500 Negroes in a municipal campaign; sometimes, it was locally believed, more. It was the only place in West Tennessee — the State's Black Belt — to permit and even encourage Democratic primary voting among Negroes.

This situation resulted not from urban liberality on the part of the white citizenship, although the city was the home and chief sphere of influence of a white man prominent in the Interracial movement. It was due probably rather to the outright strength of the Negro population, under very skillful leadership, and to peculiar conditions of State politics.

Memphis was the largest city in Tennessee, and the only large city in that western section of the State which had always been distinct in interests and politics from Middle Tennessee, centering on Nashville, and East (mountain) Tennessee. Its vote therefore was crucial in the State primary elections, important in determining Tennessee's doubtful position in national politics, and essential to the power of the Democratic faction of its own portion of the State. Thus, in Memphis every vote counted; it was often charged, indeed, that many votes were made to count several times, and that others were disregarded in the counting. As Tennessee had no unusual voting requirements beyond poll-tax payment, and no state-wide white-primary rule, it was not easy to prevent Negroes from voting.

In this political background lived a Negro population very nearly half that of the city as a whole. A large part of this group was engaged in unskilled labor, principally about the docks and freight yards, and domestic service. There was, however, commercial activity, professional life, and even wealth in the community. Beale Street as a center of Negro-owned and operated activities was as well known among Negroes as Harlem. Great influence was wielded among Memphis Negroes by Robert R. Church, a man of fifty or sixty, wealthy, connected with many Negro business ventures of the city, donor to his group of a public park in the midst of valuable urban property, and astute enough to have retained until 1928 his place on the recognized Republican State committee through all the vicissitudes of lily-white attacks and convention reform. His people credited him with colored appointments to Federal office, with acts of charity, and, perhaps most important of all, with invincible political cleverness. Even Senator Heflin of Alabama paid tribute to Church, reading a poem into the Hearings of a patronage investigation:

> "Offices up a 'simmon tree,
> Bob Church on de ground;
> Bob Church said to de 'pointing power,
> 'Shake dem 'pointments down.' "

Church could, in short, "deliver" the Negro vote of Memphis, and influence it elsewhere.[7]

Church's Republicanism as such availed him nothing in the rock-ribbed Democracy of West Tennessee. But his influence among Negro voters made him an object of interest to the factional leaders of the Democratic party. He worked for many years with Edward Crump of Memphis on behalf of the Crump machine's city, county, and State candidates, in the Democratic primaries.[8]

It is not known just how large the Negro primary vote was.

Many questionnaire replies indicate that Negroes were freely admitted into Democratic primaries on application. A most amusing colloquy occurred during the hearings of the Senatorial subcommittee on the Memphis postmastership, referred to above, between a witness and Senator McKellar of Tennessee, himself a Memphian:

> *Mr. Poole:* . . . The Negroes locally vote the Democratic ticket with Senator McKellar.
>
> *Senator McKellar:* I do not know that at all.
>
> *Mr. Poole:* You should know it, Senator.
>
> *Senator McKellar:* . . . They do not have anything to do with the primary.
>
> *Mr. Welford:* Five thousand voted in the last primary.
>
> *Senator McKellar:* I do not think so.
>
> *Mr. Poole:* Senator McKellar, it is not necessary for you to talk to Church personally, with the machine you have down there, to get the Negro vote for you.
>
> *Senator McKellar:* I have not any machine at all. There were 26,000 votes cast in the last primary, and my recollection is that I got 24,000 of them. I do not see much machine about that.
>
> *The Chair:* I call it a very effective one.
>
> *Senator Heflin:* The Senator considers that an uprising of the people.

When in 1928 an issue was made of the matter by Crump's opponents, the Shelby County Democratic committeeman announced that there was no rule barring Negroes.[9] At every gubernatorial primary the cry of Negro influence was raised against the Crump machine. In 1928, pictures were taken of blocs of Negro voters, presumably bought repeaters, at various polling places.[10] The 1930 primary and election was conceded to Governor Horton in advance because of the sudden adherence of Crump and his Negro voters in Memphis, and the nomination of a very weak Republican through the machinations of Church. The consideration for Church seems to have been a promise of reapportionment in favor of the State Republican party.[11]

This Negro leader did not, however, confine himself to

playing in the white man's political game. In 1923, Rowlett Paine, campaigning for the mayoralty, was elected partly by the help of Negro votes won on written promises of improvements in the Negro section, checking of police brutality towards Negro prisoners, etc. In the course of his administration, it seemed to his Negro supporters that he was not keeping his pledges, and when over their strong protest he had a garbage incinerator erected a few hundred yards from the Negro high school and a Negro amusement park, the Negro leadership of Memphis struck back. Under Church, a mass meeting was held to discuss grievances, and a temporary organization effected. In the 1928 municipal election, Church threw his influence for Watkins Overton, Democratic nominee for the mayoralty, risking his position in the State Republican party by refusing to support a weak lily-white candidate put up at the instigation of Paine. It was at this election that the Negro vote was built up to its maximum, and it was credited with the election of Overton. In spite of the Negro's traditional Republican loyalty, Church's influence was great enough to swing it very largely for a Democrat.[12]

A peculiar combination of circumstances thus created in Memphis a steady body of Negro voters, a skeleton organization under Church, a potential Negro electorate comparatively easy to bring into occasional action, and a valuable political contact with a white machine.

In a group of western North Carolina cities a situation existed a little more prepossessing than that of Memphis, being based less on pure opportunism, less on merely political leadership, and more on solid foundations of mutual respect and good will. These cities were Durham, Raleigh, Greensboro, and, by report, Charlotte, Salisbury, and High Point. In all of these places the Negro population was about one-third of the total, except in Raleigh, where it was more, and High Point, where it was less. Although in all of them the Negro vote was small, the Negro applicant had a fair chance, and — what represented the most decided change

— in several of them he was acceptable in the Democratic primary.

In all of these cities, except High Point, there were Negro institutions of higher learning. In Greensboro there were two. In and near Durham, in addition, were the white institutions, Duke University and the University of North Carolina. Durham, Raleigh, and Greensboro were well provided with Negro business houses and other enterprises and professional men. Durham, the headquarters of the North Carolina Mutual Life Insurance Company, was reckoned a wealthy Negro community. Greensboro was the home of the national chairman of the Interracial Coöperation movement, and published a racially liberal newspaper, whose owner, with Negro help, had been mayor of the city.[13] In Raleigh, the State capital, was the office of the commissioner of Negro education, a man of wide contacts and experience among Negroes, whom Negroes considered singularly free of racial feeling. In so far as was compatible with retaining his office at all, he was a champion of fair treatment for the race.

In Durham and Raleigh especially, favorable political (and other) conditions may be traced back very specifically to Negro leadership. This centered in the former place in John Merrick, in the latter in Berry O'Kelly.

Merrick was born a slave in 1859, worked in a brickyard for six years after the war, learning to read and write at night, and went to Raleigh to carry a hod and lay bricks for Shaw University in 1877. Here he became successively a bootblack and a barber, finally moving to Durham, where he eventually became the proprietor of his own shop. His trade brought him in contact with the white leaders of the city, including the Duke family, whom he later induced to found a Negro hospital, a training school for nurses, and other institutions for Durham's colored community. Meanwhile, he bought real estate and houses, and slowly became well-to-do. Before his death in 1920, he had been active in the founding of a successful benefit association, a bank, and an insurance company which in 1930 occupied a six-story building in Durham's best business section, and had an annual premium income of a million and a quarter dollars.[14]

O'Kelly, born during the Civil War or shortly after, was still living in Method (a Negro-owned suburb of Raleigh) in 1930. He had no formal schooling, reaching the position of bank director, commission merchant, and real estate owner from the starting-point of "trading" from behind a little stall.[15] As in the case of Merrick, his business brought him into contact with white men of influence, and a great tact enabled him to secure concessions and benefactions for his race.

Of course, these two men did not alone account for the situation of the Negro citizen in the two cities in which they worked. Both helped to open up opportunities for other Negroes to establish themselves unassailably as honest, courteous, and intelligent business men, and both fell in with white neighbors of influence who could not see why such individuals should suffer from discrimination.* They are discussed here simply as examples of what is possible in cities, and in cities only.

Atlanta, Georgia, presented a slightly different picture from either Memphis or the North Carolina cities. Its Negro

* A story from Mobile, Alabama, illustrates what a combination of Negro ability and diplomacy with white open-mindedness may accomplish outside of the political field, and shows also the limits of such coöperation. Here, a Negro dentist so impressed a white colleague that he was asked himself to attend and to bring other colored dentists to the annual meetings of the white State Dental Association. When the Negro delegation arrived at a white hotel in a large Alabama city to take part in conferences and demonstrations, the white committee in charge saw to it that they were courteously treated by the bewildered staff of the hotel, and the white dentists in general outdid themselves in professional politeness. When this had gone on for some years, the Negro dentist to whose personality the whole situation was due, asked his white friend to accept dues from the Negroes who attended the meetings. The Negro group, he explained, wished to bear their share of the expenses of the Association. Here, however, the line was drawn. It was tactfully explained that the Negroes were the "guests" of the Association, and that there was no question of "dues" or "expense." Later, with the exquisite finesse which is part of every Southern Negro's protective coloration, the Mobile dentist asked his white friend to take up the matter of Negro membership in the *national* professional organization. He pointed out that Northern Negro dentists be-

population of 90,075—33.3% of the total[16]—made much the same impression of business activity as that of Memphis. In addition, Morris Brown University, Atlanta University (a merger of three independent institutions), and the Atlanta School for Social Work gave tangible evidence to the white community of the Atlanta Negro's cultural position. The headquarters of the Interracial Commission was in Atlanta, and from Atlanta Ben Davis, many times State Republican committeeman and national convention delegate, published a Negro weekly, the *Independent*.

The 1800-odd Negroes who constituted the normal colored electorate of the city did not, however, influence municipal campaigns, because debarred by a municipal white primary in this wholly Democratic city. They nevertheless registered freely if they wished and were qualified, and greatly influenced bond-issue elections and referenda. Their activity was due in some measure to Davis. Davis belied the common reputation of Negro politicians in the South: through his organ, the *Independent*, he urged Negroes to vote on every occasion.[17]

Portsmouth and Newport News, Virginia, smaller than Memphis and Atlanta, lacking the outstanding leadership and contacts between the races which distinguished Raleigh and Durham, nevertheless have produced Negro Voters' Leagues and Forums. In both cities, colored lawyers were the moving spirits. They guided these discussion groups, and the coaching classes connected with them which prepared Negro citizens to pass the registration tests. They took to court from

longed to the national body, and asked whether it was fair that Negroes who remained in their own Southland, serving the Southern community, should be denied privileges extended to Negroes who left the South. This reasoning impressed the State body, and it was agreed to accept the *national* dues of colored dentists in Alabama for *transmission* through the regular channels to the *national* organization. The Negro dentists, however, were still not members of the State body.

The situation among Mobile physicians was quite different. The Negro group felt that it was boycotted by the white doctors. They claimed that white physicians would not consult with Negro physicians, even that white surgeons would not operate on the patients of Negro general practitioners.

time to time the cases of Negro applicants who had been asked unfair questions. One of them maintained an up-to-date file of reliable colored voters. In Portsmouth, the situation was further improved for the colored voter by a hustings-court judge, referred to by the Negroes as "an old-fashioned Southern gentleman," who in spite of a conventional attitude towards the race, made short work of any attempt at illegal suffrage discrimination. In both cities the Catholic and Jewish elements on occasion joined hands with the Negro minorities to defeat Klannish candidates. In both, nonpartisan municipal elections prevailed, which greatly increased the Negro's chance of effective voting.

These are but a few samples of the note of change sounded, however faintly, in many Southern cities. Even in otherwise unfavorable situations, some factor like those discussed above might be seen at work. In Orangeburg, a small town in South Carolina, it was believed at the Negro State College there situated that more Negroes could have registered than the few who had applied, because of the influence of the State College itself. Incentive was lacking, however, in the face of the white primary and the solid Democracy of the section. In the hostile atmosphere of Hampton, Virginia, Hampton Institute nevertheless provided a background of Negro culture and professional life in which a voters' coaching class developed, led by a young lawyer who carried protests successfully before a local judge of rigid fairness. In New Orleans, which in spite of its cosmopolitan atmosphere frowned on Negro suffrage, a branch of the National Association for the Advancement of Colored People flourished, led by a courageous colored physician, which was planning a frontal attack on suffrage discriminations in the winter of 1929. In Texas, the battle against the white primary laws was waged from El Paso and Houston; in Arkansas, from Little Rock; in Virginia, from Richmond; in Florida, from Pensacola.[18]

The note of warning against too large inferences from these cases must again be struck. What was tolerated in Orangeburg had to be won in Hampton through the courts, although both were Negro university centers. What was true of Raleigh, Greensboro, Durham, was not true of the nearby Winston-Salem, with its larger Negro population at a lower social and economic level. Montgomery, a State capital with a Negro Normal School, had few Negro voters, and these had no influence; Birmingham, a large city, had even fewer in proportion. Against Roanoke's friendly registrar and urban atmosphere must be set Lynchburg's conservatism of both whites and Negroes, although they are both in the same section of Virginia, and both showed traces of Republicanism.

The political gains made by Negroes under the urban conditions we have described were not necessarily permanent. When Merrick died in Durham, he left an able successor in charge of his insurance company, equally influential among Negroes and respected by whites. This might not have been the case. Leading Negroes of Durham in 1929 bemoaned the loss of two white friends, one of whom moved to South Carolina, another of whom, connected with one of the city's tobacco companies, was promoted to its New York offices. A change of factions in office might at any time cut off white "contacts" and deprive Negro leadership of its leverage.

We shall turn, therefore, to certain special types of elections which worked to the advantage of the Negro citizen.

III. NONPARTISAN ELECTIONS

The most important opening for Negroes occurred through the use of the nonpartisan municipal ballot. This was to be found most often in connection with a commission or city-manager form of government. Municipal officers in such a place were elected without the intervention of a white primary. Of similar import was the absence of a municipal primary by decision of the party authorities. In the case of cities with ordinary municipal primaries, independent or nonpartisan candidates appeared from time to time in connection with "clean-up" and "dry" movements. Party irregularity also could be condoned when it confined itself to contesting a mayoralty or an aldermanship.

The number of cities south of the Border States operating under a city-manager charter was in 1930 one hundred and fifteen. In 1927 there were thirty-two cities in the South of thirty thousand or more under the commission plan.[19] Of course, the Negro vote did not figure in all of these. Jackson, Mississippi, was a commission city, but its commissioners were chosen in a white primary. In Roanoke, Virginia, the first city-manager election, nonpartisan, gave the city a Council of one Republican and two Democrats. The Democratic party then exercised its option and held primaries, and after this change, the Council remained solidly Democratic.[20] The commissioners who supervise the city manager of Austin, Texas, were in 1930 unpaid; there was, therefore, no contest for the offices, and no reason for encouraging Negro voters. Formerly, when the commissionerships carried salaries, they were considered more desirable, and when several more candidates offered than places available, the Negro votes of the city were a factor in the election.[21]

In Norfolk, Portsmouth, and Newport News, Virginia, the city commissioners were elected on a city-wide nonpartisan ticket, the three or five highest candidates on the list taking office. This arrangement, which prevailed in other cities as well, made the Negro vote important, even when small, for to candidates with only moderate strength a few votes, in a warmly contested election, might mean the difference between fifth place — barely elected, and sixth place — barely defeated. The normal Negro vote was 300 in Norfolk, 250 in Newport News, and 400 in Portsmouth, with a registered "reserve" of voters that could on occasion double or more than double the Negro showing at a municipal election.[22] That their votes were solicited in a systematic, if quiet, way was not only contended by Negro leaders, but admitted by white newspaper men, interracial commission members, etc.[23] In the five largest cities of Texas, the campaign for Negro votes in municipal elections was quite open.[24] In San Antonio, there had long been "peculiar [and favorable] local conditions with respect to the colored people," as testified by the congressman from the district.[25] In Galveston, a "People's Party" prepared tickets to oppose the regular Democracy, and both invited Negro participation. Similarly in Dallas, the municipal contests were staged between candidates approved by a Citizens Association and independents. Both at election time staged campaigns among Negroes which were reported by the local newspapers. All these cities enjoyed technically nonpartisan elections — that is, there were no primaries, but simply one open contest, and no party labels appeared on the ballots.

The most striking type of Negro participation in city politics, considering Southern belief in its corrupting effects,* was in "reform" campaigns.

Savannah, Georgia, saw one such in 1923. The incumbent mayor, Stewart, ran in the Democratic primary against one Rogers, who represented a general reform — and especially a dry — group in the city. Although polling 4893 votes in the primary, Rogers was defeated — fraudulently, he claimed. He could not himself run as an independent because of the compulsory pledge all primary aspirants in Georgia must take, to accept the regular nominee. He handed on the mantle, however, to one Seabrooke, and a fierce campaign was waged to organize the Negro vote, which was thought to be about 2200. The Negro voters, in the hands of their ministers and of their womenfolk, who were in turn influenced by their white mistresses, were nearly solid behind the Seabrooke reform ticket.

As election day approached, the Stewart forces, by making "nigger-lover" charges, tried to turn this Negro support into a millstone about the reformers' necks. Crude posters ap-

* On the "corrupting" influence of the Negro vote, it is interesting to note the case of Atlanta, where Negroes had no *municipal* voting strength, and where a sensational Grand Jury investigation in 1929 and 1930 resulted in heavy fines and chain-gang sentences for several councilmen and executive officers on conviction for bribery, extortion, etc. V. *N. Y. Times*, e.g., 13 January 1930, 6 April 1930, and 12 April 1931.

peared on Negro churches and lodge buildings, bearing the device, under a skull and crossbones: "This is a white man's fight."

This called for action on the part of the Seabrooke organization. A force of vigilantes was organized to protect Negro voters at the polls, and a squadron of automobiles — some of white ownership — was gotten together to bring reform Negroes out to vote. The reformers won, by 6049 to 3952. As their first candidate, Rogers, had polled only 4893 at the primaries, all of which must have been white votes, they had increased their strength by 1156 by the time of the regular election. It was generally believed in Savannah that a great many of these votes were cast by Negroes.[26]

A year after the passage of the woman suffrage amendment, which had been much opposed throughout the South because of its effect on the Negro vote, a reform ticket was put in the field in Nashville, Tennessee, against the administration ticket, which was charged with corruption. The administration had a good deal of Negro support, because the mayor personally was friendly with Negroes. The reform group assembled the women of the city who had fought for suffrage, and challenged them to prove, by getting the Negro women out behind the reform ticket, that the Twentieth Amendment was not a menace. The challenge was accepted, and on election day maids and cooks were taken to the polls by their mistresses in automobiles. The reform group carried the day.[27]

In Fort Worth, Texas, a referendum was held on the question of adopting a city-manager charter. The proponents of the change used as their chief arguments the existing commission's alleged corruption and alliances with vice. The Negro population was interested both because of the possibility of driving the red-light district out of its own residence quarter, and because of the promise of nonpartisan elections in the new charter, in which they might share. With reformers and Negroes allied at the special election, the change was made.[28]

Thus far, we have dealt exclusively with elections to office, and have seen that the Negro vote was largest and most effective where there were contests. Another type of election also brought in the Negro vote: referenda on bonds, tax rates, amendments, city extensions, etc. Here there was of course no question of a primary.

Such referenda, which were most often bond-issue matters, therefore offered the Negro voter the same steady stimulus for registration and voting as did nonpartisan city elections. Since the Negro community had a great deal to gain in bond issues for school, paving, and other improvements, in keeping some measure of control over tax rates, etc., Negro leaders urged their group to get into politics on this account alone. White citizens, too, were often anxious to have additional support for improvements which they wished to put over in spite of an opposition based on economy, or — conversely — which they wished to see defeated in order to keep tax rates down, or for other reasons. Since the vote at referenda is often small, a few votes may mean a great deal one way or the other. In some cases, where the law required that a majority, or even two-thirds, of the property holders or eligible voters affected must vote to make the election valid, it was essential to get out every possible vote.

As these referenda did not on the surface affect "white supremacy," negrophobia did not operate in campaigns centering about them. Indeed, campaigning for Negro votes was much more widespread and open in such elections than in any other type, and more cases came up in which it could be fairly concluded that the Negro vote was the determining factor. Yet it must always be recalled that the Negro vote was on the whole small in the South; referenda, like nonpartisan city elections, were but outstanding exceptions gaining prominence against the background of Negro nonvoting.

In Negro circles, the best-known case of Negro influence on bond-issue elections was that of the Atlanta referendum of 1921.[29] An issue of four million dollars was proposed for the carrying out of a comprehensive school building plan, the first thoroughgoing scheme to be offered since the Civil War. At first, there was much opposition to it because of the effect on city taxes, and a certain degree of organization against it was effected among the Negroes of Atlanta by real-estate and and property-owning elements on this ground. The administration was anxious, however, to put it through, and went to an Atlantan of great influence among the Negro population to secure the Negro vote in its favor. The Negro group was at first not satisfied with the share of improvements offered them, and the issue was twice defeated. Thereupon a meeting was arranged between the mayor of the city and the president of the Board of Education, on the one hand, and Negro leaders on the other. The promise was given that one and one-quarter or one and one-third millions out of the total issue would go into new Negro schools and the improvement of old equipment, and thereupon the measure passed.[30] In 1926, a similar deal was made over a smaller sum; in this case, unlike the first, the promises made to the Negro leaders were not kept to the full.[31]

There were not many cities in which, like Atlanta, the Negro vote was large and active enough to make demands before delivering its ballots. Louisville, Kentucky, with its large Negro vote and bipartisan municipal politics, was one such. Here, after a squabble between a policeman and a Negro picnic party had brought about an order barring Negroes from all parks, a bond issue for park purposes was defeated. It was then proposed that a new park be developed with some of the proceeds of the issue, devoted exclusively to Negro use; this satisfied enough of the Negro voters to secure passage of the proposal.[32] When the city proposed to borrow a million dollars for its municipal university, Negro leaders objected, pointing out that they were barred from this institution under the State law. They were then promised that some of the proceeds would be set aside for a branch college for Negroes. The issue passed.[33] Other cities of the Border States fell into the same class.

Farther south, Augusta, Savannah, Durham, Greensboro,

Raleigh, and the five large Texas cities already referred to were among those which offered the best leverage for referendum power to their Negro citizens. Elsewhere, an occasional disputed proposal temporarily increased the Negro vote, and induced all hands to try to influence it. From all these places, and many others, indirect evidence indicates the unabashed presence of Negro voters at the polls at a referendum election. Sometimes one encountered a reluctant admission: "In bond elections in the past Negroes have voted . . . but they have no right to vote today for the defeat of any democrat." [34] Sometimes a straightforward news account told of a Negro political meeting, occasionally addressed by white speakers, as in the case of the Atlanta city-manager charter campaigns, the Alabama port-improvement measures, the Tampa charter revision election.[35] There were warnings of Negro power in some current issue.[36] There were stories and editorials in Negro newspapers.[37]

Even where the outcome of a referendum was not in doubt, Negro voters were often encouraged, sometimes merely to make a certainty doubly sure, but sometimes out of a spirit of fair play, or because the occasion was safe for the advertisement of "cordial relationships between the races." * Several types of appeal were made to Negro voters: the promise of a share in the proceeds of bond issues; the prospect of "better business" and of employment if construction projects were undertaken. The Negro's civic pride was sometimes appealed to; or he was reminded of the negrophobia of the people opposing the measures.

* Sometimes Negroes also carry on a dumb-show of "cordial relationships" with the whites. A Negro leader in Birmingham explained that his group had no real power even in referenda, and that about the only way in which Negroes could call themselves favorably to the attention of public officers was through some gesture like a letter of congratulation on election, or an editorial in a Negro newspaper commending some improvement scheme. If it was deemed safe, some phrase was delicately introduced such as "In view of your well-known fairness," etc., or "The colored citizens appreciate the need for such-and-such expenditures." The writer saw several letters from Birmingham officials politely acknowledging such gestures.

IV. LIMITS OF THE WHITE PRIMARY

The Negro vote was noticeably smaller outside of municipal elections, for the white primary was universal from the county unit up, and this, as we have seen, was the greatest obstacle to Negro suffrage. Nevertheless, there were situations in which the white primary gave way, and these are worth some examination.

In the Border States, the Negro was most likely to find himself free to vote in the Democratic primary. West Virginia — to all intents a Northern State in the matter of Negro suffrage — offered few, if any, exceptions to this rule. In Kentucky it may be that the blackest of Black Belt counties refused to admit Negroes to the Democratic primary. In Tennessee, we have seen that Negro Democrats were a power in Memphis; they were fairly numerous in Nashville, and tolerated to a greater or less degree in other cities and towns of Middle and East Tennessee. Arkansas, with proportionately the largest Negro population of this group, had a white primary party rule, strictly enforced from about 1924 on.

But since there existed in the Border States a well-established and active Republican party, claiming the traditional allegiance of the Negro voter, the absence of barriers to the Democratic primary did not bring any large number of Negroes into the Democratic ranks.[38] Indeed, the Negro did not so much need access to the Democratic primaries where a real opposition existed.[39]

Only North Carolina, among States south of the Border group, admitted Negroes to the Democratic primary in any number, and this only in the group of western counties whose city Negro voters we have already discussed.[40]

These four States — West Virginia, Kentucky, Tennessee, and North Carolina — had no State-wide party rule barring Negroes from the Democratic primary.[41] Elsewhere, breaches in the white primary were due to obscure local anomalies and exceptions made in favor of individuals.

In South Carolina there were in 1930 a straggling few

"Hampton Negroes" to be found at the primary polls, admitted under the qualification, supported by statements from ten white men, that they had voted for Wade Hampton in the "Redemption" election of 1876 and had been Democratic ever since. Of course, this was a rapidly dwindling group.* The tendency to stretch a point now and then in favor of a "good" Negro or a staunch supporter seemed in recent years to have decreased.[42] The *Charleston News and Courier* once advocated a "selective" admission of such Negroes as "would look on it, in some sense, as an honor." [43]

In a large gulf city, in spite of the State party's white primary rule, a little bloc of Negroes voted regularly in the municipal and county primaries for some untraceable reason.[44] In Birmingham, Alabama, a very few Negroes voted in the primary who were variously described as "Uncle Toms" by those who did not, and as "leading colored citizens" by themselves.[45]

In Texas, North Carolina, and Alabama, the Democratic party in 1929-30 split — or nearly split — over the Federal senatorship and gubernatorial nominations into Hoovercrat and "regular" factions. This resulted, in two States, in a temporary lowering of white primary bars. The Hoovercrat aspirant for the governorship of Texas, Thomas J. Love, charged the regular organization with failure to reaffirm the white primary rule during the campaign. According to a colored newspaper in Houston, four counties actually let down the primary bars for this occasion.[46] The *Dallas News*, indeed, said that it could see no reason why Negro Democrats should be barred from the party nominating machinery.[47] In North Carolina, the contest between Senator Simmons, anti-Smith Democrat, and Josiah Bailey, regular, not only increased the Negro Democratic registration where

* A Columbia editor thus bemoaned the passing of one of its members: "With the death Tuesday of Henry Dark, Columbia lost one of its few remaining 'old-time' darkies . . . For twenty years he was janitor of the county court house . . . since 1876 he had voted the Democratic ticket . . . There was a quiet self-respect about Dark that somehow distinguished him from many members of his race." (*Columbia State*, 25 November 1920.)

it already existed, but raised the suspicion that county white primary rules had been quietly suspended throughout the State.[48]

The whole question of white primary rules and the laws under which they were drawn was in 1930 ripe for final adjudication by the Supreme Court of the United States. Negro leaders had already recognized the crucial importance of this matter, now that the status of the disfranchising constitutions had been fixed.[49]

In Texas, where Negro power in Democratic primaries had in the past been considerable, several cases had been pushed through the State courts.[50] One went to the Supreme Court in Washington and gained a temporary victory for the Negro plaintiffs. The *law* specifically barring Negroes from Democratic primaries was declared in violation of the Fourteenth Amendment in a decision written by Justice Holmes in March, 1927.[51] Thereupon the Legislature of Texas, expressing in deferential language its unwillingness to defy the Court, passed a new law, reverting to the model long in use in other Southern States, whereby "Every political party in this State through its State Executive Committee shall have the power to prescribe the qualifications of its own members, and shall in its own way determine who shall be qualified to vote or otherwise participate in such political party." The Democratic party authorities followed this up immediately with a rule under which only white Democrats might participate in party affairs.[52]

Three cases were taken to the United States District Court under the new law and party rule. In all, the decisions went against the Negro plaintiffs, on the ground that the Democratic party was a private organization, and therefore not subject to the limitations of the Fourteenth and Fifteenth Amendments. The same decision was reached by the State courts in Arkansas.[53]

In Virginia, Negroes attacking the white primary rule of the Democratic party and the enabling statute of the State, won an initial victory in the United States District Court, and sustained their position in the Circuit Court of Appeals.[54] The State of Virginia, it was held in the appealed case, could not delegate to its creature, the Democratic party, the right to draw a color line in matters of suffrage which the State itself had been denied by the Fifteenth Amendment. As a result, there was a noticeable tendency, at least in the larger cities of Virginia, to admit Negroes to the State primaries after the 1929 decision.[55]

This, however, was not to be the end of the matter. From Texas and Arkansas, Negro appeals to the Federal Supreme Court were planned; from Virginia, appeals in behalf of the white primary.[56] The decision it is impossible to forecast at this writing, for there is a neat legal distinction between the Texas and Arkansas cases, and the Virginia case.

In Virginia, it was argued in behalf of the Negro Democrats that the primary was paid for out of State funds, and the courts therefore held that the party, as a creature of the State, must respect the limitations laid down by the two Civil War amendments. In Texas and Arkansas, however, the primary was conducted by party officers, and paid for out of party funds. The courts sitting in these cases on this ground decided for the validity of the white primary rule. At the time of these decisions, five Southern States had primary systems financed (and in most cases officered) by the party itself. These were in 1930 safe from Federal interference as the question then stood. The other seven needed merely to change over from the State-managed to the party-managed primary system to be equally well within the law.[57] So far, no court had held unconstitutional any white primary rule, made by a party authority, when such party conducted and paid for its own primaries — that is, was arguably a "private association."

All in all, then, the primary situation was such as to offer the Negro voter a free fight and an open field only in exceptional cases. How did he fare in ordinary elections?

V. TEMPORARY CALLS ON THE NEGRO

Every four years, Negro voters, where for any reasons there were such, cast their ballots for President of the United States. The presidential election, with the few exceptions we are to note presently, was the only election south of the Border States in which there was a contest between the major parties. Of course, until November, 1928, it had always been a foregone conclusion that the Southern States would fall in line solidly behind the Democratic nominee. Southern opinion, therefore, tolerated this quadrennial excursion of Negroes to the ballot box, as it would not have if the contests were real, as it did not in the case of other elections where there were contests. This periodical loosening of the leash by which Negro political activity was restrained resulted, all observers agreed, in a quadrennial increase in Negro registration and voting.[58] Other factors accentuated this cycle: the traditional Republican loyalty of the Negro; the seeming choice offered on the ballot, so different from "off" years when only one ticket — the Democratic — was in the field; the activity of the Republican party officials, anxious to make a good showing and impress national party headquarters.[59]

Under these circumstances, it may be asked why all Negroes — or at least as many Negroes as whites — did not vote in presidential years. The answer has already been given: as many Negroes voted as did because of the far larger number that did not. Enough Negro voters, and some Southern States might conceivably go Republican through Negro votes alone; certainly such Southern States as had a considerable white Republican electorate might easily have helped elect a Republican president every four years, and lost their strength in Democratic party councils. Moreover, once registered, the Negro voter stood armed with the right to vote in all elections. Negro voting strength in the separate States might put over Republican, third-party, or bolting Democratic State administrations under obligations to the Negro electorate, elect county and city governments, send up

Congressional delegations similarly tainted. The "Negro balance of power" stood in the way. As long as the number of Negro voters remained small, its presence at presidential elections did not especially disturb the South.

The events of the presidential campaign in 1928 illustrate in a small way what the South feared in case of a divided white electorate. With a "wet, Catholic, and Tammany" candidate at the head of the Democratic ticket, thousands of Southern Democrats were for the time being alienated from their accustomed allegiance. For the first time since the days of Populism, open organizations opposed to the regular Democracy carried on heated campaigns in Southern States. The election-day results were in doubt in all but three or four States. In the event, Mr. Hoover carried West Virginia, Virginia, Kentucky, Tennessee, North Carolina, Florida, and Texas.[60] There is no doubt but that a strenuous though quiet campaign for the Negro vote was carried on in many cities of the South. There was a Negro Democratic organization in Richmond, in Portsmouth, in Norfolk, in Roanoke, in Augusta, in Savannah, in Raleigh, in Nashville, in Memphis, e.g. Smith buttons, posters, and stickers appeared in the Negro district of Atlanta. "Goose-neck Bill" McDonald, once Republican committeeman from Texas, threw all the weight of his organization for Smith among his fellow Negroes of Texas.[61] Everywhere one heard of undercover campaigning for Negro votes by regular Democrats, by Republicans of course, and — usually from a distance, to avoid the damning "nigger-lover" charges held in readiness by the regulars — by Hoovercrats.[62] Were this state of affairs to become chronic, the Negro electorate would have to be organized and concessions made to it. This was the best guarantee that 1928 would remain for some time an exceptional presidential year.

In ordinary State and county elections the Negro vote was very small. Again the Border States were an exception; offering their electorate a choice between Republicans and Democrats in many of their congressional and State-legislature districts, a State executive ballot on which Republicans had a dim chance, and county tickets on which the odds were often against the Democrats, they automatically invoked Negro partisanship at the general election even where Negroes were locally barred from the Democratic primaries.

Only in Virginia, on two occasions, did a real contest occur in the State election sufficient to draw in the Negro voter. The first was in 1921, when lily-whitism first openly entered the field; the second was in 1929, when Hoovercrats and regular Democrats split and sent separate nominees to the November polls.

In 1921, when Henry W. Anderson secured control of the Republican State Convention for the lily-white faction, a Negro ticket was put in the field. This was not wholly a matter of rebuking the Anderson faction, nor even of preparing a show of strength to impress the national party organization. It was done after conference with the white party officials behind the Democrat Trinkle. The object was to provide an outlet for Negro indignation without compromising the Democratic ticket by a sudden adherence of Negro voters. Trinkle's ticket won, Anderson ran second, and Mitchell, the Negro aspirant for the governorship, a bad third. It was suspected that in subsequent campaigns Mitchell and his friends and successors were on occasion used for drawing Negro votes from the growing Republican opposition.[63]

The 1929 State campaign was a bitter compound of long-standing issues, new features, and heritages from the Hoovercrat bolt of 1928. An alliance was struck up between Hoovercrats and Republicans to defeat the regular Democratic nominee. There were thus two sets of candidates in the field, and the uncertainty was far greater than in 1921, for both groups looked back, one with hope and one with foreboding, to the twenty-five thousand Republican majority in the preceding national election.

There is little doubt that the Negro vote was solicited in this campaign. In Richmond credible sources ascribed to both parties the attempt to get a local Negro Republican leader quietly behind them, and to tour the State in behalf of one of the candidates. In Richmond and elsewhere, party organizations had in the 1928 national campaign established relations with Negro leaders which might easily have been renewed on this occasion.

Such were the vicissitudes besetting State politics and the Negro vote in a commonwealth with a real opposition party. Even in dyed-in-the-wool Democratic States, however, occasions arose on which every ballot counted, whether deposited by a white hand or a black. Such an election occurred in Georgia in 1929. It was the outcome of a bolt from the Democratic primary, which caused a contest at the regular election.

The Congressional seat for the Fifth District, including the city of Atlanta, fell vacant through the death of Representative Leslie J. Steele. The call for a special Democratic primary, to precede the normally merely formal election, barred Hoovercrats neither from voting nor from candidacy. It did, however, require a pledge of party loyalty from aspirants, in quite the ordinary terms. Nevertheless, Hooper Alexander, Hoovercrat, announced that he would run as an independent, for some reason conceiving himself to be barred from the primary by the "ring," through this pledge. James Hill Palmer also entered the contest as an independent, urging the evils of one-party politics and "machine control." [64]

The "Negro balance of power" issue confronted the rebels from the beginning. The regular Democratic nominee, Ramspeck, victor in the primary, recalled "the agony which followed the surrender of Lee," adverted to the "effort . . . under way by the Negroes of the North to nullify the white primary system . . . and to force upon the country social equality," compared this iniquity with the "effort . . . now being made in [this] district to destroy our white primary." [65] The dreadful charge was made direct: Alexander was "too busy courting the 'dark' vote of Fulton County to give . . . consideration" to the real issues of the campaign. Palmer, said Ramspeck, had bought the support of the Negro Republican paper, the *Independent*, edited by Ben Davis, by dropping from his speeches earlier promises to have Oscar DePriest, Negro congressman from Illinois, impeached. Both bolting candidates, added Ramspeck, were "necessarily hoping to receive the votes of the 3301 registered Negro voters of Fulton County." [66]

In the event, Ramspeck received 6759 votes, Alexander, 2537, and Palmer, 121. Only about 9500 eligibles voted out of 65,000 in the district; the three to five thousand possible Negro votes, therefore, were not to be sneezed at.[67] It is widely supposed in Atlanta that Alexander supporters at least made a quiet bid for this "balance of power"; it accords with our general diagnosis of the Negro voter's position in Atlanta.[68]

Cases of this sort must recur in the South. Office-holders will sometimes die, resign, or be promoted, necessitating a special election without benefit of primary. We have seen that in several Southern cities an "open" municipal election had created a body of Negro voters; there at least, where the custom of solicitation had developed, we may be pardoned for suspecting that this body, when need arose, was drawn into a larger sphere of electoral usefulness. The foremost Negro leader in the South assured the writer that on several occasions he had been approached for the names and addresses of Negro voters, when State contests were impending, so that they might be asked to give their votes and influence.

Whenever, therefore, two candidates appeared at an election, a bid was likely to be made for the Negro vote. Who made it, and how it was made, depended on circumstances. In 1928, Hoovercrats made it, where at all, cautiously, fearing to be tarred as "Black Republicans" by the regular Democrats, fearing to give color to charges that independency in politics would — to quote Representative Ramspeck — "bring back the agony following the surrender of Lee." In the congressional election in Georgia just described, it was the independents who played most with the Negro vote, perhaps because it was large and the hope forlorn without it, perhaps because, as we previously saw, it was customary to play with the Negro vote in Atlanta on other matters. Sometimes — to introduce a lifelike confusion into this account — perfectly good and eligible Negro voters were asked to refrain from voting, in order not to compromise some friendly candidate.[69]

It appears, then, that there were four circumstances in which there might be an appreciable Negro vote in a Southern community. One was the case of the presidential election, which may be dismissed as insignificant from the viewpoint of effective Negro political power. The two which were most significant were nonpartisan municipal elections, and referenda. Cases under a fourth heading — unexpected contests for office — while most sensational, were exceptional; they depended on such accidents as some politician's resignation or removal, death, or courage to bolt from his party. The significance of such cases could be great only in the event of a thoroughgoing party revolt in the South, like that of the eighties and nineties.

The only place in the South where the Negro had by 1930 made a real breach in the white primary system was Memphis. The largest number of Negroes voting in general elections, even under favorable urban conditions, was 3500, again in Memphis. The largest number of Negroes registered in a Southern State below the Border group was probably Virginia's 18,000 — 5.2% of the literate colored population of voting age in the State.

The matter is perhaps best summed up in the questionnaire reply of a Negro physician: ". . . where our friends need us, we vote. . ." *

* Cf. the following from the *N. Y. Times*' Texas correspondence, anent discussions in the American Legion of that State over the admission of Negroes: "It is not polite to enquire too closely into men's motives. Certainly the additional income to be gained by the Legion here through Negro memberships at a time when a child welfare and an educational program sharpens the economic need, is not its only reason for considering the problem." (7 September 1930.)

CHAPTER VIII

WHITE POLITICS IN THE SOUTH

I. PRELIMINARY CONSIDERATIONS

If previous chapters have shown anything, it is that the Negro in politics has never been and cannot be considered in a framework of abstract considerations, or of merely general political conditions. He must be studied with reference to the particular set-ups in the white politics about him.

In its recent aspects, white politics presents even greater difficulties, arising out of the nearness of the events, than the analysis of Negro voting. For developments in Negro political activity were sluggish compared with party politics, in thirteen States, finding its expression in some sort of election every year, with its concomitants of feverish campaigning, the raising of issues, the forming of temporary alliances, the calling of names, the portentous newspaper editorials — all of which might or might not signify *real* changes in political conditions and a *real* shake-up of the voting masses.

We shall confine ourselves, therefore, to white politics as it bears directly on Negro suffrage, at the expense, perhaps, of painting the whole background. This means, in effect, endeavoring to find out whether party splits or new alignments were impending in 1930 such as had in the past brought in the Negro voter.

The theoretical possibilities were three: What, from the standpoint of 1930, were the chances of new and third parties in the South? What was the likelihood for an effective Republicanism? What were the issues within the State Democratic parties which might bring about an effective and lasting cleavage among their adherents, finding expression either in independency carried to the polls, or in coherent factionalism at the primaries?

TABLE I

THIRD PARTIES IN THE SOUTH. VOTE FOR PRESIDENT, 1900-1924

State	*1900 Pop.*	*1904 Pop.*	*1908 Pop.*	*1912 Prog.*	*1916 None*	*1920 F.-L.*	*1924 Pr.-Soc.*
Ala.	4,178	5,051	1,568	22,689	....	......	8,084
Ark.	972	2,318	1,026	21,673	....	......	13,173
Fla.	1,070	1,605	1,946	4,535	....	......	8,625
Ga.	4,584	22,635	16,969	22,010	....	......	12,691
Ky.	2,017	2,511	333	102,766	....	......	38,465
La.	......	......	......	9,323	....	......	......
Miss.	1,644	1,424	1,276	3,627	....	......	3,494
N. C.	830	819	......	69,130	....	......	6,697
S. C.	......	1	......	1,293	....	......	620
Tenn.	1,322	2,506	1,081	53,725	....	......	10,656
Tex.	20,981	8,062	994	26,755	....	......	42,881
Va.	63	359	105	21,777	....	240	10,379

Source: Stanwood.

The parties were: 1900 to 1908, Populist; 1912, Progressive; 1920, Farmer-Labor; 1924, Progressive-Socialist coalition for Senator Robert LaFollette.

The 1912 column should be compared with the 1912 column of Table III, and the two together with the 1908 column of Table III, for a clear demonstration of the fact that Progressivism drew far more on Southern Republicanism than on the Democratic party. None of these parties carried a single Southern State. The combined Republican and Progressive vote of Kentucky in 1912 came within one thousand of the actual Democratic majority.

It is a truism that third parties in American politics have the merest ghost of a chance for success, save in the presence of a burning national issue. No such party was to be found on the horizon of practical politics in 1930. What the South might do with some future development was a matter outside the scope of the historian; certainly it had offered no encouragement in the recent past.

Even the agrarian movements of the eighties and nineties began in the West. The Roosevelt and LaFollette Progressive movements, much more than Greenbackism and Populism, were Western rather than Southern in their origin. Neither the 1912 nor the 1924 Progressive campaigns carried a single

TABLE II

RADICAL PARTIES IN THE SOUTH. VOTE FOR PRESIDENT, 1900-1928

State	*1900*	*1904*	*1908*	*1912*	*1916*	*1920*	*1924*	*1928*
Ala.	......	853	1,399	3,029	1,925	2,369	8.084	460
Ark.	27	1,816	5,482	8,153	6,999	5,111	13,173	429
Fla.	601	2,337	3,747	4,806	5,353	5,189	8,625	4,036
Ga.	......	197	584	1,014	967	465	12,691	124
Ky.	770	4,198	4,589	12,603	5,067	6,409	38,465	1,117
La.	......	995	2,536	5,249	292	......	......	......
Miss.	......	392	978	2,017	1,484	1,639	3,494	......
N. C.	......	124	345	1,025	490	446	6,697	......
S. C.	......	22	100	164	135	28	620	44
Tenn.	......	1,354	1,870	3,492	2,542	2,268	10,656	631
Tex.	162	3,212	8,046	26,185	18,963	8,121	42,881	722
Va.	167	274	280	870	1,127	807	10,379	430

Sources: to 1928, Stanwood; for 1928, World Almanac.

The figures are the totals for Socialist, Social-Democratic, and Socialist-Labor vote where any of these appeared in the sources. The small and recent Communist vote is not included. The large "radical" vote in 1924 is that for the LaFollette-Socialist combined ticket, which drew in many agrarian Republicans. It is interesting to note how sharply the radical vote rose for the 1912 election, the year of the Roosevelt-Progressive movement. It seems as though many Southern Republicans felt themselves unable to vote for either branch of their old party.

Southern State. The only returns giving the slightest comfort to the new parties were those of Kentucky in the Roosevelt campaign, where the Republican and Progressive vote, if combined, came within a thousand of the actual Democratic majority. The Progressive movement in both these years drew almost entirely on the feeble Republicanism of the South, very little on an assumedly discontented Democracy, as may be seen from Tables I and III.

The vote polled in the South by the radical parties has always been so small as to be negligible. Since Socialists in the most highly industrialized areas of the North had never succeeded, up to 1930, in winning more than a few mayoralties and city councils, with an occasional State Assembly and

Congressional seat from the same neighborhoods, their prospects in the agricultural and Jeffersonian South were extremely slight (Table II).

The Negro citizen of 1930, therefore, could not count on being drawn into Southern politics in his own lifetime by any third-party movement.

This narrowed the field of profitable analysis and speculation to two factors: the growth of Republicanism, and divisions over State policies among Democrats.

That Republicanism in the South would ever come into power — or even develop into a genuine and steady opposition — through the increase of Negro Republican votes was more than doubtful. In the absence of all reliable statistics, it is impossible to say whether the total Negro vote in the South increased after 1910,[1] although the circumstances under which it did grow in certain places, as has been seen, were circumstances which were coming to prevail in many parts of the South. Such local increases as occurred, were due not to efforts to build up a Negro Republican party, but to an increased Negro participation in nonpartisan elections.

II. THE SOUTH'S "NEW" REPUBLICANISM

What, then, of white Republicanism in the South? For in the light of past events, it is safe to assume that the development of bipartisan politics in the South would sooner or later draw in the Negro voter.

White Republicanism in the South, as a form of dissent in certain restricted regions, carried through into the twentieth century. Its lineage, however, was not Hamiltonian or industrial; rather did it stem from anti-Bourbonism, from the Unionism of the Civil War period, from pure Jacksonian Democracy, from a long-persistent frontier tradition. It was restricted to the white counties, and had nothing in common with organized national Republicanism but a name.[2] The mountain counties were also in many cases the center of industrialization, notably in North Carolina's textile manufacturing district; here this older Republicanism was reënforced by the tendency of manufacturers to cleave to the Northern industrial party.

A "new" Republicanism in the South, based neither on the Negro vote nor on the white counties, was much discussed, especially outside of the South, in the ten or fifteen years preceding the national election of 1928. There was supposed to be a growing consciousness in the South of the evils of a one-party system in local politics. The industrialization of the South, the diversification of agriculture, the development of extractive industries, and Northern immigration into the South, all created Republican sympathies at least on the tariff. This new Republicanism harked back to the Southern Whiggism of the eighteen-forties and fifties.

When in 1928 Herbert Hoover carried seven Southern States and rolled up a large Republican vote in the remaining six, many observers of the contemporary scene proclaimed that the end of the Solid South was in sight — that political wisdom and economic determinism had triumphed over the dead weight of tradition. But the returns of State and congressional elections in 1929 and 1930 showed how ill-founded were these prophecies. In South Carolina, Cole Blease, in spite of having been for years the idol of the poor white Democracy, went down to defeat in the Senatorial primaries as a Hoovercrat — an apostate. In Alabama, Thomas Heflin, similarly idolized as the poor man's friend, was barred from the Democratic primaries for his backsliding in 1928, and snowed under when he ran in the election as an independent. In Virginia, anti-Smith Democrats and lily-white Republicans staked their joint heritage of 1928 influence on the 1929 State ticket, and lost. In Texas, the candidacy of an anti-Smith supporter for the governorship was nipped in the first primary, two simon-pure Democrats only reaching the "run-off." A Southern Republican contingent in Congress was reduced from twenty-four to ten.[3]

This reversion from Republicanism was exaggerated by continued agricultural depression, by the stock market crash of 1929, unemployment, and hard times. When we consider, however, the obstacles to Republicanism in the South, we are led more easily to the conclusion that the 1928 election was won by anti-Catholicism and prohibition, rather than by the conversion of Southern Democrats, and that it was a freak not soon to be looked for again.[4]

A glance at the popular vote for Republican presidents in the South from 1896 onwards, stopping short of 1928 (Table III), will show how very small was the growth of Republicanism up to that point. It is a truism to say that the dead weight of effective tradition in the South had long regarded Republicanism with horror, and linked it with "niggerism." Any change in this view was contingent upon an improbable concatenation of political adjustments. In the first place, not only Southern, but to some extent Northern, Republicanism would have to be purged of its connection with the Negro. Next, large masses of Southern voters would have to be converted to Republican "principles" and to the record of the party, and this conversion effected before a switch could be made by the Democracy. Finally, new, active, and ostentatiously respectable organizations would have to be created in the Southern branch of the Republican party. Even this would probably not suffice; nothing short of an actual breakdown thoroughly discrediting the local political nabobs could wean the South away from the Democratic organizations.

It is with some diffidence that a realistic account of American political life approaches the matter of Republican "principles" *vs.* Democratic "principles," and the "conversion" of voters from one to the other. Historians as well as journalistic cynics have long pointed out the absence of standing issues between American parties, an absence emphasized in the 1928 campaign by the open conversion of the Democracy to the protective policy, the dalliance of the Republicans with government ownership and operation of certain great power resources, and the promises of both parties to the disgruntled farmer. Nevertheless, the feeling had long prevailed among Democrats that their opponents were the party of industry,

TABLE III

THE REPUBLICAN PARTY IN THE SOUTH.

VOTE FOR PRESIDENT, 1900-1928

State	*1900*	*1904*	*1908*	*1912*	*1916*	*1920*	*1924*	*1928*
Ala.	55,512	22,472	26,283	9,731	22,809	74,690	45,005	120,725
Ark.	44,800	46,860	56,760	24,297	47,148	71,117	40,564	77,751
Fla.	7,420	8,314	10,654	4,279	14,611	44,853	30,633	144,168
Ga.	35,056	24,003	41,692	5,190	11,225	43,720	30,300	99,369
Ky.	226,801	205,277	235,711	115,512	241,854	452,480	398,966	558,064
La.	14,233	5,205	8,958	3,834	6,466	38,538	24,670	51,160
Miss.	5,753	3,187	4,363	1,511	4,253	11,576	8,546	27,153
N. C.	132,997	82,442	114,887	29,139	120,988	232,848	191,753	348,992
S. C.	3,579	2,554	3,965	536	1,550	2,244	1,193	5,858
Tenn.	123,180	105,369	118,324	59,444	116,223	219,829	130,882	195,388
Tex.	130,641	51,242	65,666	28,853	64,999	114,538	130,023	367,036
Va.	115,865	47,880	52,573	23,288	49,356	87,456	73,359	164,609

Sources: to 1928, Stanwood; 1928, World Almanac.

Mr. Hoover in 1928 carried Florida, Kentucky, North Carolina, Tennessee, Texas, and Virginia. West Virginia makes a seventh Southern State. Kentucky in addition went Republican in 1896 and 1924; Tennessee in 1920.

The 1912 column of this table and of Table I shows how much of Republican strength was drawn into the Roosevelt-Progressive movement.

The only State showing a steady Republican gain is Florida. This may be due to Northern immigration.

The Republican vote rose sharply in the 1920 election. This was the Harding-Cox campaign on "No foreign entanglements," and the "return to normalcy." Both these issues seem to have attracted the Southern voter.

The Georgia and South Carolina Republican vote for 1928 is the total in each case of a "Republican" and an "Anti-Smith" official return, as follows:

	Republican	*Anti-Smith*
Georgia	63,498	35,871
So. Car.	3,188	2,670

of finance, of the northeastern seaboard and the older Middle West — of "Capital," in brief; and among Republicans conversely that the Democracy was agrarian, radical, and "unsafe" for normalcy, prosperity, and progress. This feeling must be taken into account; it accorded, indeed, with the early traditions of the two groups.

While industrialization and urbanization in the South had undoubtedly brought about a slow conversion of Southern business men to Republicanism in national politics, the great mass of voters was still untouched. Against whatever social and economic arguments Republicans might urge, were arrayed the dead weight of traditional allegiance to dead issues, and the ingrained Southern habit of voting for personalities rather than policies. In such a milieu, a politics of social and economic issues labored under more than its ordinary handicaps. Moreover, Democrats had made an easy transition, where the interests of their constituencies demanded, to that protective-tariff viewpoint which was the very essence of the quadrennial mimic party warfare. Contentedly and busily they had traded votes in Congress for the protection of Mississippi lumber, Louisiana sugar, Texas cattle and wool, and Virginia peanuts. And in 1928, the Committee on Resolutions, preparing a national platform, declared for "equalization of production costs at home and abroad," five influential Southerners concurring.[5]

Nevertheless, on its merits as the proponent — in the crude public view — of a certain social policy, the Republican party stood at some slight advantage among Southern white men in 1930, as compared with 1900. Was it taking any steps toward that basic essential of success in the South: reorganization, the casting out of the black brother, a drive for votes?

III. ACHIEVEMENTS OF THE "NEW" REPUBLICANISM

The origins of the modern lily-white movement are shrouded in the mists of obscure local factionalism. As we have seen, the term was coined in 1888 in Texas, by the Negro Republican leader Norris Wright Cuney, after riots at a State convention which he charged to white interests in the party anxious to drive out the Negro membership. In 1892, a group of white Republicans bolted from the regular Texas organization, held a convention of its own, and sent a contesting delegation to the national Republican convention. The white delegation was for McKinley; the Negro, for Allison or Reed. Cuney and his friends were turned down for the McKinley whites.[6]

The first flare-ups between Southern Republican factions to attract widespread public attention occurred in 1908 and 1912. In the latter case, the forthcoming Chicago convention was believed to be poised delicately between Roosevelt Progressives and Taft regulars. Roosevelt workers held bolting conventions in as many Southern States as they could, excluding Negroes as far as possible, and sent up contesting delegations. Almost all the contests that were fought to a finish were decided in favor of the regular "black-and-tan" organizations, who were for Taft. What followed in the national political arena is history, but here it does not concern us.

Meanwhile, the conviction expressed by Roosevelt himself in 1901 was growing in the country, namely, that the Republican party in the South was made up of politicians, mostly Negro, "who make not the slightest effort to get any popular votes, and who are concerned purely in getting Federal offices and sending to the national convention delegates whose venality makes them a menace to the whole party." [7]

On the basis of the moral issue thus presented, lily-white Republican organizations, rivaling the traditional Negro and "regular" bodies, had sprung up in every Southern State, except West Virginia and Kentucky, by the time of the 1928 convention.

The events surrounding the nomination and election of Herbert Hoover gave them additional prominence. For in view of the confusion into which the Southern Democracy had been thrown by the nomination of the wet, Catholic, and "Tammany" Smith, the time seemed ripe for a genuine Republican campaign in the South. Mr. Hoover himself seemed to have hoped that by working through lily-whites, an underground Republicanism, based on Southern industrialism and discontent with single-party politics, could be brought into the open to merge with the anti-Smith elements into a permanent and open Republican current.*

At any rate, the tide in the Republican organization seemed to be running against the "black-and-tan" regulars. Ben Davis, colored committeeman from Georgia, was given money for pre-convention expenses from a regular party source, but testified to his uneasiness over the activities of a white man, Clark Greer, who seemed to be in charge for Hoover.[8] After the election, his uneasiness was justified by his summary discharge from Republican councils by Mr. Hoover himself.[9] Perry Howard, another Negro "regular," then United States attorney and Republican committeeman from Mississippi, was allowed to bring his Hoover delegation to the convention,[10] but he walked in fear of a lily-white organization which he claimed had been encouraged by Mr. Hoover at the time of the flood relief work of 1927.[11] He was subsequently removed from his position and shorn of party power while under charges of bribery and the sale of Federal offices.[12] During the campaign, the work for Hoover was in charge of a lily-white, a recent accession to Republicanism, Lamont Rowlands. The Negro leader from Louisiana, Walter L. Cohen, was himself seated, but the other eleven delegates, all Hoover men, were lily-whites, led by the lily-white Emile Kuntz.[13] From Texas, a lily-white delegation, led by a Hoover supporter, Henry R. Creager, was seated over the protests of the Negro committeeman "Goose-Neck Bill" McDonald, and of the lone white Republican Repre-

* It was pointed out in an editorial in the *New York Times* that Mr. Hoover did not attempt to make a clean sweep of "black-and-tan" Republicanism in the convention, but got appreciable support from it (20 November 1928). It is true that no action was taken against Davis of Georgia, Howard of Mississippi, or the white "black-and-tan" Tolbert of South Carolina until after the election; the powerful R. R. Church of Tennessee seems to have been left wholly undisturbed. It is also true that alongside the white Mann committee, a Negro campaign committee functioned for Mr. Hoover, carefully kept separate from national headquarters, and instructed to leave the South alone. This body was under John R. Hawkins, financial secretary of the African Methodist Episcopal Church.

sentative Wurzback, who owed his seat to the Negro voters of San Antonio.[14]

The Hoover nomination accomplished, a separate campaign committee was created, under the chairmanship of a mysterious Colonel Horace A. Mann, to drum up the white Southern vote independently of the regular "black-and-tan" State organizations.[15] Branches of this committee clashed openly with the black-and-tan factions in Tennessee and in Texas, where the veteran Negro committeeman, William ("Goose-Neck Bill") McDonald, owner of a newspaper in Fort Worth, declared himself openly for Smith, and urged his followers to quit the "new" Republicanism.[16] Elsewhere, as we have seen, Negro leaders coöperated with Smith organizations, feeling that they had been shorn and left shivering.

Soon after the election, the Negro committeeman from Georgia, Ben Davis, was deprived of his patronage influence; the word was given out that a "clean-up" throughout the South was impending;[17] Perry Howard quit both his Federal job and his patronage refereeship in Mississippi; and finally the thunderbolt fell. At a press conference soon after his inauguration, Mr. Hoover declared that successive presidents had long wished to build up a Republican party in the South "such as would commend itself to the citizens of those States." He commended the existing lily-white State committees in Virginia, North Carolina, Alabama, Arkansas, Louisiana, Texas, and Florida. But in South Carolina, Georgia, and Mississippi, "recent exposures of abuse" in the sale of patronage "obviously render it impossible for the old organizations . . . to command the confidence of the administration . . . The duty of reorganization rests with the people of those States, and all efforts to that end will receive the hearty coöperation of the administration . . . If these three States are unable to initiate such organizations . . . the different Federal departments will be compelled to adopt other measures to secure advice as to the selection of Federal employees." [18] Postmaster General Brown, the department head with the greatest amount of patronage at his disposal, further announced that the national committeemen of the condemned States would not be recognized by him, but information as to prospective appointees sought "from citizens of the States who can be relied on to advise the Department in the public interest." Patronage committees of the sort indicated were subsequently set up, and a national committee, consisting of the Postmaster General, one of the President's secretaries, and the counselor of the Republican party, was created, to review all recommendations for office in the interests of the new policy.[19]

Hasty prophets saw in this new Republican activity the positive counterpart of the negative "break-down of the Solid South" which they professed to have seen in the election returns. Again, both events and certain general considerations prove them to have been not wrong — it is still too early to pass such judgment — but very premature.

Even before the President's announcement of a new deal for Southern Republicans, Colonel Mann, the accredited Hoover bellwether in the South, had resigned from his connection with the administration machine.[20] It was commonly supposed that his discontent was due to a lack of coöperation on the part of Postmaster General Brown, who, with an eye to the Negro Republican balance of power in his own State of Ohio and elsewhere in the North, was not giving their due to the Mann-lily-white organizations in the matter of Federal appointments.[21] At any rate, Mann called a meeting of independent Southern Republicans at Savannah in August, 1930, inveighing against the "designing political highjackers [who] invade the Southland every four years and rob her of the right to a legitimate representation at national Republican conventions." [22] But when Colonel Mann's independent Southern organization held a final meeting in Atlanta, it convened at the home of Ben Davis, Negro ex-committeeman. It had either surrendered, or been captured.[23]

The high command of the Republican party was by no means committed to the policy of whitewashing its Southern forces. The announced Hoover policy was the most expansive public gesture towards the lily-whites ever made by a responsible Republican spokesman, but there were still forces in the party which were satisfied with the manipulative power in national conventions which they derived from the irresponsible black-and-tan delegations, and who feared the effect of Southern lily-whitism on Northern Negro Republicanism.[24]

Practically, therefore, the creation of a white man's Republicanism had not gotten very far by the end of 1930. At that time there were dual organizations in several States. In Georgia, though Davis had resigned, there were contesting lily-white and black-and-tan national committeemen, the patronage advisory body not working clearly with either.[25] Although a patronage body had been set up in Mississippi, and the lily-white Lamont Rowlands was trying to enroll white voters in the party, Perry Howard was still in charge of the "legitimate" organization.[26] The white black-and-tan chieftain of South Carolina, "Tieless Joe" Tolbert, retained his party office, and the lily-white patronage committee lost its most influential members because of alleged lack of administration support.[27]

The powerful Robert R. Church still functioned in Tennessee; the Negro Collector of the Port, Walter L. Cohen, in Louisiana — although both were faced with an opposition.[28] In Arkansas, the Republican organization was controlled by men who had up to 1924 been violent in their lily-white protestations; there were now, however, Negroes on the roster of party officers, and Arkansas Negroes felt that lily-whitism was no longer serious.[29] Similarly, the Alabama organization had a lily-white at its head, but there was also at least one Negro on the State committee. Florida had a situation peculiar to herself: under the State election law, the size of the Hoover vote in 1928 brought the Republican party under the operation of the compulsory primary law, and Negro and lily-white factions in local elections were disputing before the courts the right to hold Republican primaries.[30] In Texas, the Creager lily-white faction seemed definitely on top; but it could not claim clean hands after a Senatorial investigating committee had bracketed it in 1930 with South Carolina,

Georgia, and Mississippi in venal patronage dealings.[31] It was widely believed that an alliance with a Democratic machine in southwest Texas debarred Creager from attempting to build up his party in the State.[32] That he had still to face a reckoning with his enemies was very obvious; not only the veteran Negro Republican McDonald, but the single Republican Congressman from Texas — Wurzback — were bitter against him, and Wurzback owed much of his strength to the Negro voters of San Antonio.[33]

Under these circumstances, in spite of President Hoover's striking gesture, who was to say whether the Southern Republican party of 1930 was white or "black-and-tan"? The formal decision on the almost certain contests from six States lay with the National Committee, to meet in 1932, before the next national convention.

IV. HANDICAPS OF LILY-WHITISM

Meanwhile, it must be remembered, most of the lily-white factions in the South had never been, and were not in 1930, anything more than skeleton organizations of politicians, exactly as were the black-and-tan bodies. The Border States were exceptions, and therefore do not figure in this discussion; [34] Virginia had been something of an exception since 1921, and North Carolina somewhat longer.

In Virginia in 1921 and again in 1929, the lily-white Republican party staged what were up to that time the most threatening demonstrations against Democracy that any Southern State had yet seen. Although the Republican threat was in neither case implemented by a victory at the polls, it was nevertheless remarkable for its open repudiation of Negro support and for the number of voters it was able to muster.[35] In both cases, be it noted, the battle was waged against a divided Democracy — in 1921 caused by the dissatisfaction with Trinkle, the Democratic nominee; in 1929, by the persistence of the anti-Smith Democratic organization.[36]

The mechanism of the lily-white *coup* of 1921 is interesting because typical. Simultaneously with the holding of "regular" black-and-tan local meetings, meetings limited to white men were held all over the State — held at private homes of white people or at hotels or clubhouses to which Negroes could not gain admission. From this double set of meetings, double sets of delegates were sent to the State Republican convention at Norfolk, which was also held at a white hotel. All but three Negroes were barred from the convention as lacking proper credentials. Colonel Henry W. Anderson, leader of the lily-white group, declared in a keynote speech that his party was not a Negro party, that it would not change the political or social relationships of the races in Virginia, and that Negroes could not and should not expect to hold public office. These affirmations were included in the platform, softened by a clause calling upon all citizens, white and black, to support the party they believed in, and deploring racial political solidarity as a menace.[37]

The program of this Virginia lily-white Republicanism may be reconstituted from the utterances of Colonel Anderson during the 1921 and 1929 campaigns, and from his various public addresses in the intervening years. In the first place, it should be stated that Colonel Anderson, the moving spirit of the whole development, had long been associated with the business and industrial interests of his State, and was counsel for one of Virginia's large electrical utility corporations. His party, therefore, was generally taken in Virginia to be the party of the "new" South — to be a recrudescence of whiggism, in the sense of the analogy we have drawn above. Next, he proclaimed the familiar "evils of a one-party system," and charged the Democracy with being a "ring," inefficient, extravagant, and corrupt, which could not be successfully reformed from within. Because of its control of the election machinery, Colonel Anderson claimed, this "ring" was self-perpetuating. He made much, therefore, of the necessity for the reform of the election law. This was not effectively bi-partisan, as it ought to be; and further, *the machinery designed for the disfranchisement of the Negro was actually disfranchising white voters*. For the first time, a public issue was made in the South of white disfranchisement under the new constitutions.[38] Colonel Anderson said that the required payment of three years' poll taxes cut out large numbers of white voters, and should be reduced or repealed. The needlessly complicated ballot caused the invalidation of many votes actually cast. Further, he charged that Democratic election officials increased their party's support by illegally crediting their friends with poll-tax payments not actually made, registered good "regular" Democrats without the required application in person, distributed absentee-voting ballots to housewives and other shut-ins they could count on, and refused registration to plainly qualified white voters of opposition groups on technicalities such as abounded in the election code, framed with the Negro in view. In 1921, Colonel Anderson was still able to charge the party in power with failure to reapportion the House of Assembly.

In 1929, he pointed out that "ring control" had been strengthened through changes in the constitution which decreased the number of elected officers and increased the governor's appointing power. Tax equalization — a burning issue in a section like the South which is changing over from a rural-agricultural to an urban-commercial-industrial community — also figured in his speeches, as did the usual commonplaces of State politics, such as prison reform, the modernization of county governments, etc.

A curious reversal of the accepted positions of the two major parties enlivened the 1929 campaign. The Republican Anti-Smith coalition sought to picture the Democratic candidate as an "aristocrat," claimed that it opposed the industrial development of the State at the expense of the laboring population, and made a play for the small oyster-dredgers of the shore counties by promising redress for alleged wholesale leases of oyster beds illegally held by certain large seafood corporations.[39]

In North Carolina, the lily-white Republican faction had still greater claim to be considered more than a skeleton organization. There was a larger body of white Republican voters, and a greater number of Republican candidates regularly offered at the polls than in the States farther south.[40]

Elsewhere, for lack of money and support at the polls, few Republican organizations ran candidates for State and congressional office.[41] In no case, therefore, were they active as vote-getting organizations, save in presidential years. In the exceptional campaign of 1928, they gathered in a considerable vote for the presidential candidate.* But their voting adherents in that year were most anxious to return to Democratic regularity in order to participate in succeeding State primaries, as the number and nature of bitter controversies on this point indicate.[42]

Further, in any efforts lily-white groups might make to build up a steady voting power in their respective States, they were blocked by several features of Democratic policy. For one thing, since the omnipotent Democratic primary was considered the implement of "white supremacy," known white Republicans were freely and universally admitted to a voting participation in it on the basis of their color. This was not only generally admitted in private conversation in the South, but also appeared as a matter of public record.[43] In such a primary, white Republican sympathizers had a fighting chance to influence the choice of their local officials which they would lose if they should separate themselves entirely from the Democratic party.

* The lily-white organization in Alabama—so without fixed policies were Southern politicians—after the good showing made by Mr. Hoover in 1928, in 1930 abandoned its plan to nominate a State ticket, and indorsed the candidacies of Senator Heflin for reëlection and of Hugh Locke for governor. These two men had been barred from the regular Democratic primary ballot because of their Hoovercrat activities in 1928 (see note 42). Alabama was thus treated to the spectacle of the Republican party indorsing a man—Heflin—who was one of the South's bitterest negrophobes, which ran counter to the Negro tradition of the party; and who posed always as the poor man's friend, the man of the people, the farmers' representative, which ran counter to the respectable whiggism of the "new" Republicanism. On the other side stood the Democratic party, traditionally radical and agrarian, now proclaiming the necessity of getting rid of Heflin once and for all, as a demagogue who frightened away investment and development.

For the most part, influential sources of Southern opinion were frankly skeptical of the chances of maintaining white supremacy in a two-party system, no matter how cordially they might indorse a particular lily-white, or the general theory of bipartisan politics. In the light of past events, of which of course they were fully conscious, one must credit them with a great deal of realistic insight in this skepticism. For every editorial deploring the evils of one-party politics — "There can be no debate over the fact that the long prevalence of undisputed one-party control . . . has diminished the sense of party responsibility and dwarfed our politics into personal and factional proportions . . . with slight references to political ideas or administrative policies" — some other expression, such as the following, addressed to the Mississippi lily-whites, might be found: "It is only through a continuation of [the one-party system] that the Negro can be legally kept from dominating the politics of the State . . . where the Negro can be used, there is always the temptation to use him, and politicians have no trouble squaring the matter with their consciences . . ." [44] Colonel Anderson, during his Virginia campaign of 1921, was accused of disingenuousness in repudiating Negro support, partly because of a few softening phrases disclaiming any intention to "oppress," chiefly because of his attack on the three-year poll-tax requirement for voters and on the complicated Virginia ballot.[45] When Mrs. Hoover, *pro forma*, invited the wife of the Negro Congressman Oscar DePriest (of Illinois) to a White House reception, this was seized on in the South as evidence of Republican unregenerateness.[46] So was the refusal of the Senate to confirm Judge Parker of North Carolina to the Federal Supreme Court, following protests from Negroes who objected to his racial philosophy.[47] We have already discussed the injection of the race issue into the 1928 campaign, when it was simply a question of voting Republican in that one election.

The going Democratic concerns in the South opposed lily-whitism with all their resources of publicity on other grounds than the publicly avowed one, the "Negro balance of power." Obviously, any success of State lily-whitism would constitute a proportionate threat to State Democracy, while Negro Republicanism was no threat at all. Further, the State Democracies had devious connections with old-line black-and-tan Republicanism in the latter's often shady patronage deals. Both these points were curiously illustrated in the outcome of the trial of Perry Howard, Negro Republican national committeeman from Mississippi.

Howard, together with several other active Negro Republicans of Jackson, Mississippi, was indicted in 1928 for the sale of Federal offices and for levying political contributions on Federal employees in violation of the Civil Service code. He was given a jury trial in a Federal court, and the United States attorney in charge of the prosecution protested almost tearfully that the case against Howard was water-tight and fool-proof, a view in which many spectators at the trial concurred. President Hoover was sufficiently impressed with the evidence against Howard to accept his resignation as assistant United States attorney, and the Senatorial committee investigating the sale of Federal offices in 1929-30 condemned the Republican organization of Mississippi largely because of its opinion of Howard's activities. A patronage committee, as we have said, was appointed to take over Howard's duties as patronage referee for the State. Nevertheless, Howard was acquitted.

How was it possible that this Negro politician, active in the opposition party, well-dressed, well-spoken, with money in his pockets, the very archetype of all that irritates the ordinary Southerner, seemingly caught out in a grave offense, and fighting a native Mississippi white man — Lamont Rowlands — for the control of his party — how was it possible that Perry Howard should be acquitted, as he was, by a jury of twelve white Southerners? How was it possible that Perry Howard should come into court with glowing letters from the chief justice, an associate justice, and the clerk of the State Supreme Court, and from many other Mississippi worthies, attesting to his pleasing personality, high moral standards, great ability, standing in court, etc.? [48] Why should his acquittal have caused rejoicing in the press and among the politicians of the State, as it did, and the acceptance of his resignation from Federal office be condemned, as it was? [49]

It must first be conceded that all this came about partly through the pride and interest that many Southerners take in "one of our boys," even though colored, who achieves success and bears the outward mark of ability, as Howard undoubtedly did. Partly, too, this phenomenon was due to a sense of fair play, for it was felt that the administration, prodded by the local lily-whites, was making a "goat" of Howard after many years' acquiescence in his alleged acts.*

There were, however, other factors which helped to create a sentiment favorable to Howard, and these were factors which have made the struggle of lily-whites uphill throughout the South. In the first place, in view of the Hoover vote in the South in 1928, the Democracy was anxious about future lily-white successes — especially, although unnecessarily, so in Mississippi, where the lily-white movement was in charge of a white man of unimpeachable integrity, formerly a leader of the reform wing of the Democracy. In the next place, Perry Howard had been instrumental in securing Federal appointments *for Democrats*.[50]

That close relationships long existed between Democrats and black-and-tan Republicans in the matter of Federal jobs was a commonplace of Southern political gossip. It was

* In previous footnotes this writer has attempted to put into its proper background, often overlooked, the charge that Negro politicians in the South wrongfully neglect to build up the Republican party. Without wishing to condone the sale of offices or the levying of contributions on office-holders, it is felt that this feature of Negro politicians' activities has also been dealt with a little too abstractly. What was there for a Republican official to do in the South except referee job contests? The national party organization looked to him to do this, and to keep the fences mended for convention years. If he levied toll on his beneficiaries, it will be readily conceded that he was but keeping the custom of the country, both North and South. That he should pocket the proceeds, instead of turning them over to the party's uses, is of course—where true—another matter.

established as a fact by the Senatorial patronage investigation committee of 1929-30, and is, of course, common sense.[51] This was shown through questions asked by Senator Brookhart of the Republican State Chairman of Georgia:

Q. — "What proportion [of your recommendations] are Democrats?"
A. — ". . . Outside of [the Seventh and Ninth Congressional] districts they are largely Democratic . . ."
Q. — ". . . Are contributions to the committee made by the Democratic postmasters in the same way as . . . by the Republican postmasters?"
A. — "They are all made in the same way . . . The Republican always gets the plum if he is available and qualified."
Q. — "And the large majority of them, in spite of that rule, are Democrats?"
A. — "The large majority are Democrats — we have not enough to go around."

There have never been enough Republicans to "go around" the available Federal jobs in the South, especially as many posts in many places were closed to Negroes because of prevailing public sentiment. Quite naturally, Democrats came in for favor at the hands of the Republican organizations, not necessarily corruptly; [52] and, quite naturally, Republican party officials received some token of appreciation, not necessarily corruptly, from their beneficiaries.* Thus a friendly connection was established profitable to both parties, and this friendly connection, so useful to Democrats, was menaced when one of the personalities involved — like Howard's — was threatened, and seemed about to be supplanted by a

* Consider the affidavit of a South Carolina postmaster who had received his appointment through the influence of a Negro named Dixon, allegedly in a corrupt manner: "Dixon is a colored man who was reared in the back yard of my grandmother and has known my family all his life . . . He said he would do anything he could for me and made no request of me . . . for any pay or present . . . About April 25, 1922, I received appointment as acting postmaster . . . After I took charge I felt from what I had seen in the papers that Dixon had helped me to receive this appointment and I made him a present of $25 in cash as evidence of my appreciation of what I thought he had done for me." (Postmasterships Hearings 1929, p. 301).

lily-white Republican who refused to deal with Democrats, or who had a different set of Democratic friends.

No wonder then that the Democratic organizations in the South looked askance at lily-whitism. They had everything to lose, nothing to gain: the formation of a genuine opposition, the loss of underground connections in Washington, and the eventual reëntrance of the Negro into politics, were what they foresaw in lily-white success.

We have assumed so far that lily-whitism was sincere, that it honestly and actively pursued its objectives of "cleaning up" the Southern Republican party, dispossessing the Negro membership, and gathering voters under its banners. This view has not always been held. At the time when the term was coined, Albion Tourgee wrote: "The name is a good one, and all the more stirringly appropriate, for as everybody knows, that faction thus arrogating to itself purity, capacity, and patriotism, is organized for plunder, . . . to cut the party loose from the Negro in order that they may control whatever plums of Federal patronage . . . may fall to the party organization . . ." [53]

These were extreme words. Proof of them is not forthcoming. But down through 1930, Negro Republicans in the South — prejudiced witnesses, to be sure — repeated their substance. When the observer of Southern politics in that year ran down the list of lily-white Republican names, he found few that had figured seriously in the State politics of the past twenty years. Anderson of Virginia seemed one such, the Republican organization of North Carolina yielded others, Lamont Rowlands of Mississippi was assuredly another, and certain supporters of Creager in Texas a fourth group.[54] Elsewhere the names were obscure and unfamiliar. In a gulf-state lily-white group, there was at least one politician, a Federal office-holder, of whom the Negro Republican committeeman might have said, as Cuney of Texas had said, pointing to his own opponent: "That [man] is my creature. I warmed him into life. He betrayed and stung me . . . He is my creature. I made him. I stood by him when he had not a friend. I gave him a chance to come to the front and held him up against the protests of my friends. And all the time he has been plotting to undermine me . . ." [55]

But surely, the idealist will still ask, there were genuine State issues in the South on which a Republican party could be built, State by State? There were; we shall deal with them immediately. But they must be dealt with in connection with the Democratic parties of the South, for wherever such issues emerged, they were used up, so to speak, in the heat of Democratic factional politics. Moreover, we have already made brief reference to the Southern voter's lack of interest in technical social, economic, and administrative questions in politics; on this point, too, we shall presently say more.

In sum, then, the "new" lily-white Republicanism in 1930 was real and active in North Carolina and Virginia, perhaps in Texas; in the far South it had slowly grown by fits and starts. The Hoover campaign administered a temporary stimulant. In the Border States it had hardly appeared — in Kentucky and West Virginia not at all, and in Tennessee with a dark future, because of the need for Negro votes in a sharply divided State. Everywhere it had to face the traditional fear of a "Negro balance of power" in case of bipartisan politics, powerful enemies in the Democratic organizations, and overwhelming temptations from within such as, yielded to, had discredited the "black-and-tans." Southern Republicanism in 1930 was, therefore, far from attaining that strength which might induce it or its Democratic opposition to call on the Negro for a casting vote.

V. DEMOCRATIC POLITICS

From all that has gone before, it would seem that in the period 1900-1930 there was every encouragement for the development of a politics of issues within the Democratic parties of the Southern States.

There was no lack of material in the South for an intraparty politics of intense and vital interest. The South, having long lagged behind in the provision of public education, had a whole range of questions, financial, administrative, and theoretical, connected with its school system. During its period of extreme depression, the South had perforce neglected its prisons, hospitals, and poor-relief agencies. At once the seat of the earliest prohibition manifestations, and the home of liquor manufacture both licit and illicit, the stronghold of actively "dry" Protestantism, and the seat of individualism and States'-rights theory, the South might well have divided at its primaries into dry and wet Democrats. The long continuance in power of the Democratic party gave rise to charges of "machine control" by the professional politicians, coupled with the usual accusations of graft and incompetence, and intensified by the devious election codes which — aimed at the Negro — centralized the election machinery to a high degree. Administrative changes, in line with the modern developments of political science, were also badly needed in many States: simplification and rationalization of the central government, county reform, modernization of the municipal code, the abolition of the fee system. Discontent with the prevailing legislative apportionment hung over several States.

The rapid economic and social changes which occurred in the South in this period provided a whole set of issues on which to base a rational and consistent intra-Democratic politics. There were questions of State encouragement to industry, through changes in the law of incorporation, which were in some cases cumbersome, in some even threatening; through changes in the taxation scheme. There were questions of highway improvement, in which the South had lagged, and which, with industrialization and urbanization, now assumed new importance. The textile strikes in Virginia, North Carolina, and Tennessee from 1927 to 1930 revealed the need for a general overhauling of the Southern labor codes, especially as they concerned women and children. The development of the South's large power resources raised problems of rate and service regulation, and presented the alternative of State ownership.[56] The speeding up of lumbering operations in Louisiana, Mississippi, and South Carolina called up the specter of denudation and exhaustion of resources, with its alternative of conservation and reforestation.

In this background, the Democratic parties of the Southern States might easily have divided at their primary elections into two fairly stable and consistent factions, shall we say, liberal and conservative. Each would have found its appropriate position on the possible controversies we have indicated. This did not happen.

Why had no "liberal" or "conservative," or any other stable and consistent factions formed within the Southern Democracies, finding their issues in the South's changing material culture? The Negro, for all practical purposes, was out of politics; Republicanism — except in the Border States — was a lost cause. There was no further need for a united front among all classes and interests to pursue these ancient grudges, especially as the white primary provided a rampart behind which all disagreements could be fought out free of interference from outsiders.

Foremost among the inhibiting factors was the heritage of Negro issues. "Negro domination," "white supremacy," "the Negro balance of power," had been important to the South for so long, that the use of these phrases had become habitual to the politician, and response to them automatic among the voters. The Negro question, emphasizing party loyalty, had brought about the subordination of other issues dangerous to solidarity, and stifled discussion. Racial fears still remained, a dead hand on the throttle of politics, in spite of the solid achievements of the new disfranchising techniques and the white primary.

But to ascribe the unreality of Southern politics to the racial situation alone would be superficial and unfruitful. It must also be borne in mind that Southern society was predominantly rural in character, even as late as 1930, when so many changes had already occurred. The rural South had not yet been aroused over those twentieth-century issues which were clamoring for its attention. It had little training in discussing or meeting them, either by direct experience, or by the gossip of the city market place, or even at second-hand through the medium of a good and extensive school system.

There was still another reason in Southern tradition for the backwardness of Southern politics. A Southerner of advanced views, asked to explain the intra-Democratic politics of his State to the writer, said: "The first thing required of any candidate is that he be a Methodist. If he or one of his forbears served in the Confederate Army, so much the better. And if the aspirant to office has a wooden leg, that clinches it." However exaggerated this statement, it contains a kernel of truth: personalities have always played a large part in Southern politics. Almost without exception, Southerners, white and black, when asked in 1929 and 1930 to describe the platform, the issues, the proposals, whereby one Democratic primary candidate for State office was distinguished from another, replied that it was merely a question of the "ins" and "outs," and that the decision was governed partly by the set-up of the political machine at the time, partly by the personality and associations of the candidate himself.

The reasons for this situation are worth considering, for as long as it endured both white politics and its shadow, Negro suffrage, must remain much as they were in 1930.

Certain features of Southern society have from the beginning thrown a direct emphasis on personalities in politics. The sharp class distinctions erected on the basis of slavery and land ownership, which persisted in tradition if not in fact even beyond the Civil War, made it important to one group whether a political aspirant was acceptable as a "gentleman" or not. Jacksonian democracy, cradled on the long-enduring Southern frontier, presented the antithetical "plain man of the people." The Civil War brought unblemished and preferably spectacular Southern loyalty to the fore as a *sine qua non* of political preferment. Later, Reconstruction intensified the concern with "southern-ness." [57] There followed the agrarian revolt, with its renewed emphasis on "the farmer's friend" and "the man of the people." From Reconstruction down, the Southern voter was taught that party regularity was indispensable to the salvation of the South from "Negro domination"; this added to the process of assaying candidates the test of personal loyalty to the party and to political friends. It will easily be recognized that this whole situation gave exceptionally free range to the orator-candidate, the hand-shaker, the man with "connections"; at the worst, to the demagogue.

Nevertheless, it must not be supposed that all the vital issues to which we have alluded were totally ignored during primary campaigns in favor of Negro-baiting, rebel yells, and back-slapping. Two in particular — the class issue, and the charge of "machine control" — recurred again and again; others from time to time, as occasion arose.

The historic class cleavage, somewhat altered since the agrarian revolt, still persisted in all Southern States. It was perhaps the clearest and most consistent political division to appear, even as late as 1930. Since the reunion of the New Bourbon and plebeian-agrarian factions after the Populist era — a reunion solemnized by the new disfranchising constitutions — a plebeian faction remained fairly consistently at the helm of the Southern Democratic parties.[58] This group was not wholly homogeneous, consisting as it did of small farmers and tenants, urban middle and lower classes, and the new factory proletariat of the up-country mill-villages.

Opposed to it were two other strata of Southern society. One included "the best people" and the intelligentsia, such as in South Carolina were glad to shelve Cole Blease in 1930 because of their dislike of what they considered his demagoguery and disreputableness.[59] Another embraced the "whiggish" South; what we have also called the "New Bourbons": the manufacturers, bankers, commercial magnates, and a large part of the middle class. This was the group which in Alabama rejoiced in the defeat of Senator Heflin because it felt that his record as an agrarian radical frightened investments away from the State.[60]

This cleavage appeared quite plainly from time to time in

Southern primary campaigns. Governor Henry L. Whitfield of Mississippi (1924-27), for example, was elected as an exponent of the Whig point of view and a representative of the State's "best people," a member of the "respectable" Democratic faction headed by the late Senator John Sharp Williams, as opposed to the poor-white and agrarian faction led by Senator Vardaman. Charges that he favored the "interests" played a vital part in the campaign.[61] As chief executive, he sponsored a more liberal attitude towards business, fathering acts which wiped from the statute books such agrarian restrictions as a two-million-dollar limit on corporate real-estate holdings, and sundry unenforceable but spectacular anti-monopoly laws. He endeavored to check administrative abuse of laws permitting the official inspection of private business accounts. He signed bills giving power companies the right of eminent domain. For the first time in many administrations, he kept appropriations within the limits of current revenue, and refused to permit bond issues for current expenses, thus disappointing local interests anxious for improvements at the expense of large taxpayers. That he was no blind servant of "the interests" was evidenced by his stand for income and inheritance taxation.[62]

Governor Whitfield, Senator Williams, and — until his conversion to lily-whitism — Lamont Rowlands, seconded in the press by F. S. Harmon of the *Hattiesburg American*, represented for Mississippi the New Bourbon, Whig, and intelligentsia faction in the Southern Democracies. On the other side stood such men as Senator Vardaman and Whitfield's successor, Governor Bilbo, who were both of "plebeian" origin, political children of the agrarian revolt.

But even at that, in Mississippi as in other States where the class division was discernible in State politics, the emphasis in actual campaigns was less on the specific social and economic issues involved, less on coherent and enduring platforms, than on the clash of personalities. Governor Bilbo of Mississippi, Governor Long of Louisiana, Governor Bibb Graves of Alabama, all owed their political advancement, not so much to the intellectual appeal of some agrarian or liberal philosophy, as to the personal, sentimental appeal of their humble origins, their long residence and wide acquaintance among the poor-white groups of their respective States, their forthright and old-fashioned oratorical abilities, and in the case of Governor Graves at least to strong public statements on Negro inferiority.[63] Whitfield himself, in Mississippi, rode into office on a wave of discontent with extravagance and alleged corruption, as something of a dark horse, a schoolman who had hitherto kept clear of politics.

In this background, the outlook was not bright for the development of a consistent class factionalism in the Southern Democracies, a factionalism so deep and so self-conscious that it might vitalize Southern white politics, and, vitalizing white politics, hold out to the Negro citizen the promise of his eventual reëntry into the political arena. At any moment, under propitious but fleeting circumstances, a factionalism of this sort could be suspended by the appearance of some candidate of pleasing personality and appropriate background.

Next to the class cleavage, the issue recurring most often was one familiar in American politics: "machine control," often coupled with the demand of the "younger generation" of politicians for recognition in the party councils. This was a crucial point of division among the Democrats of Virginia. Here, there existed a nebulous "Liberal Democratic" group, less a faction with primary aspirants and campaign machinery, than simply a movement of criticism. Its newspaper exponents, the *Richmond News-Leader* and the *Norfolk Virginian-Pilot*, among other matters made much of the "machine" issue, proposing as one method of reform changes in the election and registration laws. They demanded greater stringency in the handling of absentee-voters' ballots, the posting of sample ballots for the guidance of voters, the reduction of the three years' poll-tax requirement, and a simplified method of marking ballots. Such changes, they felt, would lessen the initial advantage of the "in" group at elections through control of the electoral machinery; and would increase the vote, especially by bringing in independents.[64] In North Carolina, the defeat of the veteran Senator Simmons in the 1930 primaries by Josiah Bailey, a comparatively new man, was in some measure due to the ambitions of the "younger generation," and to charges of "machine." [65]

On the whole, though, it cannot be said that "machine rule" has been a very basic or continuous issue in Southern State politics. Like the class issue, when it was raised, it was likely to be overshadowed by the personalities involved. In primary campaigns one or more of the aspirants may choose to go on the stump as "independents" who have never "taken orders" or been "subservient" to the "boss." Such candidates have very often been closely associated with the "machine" they condemn, or at best been obscure jobholders with no right to pretensions either of "independency" or "regularity." On such occasions, other candidates may choose to take their cue from this "independency" to proclaim their own "true-blue Democracy," their "regularity," their "loyalty," their "long service to the people of the State." The whole question then becomes merely an oratorical springboard chosen for its adaptability to the particular candidate's brand of public speaking, and the audience he is trying to reach. However much or little the "machine" charge may have fitted Southern Democratic organizations, the issue was not such in 1930 as to promise either a clear factionalism or a party split in any Southern State.

Behind these two recurring issues in Southern State politics — the class division and "machine rule" — trailed a host of temporary and occasional questions. Every Southern State, especially in the third decade of the century, had its struggles over road improvements. Most had elections fought in large measure over the question of free school texts. Two at least struggled with reapportionment measures.[66] All the other fiscal and administrative changes agitating Northern and Western States during the period were taken up at one time or another by some Southern group. But most of these proposals could hardly be hammered into place in a consistent factional rivalry. A plea for free textbooks for school children, for example, equally well became the representative of the horny-handed farmer, and the apostle of the "new" urban and industrialized South. As a result, such occasional issues were simply seized on for indorsement or dissent by one, two, three, or all primary aspirants at one election, and often, whether disposed of or not, forgotten for some more promising appeal at the next.

All the issues, then, which the historian might have expected to find in a changing community like the South, actually appeared in its politics. In fundamental *interests*, the South was no more solid in 1930 than it had ever been. But these issues appeared only spasmodically — even deep-lying and historical issues like the class cleavage. They were obscured, if not obliterated, by personalities. They were kept from the light of reason by racial fears. Out of them there had not yet arisen in the South a realistic politics openly concerned with social and economic welfare. As a body of voters, the South, if not solid, was at any rate inchoate.

CHAPTER IX

CONCLUSIONS

The early chapters of this story have attempted to make clear the nature of white political divisions in the South, and to set them in their background of the plantation system and Negro slavery. Before the Negro became a political factor as the result of the Civil War and Reconstruction, the South was the scene of bipartisan politics normal in its outlines, but embittered by the social and economic divisions arising out of its "peculiar institution." The threat to slavery and to racial equilibrium which the South saw in the election results of 1860 created the Confederacy, a Southern nation effectively, if not unanimously, united to maintain the racial *status quo.*

For a brief period, after slavery had been destroyed but not yet replaced by a new régime, bipartisanship again raised its head in the South. But when Reconstruction, in the vivid Negro figure, put the bottom log on top, the white South again united to restore the first desideratum of all white Southerners — "white supremacy." White supremacy, however, demanded a solid front against the now enfranchised Negro, and this could not be maintained during the agricultural depression of the eighties and nineties, especially in the background of the earlier white divisions in the South. The white South divided, and the Negro became a balance of power between the factions. This was among the reasons for the collapse of the agrarian revolt in the South, and the disappearance of a small farmers' party as a separate fighting body in Southern politics. Around 1900, all factions united in a white man's party once more, to put the Negro finally beyond the pale of political activity, in seven States by means of detailed and stringent constitutional measures.

What changes occurred in the political life of the South after 1900?

In the first place, the new constitutions provided a sure and regularized means of Negro disfranchisement in seven States. They did not disfranchise all Negroes, but those who retained the vote were exceptional. Nor did they absolutely guarantee the South against the renewed use of Negroes by an administration machine, since the suffrage tests provided for could as easily be interpreted to admit Negroes as to reject them. They did, however, prevent the injection of large masses of Negroes into the electorate by an opposition group, not in control of the suffrage administration. Without the constitutions, the divisions in the South over Smith and Hoover in 1928 might have brought about a marked increase in the Negro vote, and reawakened the sleeping "Negro domination" and "balance of power" issues. In the States unprovided with constitutional devices of the literacy, "understanding," and "character" types, more Negroes undoubtedly voted; but the number was kept low through the operation of public sentiment and Negro apathy, and in some cases of intimidation — the same factors, indeed, which elsewhere gave their peculiar administrative bias to the disfranchising constitutions.

Constitutional disfranchisement was supplemented by the white primary rules of the Democratic parties, coupled with the technical requirement of registration for primary eligibility. These rules, made under authority granted by the States, had not yet been finally passed on by the Federal Supreme Court. If they should ever be voided, Negroes could still be kept from the primaries by a strict enforcement of the legal prerequisite of registration. Nevertheless, if ever intra-Democratic politics became bitter enough, Negro voters could be introduced into the primaries, easily by the faction in control, with much difficulty by the dissidents.

As long as the South continued loyal to the Democratic party, there was no occasion to call on the much-feared Negro vote. In 1930, this loyalty was still unshaken for practical purposes. If it were to break down, the precedent of the agrarian revolt and of the contemporary *local* use of Negro voters pointed to a reëntrance of the Negro into politics.

So far as white citizens were concerned, the new constitutions, with their complicated franchise requirements, discouraged many white voters from attempting to register. Failure to register technically involved ineligibility for both primary and general elections. But the white applicant for a primary ballot was seldom required to produce evidence of registration. In any case, the constitutional tests were loosely interpreted for the benefit of whites who presented themselves for registration. While the registrars had the power, under the constitutions, to make it extremely difficult for any voter to qualify, regardless of race or color, very few charges of white disfranchisement, either at primary or general elections, were made in the South after the agrarian revolt.

The Democratic one-party system, therefore, was the condition of continued Negro disfranchisement under the new constitutions; but the new constitutions also tended to preserve the one-party system, for they strengthened the hold of the Democratic machines in the face of any revolt which might occur, by giving them control over the admission of a Negro voting balance, and perhaps by enabling them at some future time to discriminate among white voters.

The Negro was not faring well under "white supremacy," as compared with the dominant group, although, indeed, he was faring better than he once had. Negroes themselves felt that they could put the ballot to good use if they could get it.

Thus in North Carolina, at once one of the most advanced of Southern States and the home of prosperous Negro communities, with a Negro population 29% of the total, there was a marked disparity between the educational facilities provided for the two races. Only twenty-six out of the State's hundred counties provided organized Negro welfare work at public expense, employing only twenty workers.[1] The lack of sanitary facilities, of paving, of street lighting in Southern Negro quarters, was obvious to the most casual visitor.

North Carolina Educational Statistics, 1928

	White	*Negro*
School Population	682,710	312,412
Number of Teachers	17,973	5,959
Average Term in Days	152.7	137.4
Average Teachers' Salaries (monthly)	$117.20	$70.00
Average Value of Schoolhouses	$23,369.00	$4,215.00

The Negro's votelessness reacted unfavorably on his general social and economic welfare in more subtle ways than in matters, like the above, involving appropriations. His position in court was not so secure where he had no control over the choice of magistrates and state's attorneys.* He had no redress against police brutality or arrest on flimsy suspicion. He was even put at a disadvantage in getting work. In a city with a large Negro electorate, no such ordinance would ever have been offered as Atlanta's attempt to forbid colored barbers from bobbing white women's hair. In Augusta, a Negro blacksmith of acknowledged skill observed that the mules of a large trucking concern were no longer sent to him for shoeing; upon asking why, he was told that the owner was a candidate for the mayoralty nomination and had turned the job over to a white man who could vote and bring out other voters. If Jim-Crowism could coexist with Negro political power, Negro leaders could still at least secure better enforcement of the "*equal* though separate accommodations" provisions of the law.

The factors tending to "liberalize" the Southern attitude towards Negro suffrage have already been fully discussed. They depended chiefly on the economic advance of the South, bound up, for the time being, with industrialization. They included urbanization, increased educational facilities, decreasing economic competition as new and more jobs became available, and a higher standard of living. These factors

* "The Negro's political impotence was pointed to as a factor in the indifference of officers toward the prosecution of mobs," by the Southern Commission on the Study of Lynching. V. *N. Y. Times*, 10 November 1931.

had already made themselves felt. It was growing comparatively easy for Negroes to register in cities. The number of obviously well-schooled Negroes was increasing, as were Negro property owners and business and professional men. A change in white opinion manifested itself in such organizations as the Interracial Coöperation Commission, and in the appearance of protests against lynching and other forms of repression and discrimination — even against suffrage restrictions themselves.

Such liberalizing factors were on the increase in the South from the turn of the century to 1930. Were it not for the continued one-party political situation, therefore, it would be reasonable to suppose that the number of voting Negroes increased after the first flush of disfranchising activity engendered by the passage of the new constitutions. Certainly it is probable that Negro suffrage in various types of nonpartisan elections increased. As the development of the South continues, it may well be that Negro suffrage will markedly increase, especially if bipartisan politics should be built up.

It cannot be definitely shown that Negro suffrage gained in the South between 1900 and 1930. No statistical evidence exists, and a certain number of Negroes always voted, under varying circumstances, from Reconstruction on. Nor is it possible to say unequivocally that the social and economic advances of the Negro in the twentieth century had a directly favorable effect on Negro suffrage. For, during our investigations in 1929 and 1930, it did not always seem to follow that propertied and educated Negroes were admitted to the polls, although where there were many such — i.e., in the cities — a greater political freedom seemed to exist than in backward districts.

It would be a mistake, also, to assume that the Negro vote in the South was all set for a slow but steady increase in 1930, because of the growing urbanization of the South, the spread of education, the appearance of "liberal" organizations of native origin, and the social and economic advances of the Negroes themselves. The very increase in Negro voting that such changes implied might bring into play its own check: the possibility of making an issue once more of "Negro domination" or the "Negro balance of power."

While the social and economic changes taking place in the South in the twentieth century undoubtedly created situations favorable to racial tolerance, they also carried in them the seeds of discord. As the Negro was drawn into the city, industrial competition between the races increased. During the depression of 1930, an organization of "Black Shirts," covering white skins, initiated a drive in Atlanta against employers who preferred Negro to white labor. The competition of cheap Negro labor and the possibilities of Negroes as strike breakers had already been demonstrated in the North, with the result of causing racial feeling and even riots. The industrialization of the South might as easily lead to situations like the East St. Louis riots, gravely intensified and on a much larger scale, as to racial peace through prosperity and education.

While many changes had occurred in the South, therefore, they had not yet had much effect on the situation created by the new constitutions. What little effect they had had, moreover, was erratic — here, "Uncle Tom" Negroes could register; there, substantial Negro business or professional men, for example. And in the background of Southern sentiment and tradition, it was still easily possible in 1930 for some adverse factor, some racial difficulty, some negrophobe politician, to set "liberalism" back, to check it, to prevent for a long time its further development.

APPENDICES

APPENDIX I

THE NEGRO SUFFRAGE QUESTIONNAIRE

The questionnaire exhibited as Table I on a succeeding page was sent out in the Spring of 1930 to 8806 colored citizens, of both sexes, in the States of Alabama, Arkansas, Florida, Georgia, Kentucky, Louisiana, Mississippi, North and South Carolina, Tennessee, Texas, and Virginia. West Virginia, at some points in the foregoing text considered as a Southern State, was omitted, because field investigation had already revealed that this State was to all intents and purposes a Northern State from the standpoint of Negro suffrage. Details as to the number sent and returned are given in Table II.

The original sample sent out was small; the returns smaller still. This was necessarily the case, for only such Negroes could be questionnaired, as were listed, with addresses, in some sort of directory. The source of names and addresses was chiefly the alumni lists of the leading Negro institutions of higher learning, both collegiate and technical, Negro professional schools, and the directories of various national, State, and local Negro professional associations (doctors, dentists, lawyers, teachers). After returns had come in from a sample list, not all the women on the remaining lists were questionnaired; they were in some cases in a large majority, but their rate of return was very low.

The use of the sort of lists indicated was further prompted by the thought that the groups therein represented were *prima facie* able to meet any reasonable voting prerequisite put upon them, and that as leaders of their race they would be more than usually willing to take the trouble of filling in and returning the questionnaire.

As a result of the special nature of the sample, several factors unexpectedly weighted the results in the direction of showing a large number of Negro voters for the South as a whole; 68.5%, as exhibited in Tables V and VII. One was the high literacy, general capacity, activeness, and comparative economic security indicated by the very sources of the list. The comparative economic security of the group questionnaired is further indicated in Table IV, showing the occupational distribution of the returning Negroes, as is, also, its literacy and intellectual capacity—v. the number of professional persons included, e.g., Table IV, Groups A, B, C. Another factor weighting the tabulation in the direction of a large Negro vote is to be found in the large proportion of returns—56.2%—from large towns and cities (see Table III). As has been explained in the foregoing text, both the opportunity to vote and the value of the vote for Negroes is greatest in the cities of the South. It also seems probable that a very large number of the 88% of subjects not returning, failed to take the trouble because of the very political apathy the actual tabulation shows, or from a feeling of guilt at never having attempted to vote; in a few cases, fear may have been the motive for silence.

For these reasons, because of the smallness of the sample, and also because of the writer's findings in the actual Southern field, it is felt that the total percentage of Negroes voting shown in the tabulation—68.5%—*very greatly exaggerates the real condition* of the mass of Negroes with respect to political activity.

It will be observed that not all the questions asked in the schedule (Table I) have their counterpart in the tabulations. In some cases it will be obvious that the question was asked merely to establish the eligibility of a given return (e.g., age). For others, the whole return was so small as to make minute separation impracticable and worthless (e.g., county and town of residence; and sex). Party affiliation is not tabulated (nos. 12–14) because the overwhelming majority of returns gave "Republican," with a scattering of perhaps a dozen Democrats, "Independents," and one Socialist. Poll-tax payment and registration are asked about separately, but tabulated together, since the two acts *together* are the usual voting prerequisite.

No dates of registration or voting are given, for not enough replies specified dates clearly. The returns were tabulated under "Registered," "Registered and Voting," and "Refused Registration and/or Voting," as the table headings indicate, "*at any time.*" There are, therefore, returns which are tabulated both under "Registered," etc., and "Refused Registration," etc. An effort was made to exclude from the classification "Registered and Voting" the returns of older persons whose political activity seemed to have been confined to periods antedating the disfranchising constitutions of the respective States.

The questions regarding primary voting (nos. 21–23) were much misunderstood. The object was to discover how many colored citizens had applied for a Democratic primary ballot and been positively refused by the officials in charge. In some cases, the answers were clear to this effect; in some, they very clearly indicated that the prevention had been negative, in such answers as "Not allowed here," "White primary rule prevents," etc. But in most cases the replies were ambiguous; there was no possibility of telling whether the "prevention" had been active or merely negative. Since in many cases, also, the question was not answered at all, we have preferred to tabulate, under the party label, the actual colored voters at primaries (Table V). This number is of course small.

Similarly with questions 24 to 30. It was desired to test quantitatively the otherwise quite well-established theory that Negroes were freer to vote in Presidential elections, at referenda, and to an extent in city elections, than in the primary-governed Congressional, State, and county elections. Many returns indicated that this was the case, although some also stated emphatically, "I vote in all elections." For the most part, however, these details were either omitted entirely, or the questions were answered in a manner indicating that the respondent thought them to refer to his place of residence, rather than his sphere of political activity. "Registered and voting at any time," therefore, means also "in any kind of election," except, of course, the primary.

This fact also has its bearing on the large percentage of Negro voters shown by the tabulation as a whole. Many of the 68.5% voting never cast a ballot save at an occasional bond-issue election; many more, also, voted once or twice in a long period of years.

Although the sample is so small and so specialized in its scope, it is still permissible to point out several features of the tabulation, because they correspond so closely to the findings described in Part II of the main body of the text.

1. The States ranking lowest in Negro suffrage were the States ranking lowest in white population ratio, in literacy, and —to a lesser degree—in urban ratio (Table VII).

2. The States ranking lowest in Negro suffrage were also those having disfranchising constitutions (Table VII).

3. Among Negro non-voters, more than three times as many never attempted to vote, than were prevented from registering and/or voting (Table V).

4. Among the reasons for never attempting to vote, the uselessness of the attempt ranked highest, unfavorable public opinion next, and the fear of humiliation or threats third. These three factors together account for almost half the number of those never attempting to register and/or vote. The column "No explanation" is excluded from this summary (Table VI).

5. Although the questionnaire touched, presumably, on a grievance among Negro citizens, the returns were only 12.3%, including a limited follow-up; or little better than the run of returns to questionnaires. This perhaps points to "apathy" and discouragement, especially in connection with Points 3 and 4 above (Table II).

6. The return for men was 15.1%; for women, 5.0%. This perhaps represents the comparative interest of the sexes in politics; although it must also be borne in mind that "humiliation," "threats," and unfavorable public opinion probably bear more heavily on Negro women than on Negro men.

TABLE I

THE QUESTIONNAIRE

(If You Have Already Filled Out and Returned One of These Blanks, Destroy This)

1. Age, over 21 ☐ Under 21 ☐ 2. Sex, Male ☐ Female ☐

EDUCATION: (Check all you have attended)

3. Grade School ☐ 4. High School ☐ 5. Trade or Agricultural School ☐ 6. College ☐ 7. Professional School ☐

RESIDENCE:

8. State.......... 9. County.......... 10. Town ....
11. Business ....

PARTY:

12. Republican ☐ 13. Democratic ☐ 14. Independent ☐
15. Did you pay poll tax last year?.... 16. Have you ever paid poll taxes?.... Give places and dates: ....
....
17. Are you a registered voter now?...... 18. Have you ever applied for registration as a voter?...... Regularly?...... Or give places and dates: ....
....
19. Have you ever been registered as a voter?........ Regularly?........ Or give places and dates: ....
....
20. If not, for what reasons? ....
....
21. Have you ever voted in a primary?...... 22. What party?.......... Regularly?........ Or give dates and places:..........
....
23. Have you ever been prevented from voting at a primary? .... What party?.......... What were the circumstances?......
....
24. Did you vote at the 1928 general election?............ 25. Have you ever voted at a general election?........ Give places and dates below:
26. National ☐ .... 27. State ☐ ....
28. County ☐ .... 29. Town or city ☐ ....
30. Special ☐ (State whether bond issue, assessments, improvements, etc.)
....
31. Have you ever been prevented from voting at a general election? ...... What were the circumstances? ....
....
32. Have you ever contested your right to vote before a court, election commissioners, etc.? ....What were the circumstances? ....
....
Results: ....
....
33. Comments: ....

TABLE II

QUESTIONNAIRES SENT AND RETURNED, BY STATES

State	Number Sent			Returns					
				Number			Per cent		
	Men	*Wmn.*	*Total*	*Men*	*Wmn.*	*Total*	*Men*	*Wmn.*	*Total*
Ala.	653	386	1,039	129	16	145	19.8	4.1	13.9
Ark.	256	72	328	34	4	38	13.2	5.6	11.6
Fla.	437	78	515	47	5	52	10.8	6.0	10.1
Ga.	727	192	919	92	7	99	12.7	3.6	10.7
Ky.	277	90	367	34	5	39	12.3	5.6	10.7
La.	420	294	714	64	18	82	15.2	6.1	11.5
Miss.	304	60	364	75	1	76	24.7	...	21.4
N. C.	650	246	896	92	8	100	14.2	3.3	11.2
S. C.	516	140	656	103	12	115	20.0	8.6	18.1
Tenn.	592	157	749	59	1	60	10.0	...	8.0
Tex.	510	221	731	83	9	92	16.3	4.1	12.6
Va.	1,007	521	1,528	146	38	184	14.5	7.3	12.0
Total	6,349	2,457	8,806	958	124	1,082	15.1	5.0	12.3

The initial return for Alabama, Mississippi, and South Carolina was so small that a follow-up was sent, to men only; resulting in an increase of about 10% in the returns.

TABLE III

URBAN DISTRIBUTION OF RETURNS

State	*Total return*	*Returns from cities 25M and over*	*Returns from cities 10–25M*	*Total urban return*	*Per cent return urban*
Ala.	145	46	20	66	45.5
Ark.	38	8	7	15	39.4
Fla.	52	32	14	46	88.4
Ga.	99	56	18	74	74.7
Ky.	39	18	12	30	76.9
La.	82	30	12	42	51.2
Miss.	76	9	19	28	36.6
N. C.	100	48	16	64	64.0
S. C.	115	42	11	53	46.1
Tenn.	60	38	5	43	71.7
Tex.	92	49	16	65	70.6
Va.	184	86	8	94	51.0
Total	1,082	462	146	608	56.2

The urban classification of places is based on the Census of 1930, Population Bulletins, 2nd series.

Thirty of the seventy-four Georgia urban returns are from Atlanta, and Norfolk and Richmond account for 24 each, or 48 out of 94 Virginia returns.

TABLE IV

OCCUPATIONAL DISTRIBUTION OF RETURNS

Group A: Medicine, etc.

Dentists	80	
Nurses	5	
Optometrists	1	
Pharmacists	33	
Physicians	230	
"Professional"	2	
Total		351
Per cent		32.4

Group B: Teaching, etc.

Editors	8	
Librarians	4	
Ministers	59	
Social Work	8	
Teachers, sub.	224	
Teachers, sup.	113	
Total		416
Per cent		38.4

Group C: Misc. Professional

Dietitians	2	
Matrons	2	
Lawyers	39	
Undertakers	6	
Total		49
Per cent		4.5

Groups A, B, and C

Total	816
Per cent	75.1

Group D: Business

Accountants	1	
Banking	6	
Contractors	9	
Insurance	26	
Merchants	10	
Real Estate	8	
Stenog., clerks	11	
Total		71
Per cent		6.6

Group E: Craftsmen

Barbers	1	
Blacksmiths, tinsmiths, mechanics	8	
Bricklayers	3	
Carpenters	3	
Dressmakers	1	
Engineers, bldg. supts.	5	
Plumbers	2	
Printers	4	
Shoemakers	1	
Tailors	6	
Total		34
Per cent		3.1

TABLE IV (*Continued*)

Group F: Semi-, Unskilled Labor		
Draymen	1	
Federal employees	13	
Housewives	8	
Laborers	1	
Railroadmen	1	
Cleaners and Pressers	1	
Total		25
Per cent		2.4

Group G: Farmer		
Total		29
Per cent		2.7

Group H: Miscellaneous		
Billiard Parlor	1	
Musicians	1	
Not Given	105	
Total		107
Per cent		9.9

RECAPITULATION

Group	*Returns*	*P.C. of total return*
A, B, C: Professional	816	75.1
D: Business	71	6.6
E: Craftsmen	34	3.1
F: Semi-, Unskilled Labor	25	2.4
G: Farmers	29	2.7
H: Miscellaneous, and Not Given	107	9.9
Total	1,082	100.0

The eight groups were constructed partly with a view to a logical classification of similar occupations, partly to the amount of schooling and skill required, partly to the social standing given by the occupation both in white and colored circles. This involved some difficulties and overlappings. Thus in Group D, Business, some of the Bankers, Merchants, and Real Estate dealers returning were recognizably fairly wealthy men. There was much overlapping among Teachers, Farmers, and Ministers; less among Teachers and Merchants. In these cases, the tabulation classified as Teachers or Ministers, rather than Farmers, because it was felt that the professional rank added a cubit to the social status of the individual, and must often imply some special training.

In Group A, the class "Professional" were probably medical men.

In Group B, subordinate teachers are teachers in elementary and secondary schools; superior teachers, principals and supervisors at any grade, and teachers and administrators in Institutes, colleges, etc.

In Group F, Federal Employees were with two or three exceptions letter carriers.

TABLE V

POLITICAL ACTIVITY, BASED ON RETURNS, BY STATES

State	Returns	Voters at any time			Refused same		Apathetic		Primary voters			Contests
		Rg.	*R. V.*	*Per cent*	*No.*	*Per cent*	*No.*	*Per cent*	*R.*	*D.*	*Not stated*	
Ala.	145	68	64	44.1	27	18.6	63	43.4	7	15	1	1 pend'g 1 lost
Ark.	38	35	29	76.4	2	5.3	5	13.1	..	7	..	......
Fla.	52	44	41	78.8	..	..	10	20.0	4	..	..	......
Ga.	99	95	89	89.9	3	3.0	10	10.0	6	2	2	1 lost
Ky.	39	39	39	100.0	..	..	..	..	30	1	..	......
La.	82	33	24	29.3	10	16.7	48	58.5	16	..	..	......
Miss.	76	46	35	46.0	5	6.6	32	42.1	1	..	..	......
N. C.	100	82	76	75.0	10	10.0	13	13.0	15	16	3	......
S. C.	115	78	67	58.3	9	7.8	32	27.8	7	6	1	......
Tenn.	60	56	55	93.2	1	1.7	2	3.3	26	10	..	......
Tex.	92	85	79	85.9	1	1.1	6	6.1	6	13	3	......
Va.	184	150	143	77.7	8	4.4	33	17.9	8	27	1	1 won
Total	1,082	811	741	68.5	76	7.0	254	23.5	..	97	..	.....

"Rg." means "Registered"; "R.V.," "Registered and Voting." The percentages in all cases are calculated on the returns. Under "Primary voters," "R" means "Republican"; "D," "Democratic."

The Republican primary voters fall into two classes: (1) Voters in regular Republican primaries in States with an active Republican party: Kentucky, Tennessee, and the western counties of North Carolina. (2) Voters in occasional Republican primaries called to create an impression on the national party (Louisiana, e.g.), and voters at Republican mass meetings, conventions, and unofficial and unregulated primaries (Georgia, Mississippi, South Carolina, e.g., where there was no official Republican primary). In Florida, the Republican party came under the operation of the State primary law in 1929, by reason of the large Hoover vote the year before. Most of the Democratic primary voters were in large cities.

In Arkansas and Texas, tax payment constituted registration. In Kentucky and Tennessee, registration was limited to certain large cities.

TABLE VI

APATHY OF COLORED CITIZENS, BY STATES, ACCORDING TO REASONS GIVEN

Reasons	*Ala.*	*Ark.*	*Fla.*	*Ga.*	*Ky.*	*La.*	*Miss.*	*N.C.*	*S.C.*	*Tenn.*	*Tex.*	*Va.*	*Total*
No real choice	2	..	..	..	..	5	3	..	8	..	2	3	23
Sure of refusal	19	2	2	2	..	17	10	1	2	1	..	5	61
Political cynicism	1	..	2	..	..	1	..	..	1	..	..	..	5
Humiliation, threats	6	..	3	..	..	2	1	1	1	..	1	1	16
Tax too much	2	..	..	..	..	..	..	..	..	..	..	..	2
Public opinion	12	..	..	2	..	11	7	1	4	..	2	1	40
Too few Negro voters	3	..	..	..	..	..	..	2	1	..	..	..	6
No explanation	18	3	3	6	..	12	11	8	15	1	1	23	101
Total	63	5	10	10	..	48	32	13	32	2	6	33	254
Per cent	43.4	13.1	20.0	10.0	..	58.5	42.1	13.0	27.8	3.3	6.1	17.9	23.5

The numbers being so small, no attempt at a per-cent distribution of the reasons has been attempted.

Alabama required payment of all poll taxes due from age 21 to time of registration or exemption from tax.

The percentage given is that of Table V, based on *total* returns.

TABLE VII

THE STATES RANKED ACCORDING TO NEGRO VOTERS, WITH A COMPARISON OF CERTAIN SOCIAL STATISTICS

State and rank	P. C. *Negroes voting*	P. C. *Negroes refused*	P. C. *apa-thetic*	POPULATION, 1930		
				P. C. *urban*	P. C. *literate*	P. C. *white*
1. Ky.	100.0	..	..	30.5	93.4	91.3
2. Tenn.	93.2	1.7	3.3	34.2	92.8	81.7
3. Ga.*	89.9	3.0	10.0	30.7	90.6	63.2
4. Tex.	85.9	1.0	6.1	41.0	93.2	73.5
5. Fla.	78.8	..	20.0	51.7	92.9	70.5
6. Va.*	77.7	4.4	17.9	32.4	91.3	73.1
7. Ark.	76.4	5.3	13.1	20.6	93.2	73.4
8. N. C.*	75.0	10.0	13.0	25.5	90.0	70.5
9. S. C.*	58.3	7.8	27.8	21.3	86.1	54.3
10. Miss.*	46.0	6.6	42.1	16.8	86.9	49.6
11. Ala.*	44.1	18.6	43.4	28.1	87.4	64.3
12. La.*	29.3	16.7	58.5	30.9	86.5	62.7
Total	68.5	7.0	23.5	...	...	...

The population figures are those of the 1930 Census; the literacy for the population 10 years and over; the per cent urban includes places from 2,500 up.

The starred States are those having disfranchising constitutions; the others have not.

A few seeming anomalies should be noted: Georgia's position as no. 3, when her white population ratio and literacy should make her no. 8, is explained by the fact that most of the Georgia returns are from Atlanta, which was a favorable place for Negro suffrage (v. this Appendix, Table III; and above, pp. 143-144, 150-151, 160-162). Arkansas's low position, compared to other Border States and States with a simple poll-tax requirement, is probably due to her low urban ratio and the considerable extent of her Black Belt. Florida's urban ratio jumped from 34.6 in 1920 to the present 51.7. Louisiana's urban ratio is accounted for by New Orleans, the largest city in the South. New Orleans had considerably more than half of the State's urban population: 458,762 out of 833,532. Apart from New Orleans, therefore, Louisiana was nearer Mississippi in urban ratio than the figure given indicates. The Negro population is chiefly in the rural parishes.

APPENDIX II

VARIOUS REGISTRATION STATISTICS

TABLE I: LOUISIANA OFFICIAL REGISTRATION
TABLE II: ALABAMA OFFICIAL REGISTRATION, 1908
TABLE III: NEGRO REGISTRATION FROM MISCELLANEOUS SOURCES, COMPARED WITH NEGRO POPULATION AND LITERACY

TABLE I

LOUISIANA OFFICIAL REGISTRATION

a. Total Registration for the State, white and Negro, and for New Orleans.

PRESIDENTIAL ELECTION YEARS	STATE-WIDE REGISTRATION		NEW ORLEANS ONLY
	White	*Negro*	*Negro*
1896	164,088	130,344	14,153
1900	125,437	5,320	1,482
1904	106,360	1,718	660
1908	154,669	1,885	480
1912	165,082	1,704	757
1916	201,745	1,772	597
PRESIDENTIAL AND CONGRESSIONAL YEARS			
1918	144,095	735	420
1920	257,282	3,533	2,599
1922	191,191	598	459
1924	317,136	955	746
1926	274,532	988	907
1928	363,057	1,960	1,723

Note the 96 per cent decrease in Negro registration between 1896, the last year before the enactment of the disfranchising constitution, and 1900, the first registration year after.

The second half of the table shows plainly the increase in registration in presidential election years.

There was an unusually large increase in the Negro vote, mostly in New Orleans, in 1920, the year in which national woman suffrage became effective. A "drive" among New Orleans Negroes helped this tendency along.

The last column indicates how large a proportion of Negro registration takes place in the city of New Orleans.

The 1920 Census figures for New Orleans should be compared with the registration of that year: Negro population 21 years and over, 63,980; of whom the literate group numbered 45,912.

Dr. DuBois made the following tabulation, based on the 1920 Census, the 1924 registration, and his own estimates, in *Crisis*, vol. xxxv, p. 296 (Sept., 1928):

Negro Population, 21 yrs.	359,251
Literate	129,271
Farm owners, approx.	10,000
Other home owners	28,906
Other property owners	unknown
Total qualified Negroes	168,177 at least.
Total Negro Registration	980
Total White Registration	274,592

b. Population, Literacy, and Registration, 1920, of the Two Whitest and the Two Blackest Parishes.

White Parishes	White Pop. of Voting Age		Negro Pop. of Voting Age		Registration	
	Total	*Literate*	*Total*	*Literate*	*White*	*Negro*
Cameron	1,529	1,010	243	110	590	0
Livingston	4,249	3,726	836	484	2,171	2
Black Parishes						
E. Carroll	875	857	5,570	3,151	486	2
Tensas	932	865	5,637	1,954	636	0

c. Parishes having no Negro Registrants.

1900:	8	1916:	20
1904:	16	1920:	28
1908:	14	1924:	35
1912:	20	1928:	42

In 1896, before the enactment of the new constitution, there were, on the other hand, 26 parishes in which Negro registrants were in the majority.

Sources: Besides *Crisis* and the 1920 Census, the Biennial Reports of the Secretary of State to the Governor, 1895-1929. These give Negro and white registration figures by parishes.

APPENDIX II

TABLE II

ALABAMA OFFICIAL REGISTRATION, 1908, COMPARED WITH POPULATION AND LITERACY

NEGRO POPULATION

County	*Per cent Negro*	*No. Males 21 Yrs., Literate*	*Registration (Negro)*
Autauga	58.5	1,521	35
Baldwin	28.1	808	206
Barbour	62.5	2,054	46
Bibb	33.8	1,493	59
Blount	5.5	172	..
Bullock	84.0	2,628	14
Butler	53.0	1,715	2
Calhoun	27.5	1,739	151
Chambers	51.8	2,104	28
Cherokee	12.9	310	27
Chilton	20.5	708	1
Choctaw	62.2	1,184	29
Clarke	55.9	2,044	158
Clay	12.6	352	..
Cleburne	5.3	83	..
Coffee	22.1	692	..
Colbert	38.1	1,303	22
Conecuh	47.0	1,205	7
Coosa	37.6	669	not given
Covington	24.9	1,553	3
Crenshaw	32.2	1,045	..
Cullman	1.9	110	4
Dale	26.9	729	11
Dallas	81.5	4,808	55
DeKalb	3.0	114	not given
Elmore	46.9	1,799	55
Escambia	29.5	875	55
Etowah	17.4	1,324	39
Fayette	11.5	241	8
Franklin	9.5	296	12
Geneva	16.4	592	30
Greene	86.7	1,630	104
Hale	78.9	2,262	92
Henry	48.5	1,054	..
Houston	29.6	1,424	..
Jackson	9.5	411	73

TABLE II (*Continued*)

NEGRO POPULATION

County	*Per cent Negro*	*No. Males 21 Yrs., Literate*	*Registration (Negro)*
Jefferson	40.0	21,408	376
Lamar	18.2	376	7
Lauderdale	22.9	985	76
Lawrence	31.5	891	49
Lee	59.8	1,853	12
Limestone	38.2	987	28
Lowndes	88.2	2,512	57
Macon	84.6	2,611	69
Madison	40.2	2,416	112
Marengo	77.3	2,903	304
Marion	3.0	66	25
Marshall	4.8	189	..
Mobile	42.9	6,875	193
Monroe	57.9	1,499	40
Montgomery	69.2	8,265	69
Morgan	24.3	1,268	60
Perry	78.5	2,516	90
Pickens	51.7	911	112
Pike	46.9	1,633	26
Randolph	23.2	777	13
Russell	77.9	1,967	191
St. Clair	17.5	654	50
Shelby	28.4	1,112	19
Sumter	81.3	2,062	57
Talladega	48.1	2,093	81
Tallapoosa	36.9	1,140	33
Tuscaloosa	40.0	2,754	165
Walker	17.7	1,528	4
Washington	42.0	824	56
Wilcox	81.6	3,026	41
Winston	0.4	22	1
Total	42.5	121,159	3,742

Sources: Population figures of 1910 from "Negro Population . . . 1790-1910"; registration figures from Alabama Dept. of Archives and History, "Official and Statistical Register," 1920, 287-88. "No registration statistics subsequent to 1908 have been assembled" (p. 287).

APPENDIX II

TABLE III

REGISTRATION STATISTICS FROM MISCELLANEOUS SOURCES, COMPARED WITH NEGRO POPULATION AND LITERACY

Place	*21-Year Old and Literate Negro Population, 1920*	*Negro Voters at any time, 1920–1930*
ALABAMA	269,847	3,500
	Certain Counties	
Chilton*	1,345	3
Covington*	2,393	2
Cherokee *	570	5
Clay *	914	1
DeKalb *	252	0
Cullman *	163	2
Macon *	5,396	65
Walker *	3,169	12
Washington *	1,472	25 to 30
	Certain Cities	
Birmingham	33,645	300 to 400
Mobile *	11,344	193
Montgomery *	8,140	38 to 50
ARKANSAS	*Certain Cities*	
Little Rock	10,196	4,000
Hot Springs	1,764	1,100
FLORIDA	*Certain Cities*	
Daytona Beach		1,000
Jacksonville		1,200
GEORGIA	369,511	10,000 at most
	Certain Counties	
Chatham	22,678	900
Clarke *	4,299	179
Floyd	3,016	274
Fulton (incl. Atlanta) *	34,306	2,282 to 7,341
	Certain Cities	
Atlanta *	31,943	200 to 500 (city elections only)
Augusta	10,397	900 to 1,000
Macon *	10,595	"few hundred"
Savannah	19,672	700 to 800

TABLE III (*Continued*)

Place	*21-Year Old and Literate Negro Population, 1920*	*Negro Voters at any time, 1920-1930*
MISSISSIPPI	290,782	850
	Certain Counties *	
Adams	5,206	38 (incl. Natchez, *q.v.*)
Copiah	4,390	1
Forrest	2,824	10
Hinds	12,154	60 (incl. Jackson, *q.v.*)
Holmes	8,608	30
Humphreys	5,095	0
Lauderdale	6,013	140
LeFlore	9,782	40 to 50 (incl. Greenwood, *q.v.*)
Lincoln	2,577	5
Madison	6,402	12
Marshall	5,565	40
Rankin	2,964	0
Scott	1,873	25
Sharkey	3,745	0
Simpson	1,781	75
Sunflower	11,432	20
Warren	8,278	185 (incl. Vicksburg, *q.v.*)
Washington	14,583	148
Yazoo	8,582	6
	Certain Cities	
Greenwood	1,896	6
Jackson	4,182	50 to 100
Natchez	2,821	under 100
Vicksburg	3,774	75 to 100
NORTH CAROLINA	*Certain Cities*	
Asheville	3,360	100 to 200
Durham	3,105	500 to 700
Greensboro	2,678	500 to 700
Raleigh	3,897	582
Shelby	139	2 to 6
Winston-Salem	9,452	326
SOUTH CAROLINA	*Certain Cities*	
Columbia *	6,587	175 to 800
Charleston *	14,199	500 to 700

TABLE III (*Continued*)

Place	21-Year Old and Literate Negro Population, 1920	Negro Voters at any time, 1920–1930
SOUTH CAROLINA—*Cont.*	*Certain Cities*	
Edgefield *		11
Greenville	3,448	45
Orangeburg	1,303	60 to 70
Spartanburg	3,331	100 to 200
TENNESSEE		
Memphis (city)	34,336	4,500 (normally)
Fayette (co.)	6,399	50
Haywood (co.)	4,943	"none or few"
TEXAS	*Certain Cities*	
Dallas	14,239	1,400 to 1,600
Ft. Worth	9,861	3,500
Houston *	19,829	5,000
San Antonio	8,597	3,000 to 5,000
VIRGINIA	248,347	12,000 to 18,000
	Certain Counties	
Elizabeth City	4,033	365
Henrico *	2,208	200 to 460
Princess Ann	2,049	18
	Certain Cities	
Abingdon *	207	"about 50"
Bristol	496	100
Charlottesville *	1,360	20 to 30
Danville	2,164	300
Hampton	1,063	75
Newport News	7,760	250 to 900 (1928)
Norfolk *	23,746	300 to 700
Petersburg	5,895	119
Portsmouth	10,651	382 to 761 (1928)
Richmond *	28,009	700 to 1,000
Roanoke *	4,398	500 to 1,000

Sources: The population figure is calculated from the Census of 1920. The places marked with a star show "official" voting figures; the others are the estimates of responsible persons in the field in a position to know. The estimates were always checked by asking several persons in each locality for a statement.

"Official" figures include the following: actual registration or poll-tax lists seen by the writer; lists published in a newspaper in accordance with the law; the estimates of registrars when these seemed reasonable and checked with other sources. The Alabama county figures are those given Dr. Monroe Work of Tuskegee Institute, in writing, by the probate judges of the respective counties. The Mississippi county figures were published in *Crisis*, September, 1928; Dr. DuBois "had county records examined."

APPENDIX III

SOUTHERN ELECTION LAWS, 1930

ALABAMA

Suffrage Qualifications

Residence: Two years in the State, one year in the county, three months in the election district.

Taxes: Poll tax, $1.50 annually; due 1 Oct.; paid up for whole period of liability; no proceedings to collect. All land taxes for preceding year.

Property: Forty acres of land assessed at $300, voter's or voter's wife's. Educational alternative.

Education: Read and write any article in U. S. Constitution, unless disabled. Property alternative.

Character: Regular employment for greater part of preceding year, unless disabled. Registrars may require an oath to five years' previous residence, and names of employers during that period. For false oath, 1 to 5 years in penitentiary.

Appeals: Persons refused may appeal within thirty days, without depositing costs, in circuit court; final appeal to Supreme Court.

Primary: Only registered voters may participate in any primary or any other method of party action of any party or faction. Party may make further qualifications. Democratic party rule bars Negroes.

Registration Procedure

Officials: Three in each county, appointed by Governor and two State officials for four years; removable by same without reason given.

County probate judge, elected, also has registration duties.

No provision for bipartisanship.

Time: Counties: Odd Decembers, even Januaries.
Precincts: October-December, odd years.

Term: Permanent.

Refusal: County Board may refuse registration if not reasonably convinced of voter's qualifications.

Purging: By County Board or probate judge, on notice to voter; hearing granted.

Primary Regulations

Status: Primaries held at public expense, officered by State election officials.

Scope: Not obligatory. Optional for parties casting 25% of total vote. Nominates for public or party office.

Time: Presidential years: 2 Tue. in May; other even years, 2 Tue. Aug.

Election Procedure

Time: 1 Tue. after 1 Mon. Nov.; various officers in different years.

Ballots: Official ballots only.

Voter marks names wanted; 5-minute limit in booth.

Candidates put on by primary, party or factional assembly, or petition.

Officers: Three inspectors, two clerks at each voting place; returning officer for precinct; watcher for each party with candidates.

Probate judge, sheriff, and circuit court clerk in each county appoint officers from lists submitted by parties with candidates, at least two from each list. Appointing officers elected. Election officers appointed for one election.

Voters' Tests: Voter need not show certificate of registration or poll-tax receipt if name is on respective lists.

Challenges: Any qualified voter or official may challenge. Challenged person must swear as follows: that facts of challenge are false; that he is qualified, stating age, non-criminality, registration, poll-tax payment, names of two identifiers, residences for last 12 mos.; that he has not and will not vote in other precincts. Must also present affidavit of similar tenor from a person known to inspector as a qualified voter. Inspector must warn challenged person of perjury penalty, 1-5 years in penitentiary.

ARKANSAS

Suffrage Qualifications

Residence: Twelve months in the State, six months in the county, one month in the district.

Taxes: Poll tax, $1.00 annually, payable January-July preceding election.

Primary: Only regular voters eligible. Democratic rule bars Negroes.

Registration Procedure

The Constitution forbids the enactment of registration laws. The poll-tax paid list and the presentation of the poll-tax receipt provides a check on the eligibility of voters.

Primary Regulations

Status: Primaries held at party expense, officered by party officials. County committees select judges and clerks.

Scope: Optional for all parties. Elects county party officers and delegates to county conventions. City, town, and township nominations may be made by primary.

Time: 2 Tue. August preceding election.

Election Procedure

Time: 1 Tue. after 1 Mon. of Nov., even years.

Ballots: Official only. Voting machines permitted.

Voter scratches all unwanted names; 5-minute limit in booth.

Races to vote alternately.

Officers: Governor, Secretary of State, and Attorney-General constitute State Board of Election Commissioners. They appoint County Election Commissioners, who in turn appoint three election judges in each precinct. Judges appoint two clerks. All appointed for each election. Commissioners and judges shall not all be of same party "if competent persons of different politics can be found."

Voters' Tests: Voter must exhibit poll-tax receipt, and his name must appear on tax-paid list. If voter has not receipt, need only state that he has not voted and will not vote again at this election. If judges doubt his identity, may require oath or satisfactory evidence.

FLORIDA

Suffrage Qualifications

Residence: One year in State, six months in county, or city.

Taxes: Poll tax, $1.00 annually, payable by 4 Saturday before election.

Property: For bond elections only: voter must be qualified and property owner.

Other: Applicant for registration must swear to age, residence, and non-criminality. Perjury penalty, up to 20 years in prison.

Primary: Only registered voters may participate. Party authorities may make further qualifications. County party rules bar Negroes.

Registration Procedure

Officials: One supervisor per county, appointed by Governor; one registration officer per election district and as many deputy supervisors as deemed necessary, appointed by supervisor. Removals by same authorities.

Tax collector may register on affidavit when poll tax is collected. Tax collector elected.

Separate registration for primaries; same officers.

Time: For elections: from 1 Mon. Aug. to 2 Sat. of month preceding election.

For primaries: 1 Mon. March to 1 Mon. April in election years.

Books closed between registration periods.

Term: Two years, in cities; elsewhere permanent.

Purging: By supervisor or county commissioners; wrongful erasures to be corrected on application to supervisor; appeal to county commissioners.

Primary Regulations

Status: Primaries held at State and county expense, officered by State election officials.

Scope: Obligatory on all parties polling 30% of vote cast, in respective districts. Nominates all candidates except municipal, where optional with parties. Elects State,

Congressional-district, and county party executive committees.

Time: 1 Tue. after 1 Mon. June of election years.

Election Procedure

Time: 1 Tue. after 1 Mon. Nov.

Ballots: Official only.

Voter marks names wanted; 5-minute limit in booth. Names put on by primary, convention, or petition.

Officers: Three inspectors, one clerk, per polling place; more in large centers. Appointed by County Commissioners for each election. Must not all be of same party. (County Commissioners elected.)

Voters' Tests: If name not on registration book, voter must show registration certificate, whereupon election officers may permit vote if satisfied that certificate "properly" identifies.

Challenges: Communicated to inspectors through sheriff.

Inspectors must prevent repeating and refuse the vote of unqualified persons.

GEORGIA

Suffrage Qualifications

Residence: One year in the State, six months in the county.

Taxes: All poll and other taxes for which liable must be paid 6 months before election.

Property: Forty acres on which applicant resides, or $500 tax-assessed property. Education or character alternatives.

Education: Able to read in English any paragraph of U. S. or State constitution and write same when read by registrar, or if disabled to give reasonable interpretation thereof when read by registrar. Property or character alternatives.

Character: Of good character and understanding duties and obligations of citizenship under a republican form of government. Property or education alternatives.

Understanding: Implicit in education and character clauses.

Appeals: Person refused may appeal to registrars, who return plea to superior court for regular trial. Pending decision, registrars' decision valid.

Primary: Only qualified and duly registered persons may vote in primaries, or participate in conventions of any party. Party may make additional qualifications. Democratic party rule bars Negroes.

Registration Procedure

Officials: Three registrars in each county, appointed for two years by superior court judge, and removable by him at pleasure. Superior court judge elected. Not all to be of "one . . . political interest or party." County tax collector and clerk may also register; both elected.

Time: Registration closes six months before election.

Term: Permanent, but subject to examination on qualifications every two years. City-election registration for one year.

Refusal: Tax collector shall refuse to register persons when he is not satisfied of their qualifications.

Purging: By tax collector, with county ordinary and superior court clerk; also by County Board of Registrars; one day's notice to voter, and hearing.

Primary Regulations

Status: Primaries held at party expense, officered by managers appointed by party under party rules.

Scope: Not obligatory.

Time: 2 Wed. Sept. election years.

Election Procedure

Time: 1 Tue. after 1 Mon. Nov. even years; except justices of the peace: 1 Sat. December every fourth year; and municipal officers, 1 Thu. Jan.

Ballots: Official ballots only. Voter scratches all unwanted names. Names put on by filing of candidacy with county ordinary or Secretary of State.

Officers: Three managers, one of whom must be county ordinary or justice of the peace, and three clerks. No provision for bipartisanship.

Voters' Tests: Only voters appearing on list given to managers by county registrars may vote. Persons refused may have hearing before Board of Registrars, who will examine qualifications directly or by other evidence on oath.

Challenges: Challenged voter must swear in writing to his name, qualifications, residence for past 6 months, and aliases. False oath on challenge constitutes perjury, entailing 4-10 year penitentiary sentence.

KENTUCKY

Suffrage Qualifications

Residence: One year in the State, six months in the county, 60 days in the district.

Taxes: Poll-tax prerequisite only in certain cities according to their charters.

Primary: Only qualified voters may vote in primaries; must be registered in cities where registration is required, and registered as party members.

Registration Procedure

Registration is limited to cities of 1st to 4th class; i.e., of 3000 population or more.

Officials: Two judges, one clerk, one sheriff of elections, and one challenger for each party, per precinct.

Appointed by County Board of Election Commissioners from lists which party executive committees may supply, for one year; removable by same for cause, but not within five days of registration. These precinct officers must represent parties as nearly as possible equally, over the county as a whole.

Separate primary registration, by same officers.

Time: For elections: 2 Mon. Sept., 1 Tue. and Wed. Oct., annually.

For primaries: 14th day preceding primary, for voters prevented from attending regular registration, or reaching voting age meanwhile.

Term: Permanent.

Refusal: Registrant must show right to registration. Upon challenge, board may call up to three persons for examination as to voter's qualifications.

Appeals to circuit court.

Purging: At request of party county executive committee, Tue. after 1 Mon. Oct., by two officers per precinct, one from each party, or by county court at request of a voter. Hearing granted; if purgers disagree, hearing *de novo* in county court, with appeal to circuit court.

Primary Regulations

Status: Held at public expense; officered by State election officials.

Scope: Obligatory on parties polling 20% of State presidential vote. Nominates State executive officers, and county commissioners in commission-governed counties.

Time: 1 Sat. August annually.

Election Procedure

Time: 1 Tue. after 1 Mon. Nov.

Ballots: Official ballots only. Voter marks names wanted. Names put on through primary, convention, or petition. Three-minute limit in booth if voters are waiting.

Officers: In precincts, same as for registration.

County Board of Election Commissioners consists of county sheriff (elected), and two members appointed by State Board of Election Commissioners, one from each of five-name lists submitted by county party executive committees.

State Board of Election Commissioners consists of clerk of court of appeals (elected), and two members appointed by Governor from each party, on recommendation of State Executive Committees.

All appointments for one year.

Voters' Tests: (In cities with registration only) Name must appear in voters' book.

(In any election district) If person offering to vote is unknown to election officials, he may be questioned on oath as to qualifications. In case of disagreement, voter must sign affidavit showing residence, address, two nearest neighbors, and non-conviction of disfranchising crime.

Challenges: Party challenger or any voter may challenge in writing. Proceedings as under "Voters' Tests." False subscription to challenge oath is felony, entailing 2-10 years in penitentiary.

LOUISIANA

Suffrage Qualifications

Residence: Two years in State, one year in parish, four months in municipality, three months in precinct.

Taxes: Poll tax, $1.00 annually, paid for two preceding years by 31 December. No proceedings to collect.

Property: Required only for participation in bond-issue elections.

Education: Applicant shall demonstrate his ability to read and write by written application for registration on prescribed form, under oath. Penalties for false swearing not clear, but range between six months' and five years' imprisonment, with or without hard labor. Character and understanding alternatives.

Character: Good character obligatory. But illiterate may qualify as of good character and reputation, and well disposed to the good order and happiness of the U. S. and the State, and must take special "understanding" test.

Understanding: Obligatory to understand duties and obligations of citizenship under a Republican form of government, and to read and give a reasonable interpretation of U. S. Constitution. But illiterate may qualify under "character" clause (above), and understanding, upon having any section of U. S. or Louisiana Constitution read to him.

(Note: The Constitution is not at all clear as to how far "character" and "understanding" is obligatory on all voters, and how far all requirements, including education, are alternatives.)

Appeals: Person denied registration may have two trials in district court, without costs.

Primary: Only registered voters may participate in primaries or conventions. Parties may prescribe other and additional requirements. Democratic party rule bars Negroes.

Registration Procedure

Officers: One registrar for each parish, appointed by parish authorities (elected). A State Board of Registration consists of Governor, Lt.-Governor, and Speaker of House. Any two of State Board may remove registrar at will. New Orleans registrar appointed by Governor.

Time: Registrar must keep office open at all times, save in New Orleans, where registration closes 30 days before election.

Term: Life; save in New Orleans, where new registration every four years.

Refusal: Registrar may refuse; see "Appeals" above.

Purging: By registrar, of own motion or on voter's appeal. Five days' notice given to show cause why name should not be stricken off. Challenged registrant may show qualifications by affidavit signed by three voters. Persons stricken off by a court order may appeal to usual next court.

Primary Regulations

Status: Primaries held at public expense, but officered by party commissioners, named by parish party executive committee from nominees of candidates.

Scope: Obligatory on parties casting 5% of State vote, except in cities, towns, and villages of less than 5000 population, where optional.

Elects all party officers; nominates all candidates.

Time: U. S.—2 Tue. Sept. before election.
State—3 Tue. Jan. before election.
City—60-70 days before election.

Election Procedure

Time: State and parish—Tue. after 3 Mon. April.
City—Tue. after 2 Mon. June.
Orleans parish only—Tue. after 1 Mon. April.

Ballots: Official only.

Voter marks names wanted. Three-minute limit.

Names put on by primary or petition.

Officers: Three commissioners and one clerk per parish, appointed by parish Board of Election Supervisors for each election from lists sent up by parties. "In so far as is practicable, the commissioners . . . shall . . . equally represent all the political parties." Parish Board consists of registrar and two members appointed by Governor.

Voters' Tests: Voter must state name, residence, and occupation, show registration paper and tax receipt, and be on commissioners' list. If name accidentally left off list, voter must give affidavit of qualifications. Orleans only—if voter's registration paper is lost, but name is on list, may vote on affidavit of five voters.

Challenges: Commissioners examine challenged voter on oath; if satisfied, he may vote; but in any case he must establish his identity and right to vote by affidavits of two bona fide residents of ward, taken before one of the commissioners. Perjury penalties.

MISSISSIPPI

Suffrage Qualifications

Residence: Two years in the State, one year in the district, four months in cities.

Taxes: Poll tax, $2.00 annually; this and all other taxes must be paid for two years preceding election by 1 Feb. preceding election. No criminal proceedings to collect poll tax.

Education: Must be able to read any section of the constitution. Understanding alternative.

Understanding: Must be able to understand any section of the constitution when read, or give a reasonable interpretation thereof. Education alternative.

Primary: Registration "essential and necessary qualification to vote at any and all elections." State party executive committee may make rules excluding voters. Democratic party rule bars Negroes.

Registration Procedure

Officers: Clerk of circuit court in each county (elected), unless he is improper person. Registrar may appoint one deputy.

Where registrar is not clerk of circuit court, he is appointed by State Board of Election Commissioners.

Municipal registrars appointed by Mayor or Board of Aldermen.

Time: Registration closes four months before election. Registrar must spend one day in each precinct during eight months of registration period.

Term: Permanent.

Appeals: Voter denied registration may appeal in five days to county election commissioners. Their decision final on facts, but appeal to court on law. No costs save on appeal.

Purging: At demand of another voter, or by County Election Commissioners; various dates; County Election Commissioners determine; appeal to courts on law only.

Primary Regulations

Status: Primaries held at party expense; officered by managers appointed by party officials.

Scope: Seemingly obligatory, although no Republican primaries held. Nominates all State and lesser officers; elects party convention delegates, State and county, who choose party executives; and in case of State convention, appoints national convention delegates, and nominates presidential electors.

Time: U. S. Congress and State judiciary: 3 Tue. Aug. Other nominations: 1 to 10 Aug. preceding regular election, date set by State party committee.

Party convention delegates: ten days' notice from county party committees.

Election Procedure

Time: State and national: 1 Tue. after 1 Mon. Nov.

Municipal: 2 Tue. December; except certain commission cities, on 2 Mon. August.

Ballots: Official ballots only.

Voter marks names wanted; 10-minute limit unless other voters waiting, when 5 minutes.

Names put on by primary or petition.

Officers: Municipal: 3 commissioners appointed by Mayor and Aldermen.

Counties: 3 managers, election bailiff, and 2 clerks per election district, appointed "prior to elections" by County Election Commissioners (except clerks, appointed by managers). 3 County Election Commissioners, appointed by State Board of Election Commissioners two months before national elections. State Board consists of Governor, Secretary of State, Attorney-General.

County Boards not to consist all of one party, "if men of different parties can be conveniently had in the county"; also a provision that parties not holding primaries are not to be represented.

Voters' Tests: Voter must produce evidence of tax payment, and be on registration books.

NORTH CAROLINA

Suffrage Qualifications

Residence: One year in State, four months in district.

(Changed in 1920 from two years in State, six months in county, and four months in district.)

Taxes: None since 1920. Prior to that, annual poll tax of $1.43 required, payable for current year on or before 1 May.

Property: Constitution forbids property qualifications.

Education: Able to read and write any section of State constitution in English, and prove same to satisfaction of registrar. A form is prescribed for an oath of loyalty and attestation to qualifications.

Primary: Only qualified and registered voters, registered as affiliated with a party, may participate in primary. Election officers decide any challenge based on voters' affiliation with party, without appeal.

County party rules bar Negroes from Democratic primary, save in certain counties. *V.* text, Chapter VII, pp. 141-142, 153 above.

Other: Registrant must answer "any material question."

Registration Procedure

Officers: One registrar per ward, township, or precinct, appointed for two years by County Board of Elections, and removable by same "for any satisfactory cause."

Time: Books close 2 Sat. before election; must be open for 21 days before that date. Seven days longer allowed in towns and cities.

Term: Permanent; but County Board of Elections may order new registration for any precinct.

Purging: Ordered by County Board, or may be initiated in cities by registrar or any elector. Carried out by registrar and election judges for precinct. Challenged person examined on qualifications under oath, with at least one witness, who must be a voter. Challenged person's name may still be removed after oath, if authorities not satisfied he is a legal voter.

Primary Regulations

Status: Primaries held at public expense, officered by regular election officials.

Scope: Obligatory on all parties having candidates in 1914, and any others on petition of 10,000 legal voters.

Nominates all elective officers.

Time: Municipal: 2 Mon. preceding election.

Others: 1 Sat. June preceding elections.

Election Procedure

Time: Tue. after 1 Mon. Nov.

Ballots: Official ballots only, separate for each party, but without party emblems. 5 or 6 ballots for each party for various groups of officers.

Voter marks wanted names.

Names put on by primary, or nonpartisan petitions.

Officers: Governor appoints State Board of Elections, 5 members, not more than three from one party.

State Board appoints County Board, 3 members, not more than two of one party; State party chairmen recommend names.

County Board appoints two judges, one from each list of 3 names submitted by party county chairmen, for each precinct; registrar constitutes third precinct officer. All appointments for two years. County Board may remove precinct officials "for any satisfactory cause."

Voters' Tests: List made up in May preceding election.

Challenges: 1 or 2 Sat. before election. Procedure as under "Purging" above.

SOUTH CAROLINA

Suffrage Qualifications

Residence: Two years in State, one year in county, four months in districts, cities, or towns.

Taxes: Annual poll tax must be paid 6 months before election. By implication, all other taxes for which liable.

Property: Ownership and payment of taxes on $300 property in S. C. for preceding year. Education alternative.

Education: Read and write any section of constitution. Property alternative.

Appeals: Person denied registration may appeal to judge of common pleas, thence to Supreme Court *de novo.*

Primaries: Residence: two years in State, six months in county, 60 days in party club district. Separate enrollment in party clubs required. Parties may prescribe "any additional requirements and safeguards," save (N.B.) educational or property requirement.

Negroes applying for Democratic party enrollment must, under party rule, bring affidavit of ten white men showing that applicant voted for Wade Hampton for governor in 1876, and for Democratic candidates ever since.

Registration Procedure

Officers: County Board of Registration of three members; district Supervisor of Registration; appointed by Governor for two years; Supervisors in cities by Mayor or Intendant. No provision for bipartisanship.

Time: All registration books close 30 days before elections. Separate registration required for participation in city elections.

County books open 1 Mon. to 1 Wed. of each month, also 1-15 August in counties of more than 50,000. In election years, registration officer visits every town, village, or industrial settlement, giving two weeks' notice.

Special provision for certain large city-manager cities.

Term: Ordinary registration, 10 years; municipal registration, one year.

Purging: By County Board of Registration 10 days before election. Seemingly no hearing provided; appeal to Common Pleas.

Primary Regulations

Status: Seemingly held at party expense, save in certain cities for municipal primaries; officered by party officials.

Scope: Not obligatory, although recognized in certain statutes compelling Governor to appoint certain local officers in accordance with Democratic (sic) primary results.

Nominates all U. S., State, and county officers, and municipal officers in certain places by statute.

Elects party ward club officers, delegates to county and city conventions, county and city executive committees. County convention in turn elects county chairman, delegates to State conventions, and State executive committee.

Time: Nominations: Last Tue. Aug.

Party officers variously: 4 Sat. April (election years); 2 or 12 Tue. before municipal elections, or last Wed. April before same (other years).

The South Carolina primary system is unique among Southern States. The basis is the ward party club, in which all primary voters must be enrolled. This enrolment is separate from voting registration; voting registration is not required for it; indeed, the legal qualifications for enrolment are at some points contradictory of the registration requirements. *V.* "Primary" under "Suffrage Qualifications" above. Party enrolment is required to take place 1 Tue. June to 4 Tue. July of election years. Party officers have complete charge of this enrolment, including purging and contests. The law states that the primary shall be conducted "in the manner prescribed by the Constitution and rules of the political party."

Election Procedure

Time: 1 Tue. after 1 Mon. Nov.

Ballots: Seemingly no official ballot. Separate party "tickets."

Separate ballots for Federal officers, State and county officers, and referenda, each with own box.

Ballot in wrong box not counted.

Officers: Governor appoints for each county a three-member Board of State and County Election Commissioners, and

Board of Federal Election Commissioners, who hold office until succeeded. Respective Boards appoint 3 managers each for appropriate elections per polling place.

City elections are supervised by three managers appointed ten days before election by Mayor and Aldermen or City Council.

Voters' Tests: Certificate of registration to be shown at polls; and proof of tax payment, for which receipt conclusive. Election commissioners also have registration books.

TENNESSEE

Suffrage Qualifications

Residence: Twelve months in the State, six months in the county.

Taxes: Poll tax, $1.00 annually, paid 30 days before election.

Primary: All persons may participate who are qualified to vote at next general election; must produce evidence of poll-tax payment, and of registration where registration is required. Must be bona-fide and affiliated members of party, and declare allegiance at polls.

Parties may prescribe additional qualifications.

Democratic rule in certain counties bars Negroes.

Registration Procedure

Registration is restricted to towns, cities, and civil districts of 2500 population, and counties of 50,000, or more. There are a few additional divisions by special legislation. City-manager commissioners may provide for registration for local elections.

Officers: Two registrars per ward or other division, only one of a party, appointed 90 days before elections by County Election Commissioners.

Time: From 2 Mon. Aug. of election years for ten days not including Sundays. Supplementary registration for 3 days before the 20th day preceding elections. Registration must have been completed at least 20 days before election in which voter wishes to participate.

Term: Two years, except in cities 2500-5000, where 4 years.

Refusal: If registrars disagree as to voter, issue certificate marked

"The Registrars disagree," whereupon registrant goes to County Election Commissioners, who indorse "Approved" or "Disapproved."

Purging: By registrars.

Other: Applicant unknown to registrars must swear to age, specific address, landlord, place of business or employment, vocation, marital condition, origin, naturalization, and that he is not disqualified. False swearing constitutes perjury, with penalty up to ten years' imprisonment; unqualified registration entails maximum $50 fine and/or 30 days' imprisonment.

Primary Regulations

Status: Primaries held at public expense, but officered by party officials in manner similar to general elections.

Scope: Obligatory on parties casting more than 10% of vote for Governor.

Nominates for Congress, State Legislature, governorship, and Railroad Commissioner; for commissioners of commission cities; may in discretion of proper party executive committee nominate for county or district office.

Elects two men and two women from each Congressional district to State Executive Committee, for two years.

Time: State and national officers: at general election for judicial and county officers, i.e., 1 Thu. Aug.

County and district officers, where such primary held: at time decided by proper party executive committee.

City commissioners: 2 Tue. April.

Election Procedure

Time: Congress, State Legislature, Governor: 1 Tue. after 1 Mon. Nov.

Judicial and county officers: 1 Thu. Aug.

Commission cities: 2 Tue. May. Other municipalities may set own election time.

Ballots: In counties of 50,000, and towns of 2500, or more: Official and nonpartisan ballot; voter marks wanted names; 10-minute limit if no one waiting, else 5 minutes. Names put on by primary or petition.

In other counties and towns:

No official ballot; party "tickets"; voter drops wanted ticket in ballot box.

Officers: Legislature appoints 3-member State Board of Elections, 1 new member every two years; not more than two to be of same party.

State Board appoints 3 County Election Commissioners, for two years, not more than two to be of same party.

County Election Commissioners appoint 3 judges for each voting place, for each election; not more than two to be of same party; and two clerks, one from each party.

Voters' Tests: Registrars present at polls with lists; judges have tax-paid lists. Voter must show receipt or make affidavit either of payment, or of appearance of name on list. *V.* "Other" under Registration Procedure above.

Challenges: Challenged voter examined on qualifications, under oath, by election judges, who may also require "any other" answers they think material. Judges may swear in bystanders as witnesses. If judges satisfied, challenged party may vote. Ten-year perjury penalty.

TEXAS

Suffrage Qualifications

Residence: One year in the State, six months in the county and district.

Taxes: Poll tax, $1.50 annually, paid between 1 Oct. and 1 Feb. preceding election.

Property: In cities and incorporated towns only: Only payers of property taxes may vote on questions of expenditure and debt assumption.

Primary: Voter must be fully qualified to participate in primaries, or in legally established county mass conventions for selection of national convention delegates. Party may prescribe additional qualifications. Democratic party rule bars Negroes, although some counties disregard the rule.

Registration Procedure

Poll-tax payment constitutes registration. Receipt is in affidavit form, making oath of applicant's qualifications. Registration is, therefore, annual. Tax collector elected in each county for two years. False swearing on registration form constitutes perjury, entailing 2 to 5 years in penitentiary.

Primary Regulations

Status: Primaries held at party expense, officered by party officials.

Scope: Nominations: Obligatory on parties polling 100,000 or more, for State and Federal office, on all parties for county or lesser offices; optional for municipal office and for smaller parties.

Elections to party office: Obligatory on all parties for State convention delegates in years when State convention selects national convention delegates. Obligatory on all parties polling 100,000 or more, for county executive committee, county convention delegates. County convention selects State and district convention delegates; State convention elects State chairman and members of State Executive committee. Optional for smaller parties save as noted.

Time: 4 Sat. July even years; if no majority, run-off 4 Sat. Aug., except municipal: 10 days before election. County mass conventions for all parties in presidential years, 1 Sat. May.

Election Procedure

Time: 1 Tue. after 1 Mon. Nov., except municipal: 1 Tue. Apr.

Ballots: Official only. Voter scratches out all unwanted names or party lists.

Names put on only in accordance with law; *v.* "Primary Regulations—Scope" above. Provision for convention and petition procedure for small parties where permissible.

Officers: Two or four judges, two or four clerks, one supervisor per party per precinct according to size; from different political parties "if practicable." Judges appointed by (elected) county commissioners, clerks by presiding judge, supervisors by party county chairmen; for each election.

Voters' Tests: Voter must show poll-tax receipt; may swear to qualifications if receipt lost; perjury penalty, 2-5 years in penitentiary.

Challenges: Any qualified voter may challenge. Challenged party must then swear to qualifications before election judges. In cities or towns of 10,000 or more, oath must be supported by oath of "well-known resident of ward." Perjury penalties.

VIRGINIA

Suffrage Qualifications

Residence: One year in State, six months in county or municipality, thirty days in district.

(Changed in 1928 from two years, one year, and thirty days.)

Taxes: Poll tax, $1.50 annually, paid for the three years preceding election, six months before election date. No proceedings to collect till three years past due.

Property: General Assembly may prescribe property qualification for county, city, or town elections.

Education: Applicant for registration, unless disabled, must "make application to register in his own handwriting, without aid, suggestion, or memorandum, in the presence of the registration officer, stating his name, age, date and place of birth, residence and occupation at the time, and for the next preceding year, and whether he has previously voted, and if so, the State, county, and precinct in which he voted last."

Other: Applicant must answer any and all questions affecting his qualifications, on oath; answers made part of registration record. (This clause is employed as an "understanding" test in certain places; *v.* text above, Chapter VI, pp. 117-118.) Perjury penalties not clear, but between 1 and 10 years' imprisonment and/or $1000 fine.

Primary: Only registered and qualified voters may participate in primaries; must be party members; party may make additional rules. Democratic rule bars Negroes.

Registration Procedure

Officers: One registrar in each election district, appointed for two years by County Electoral Board. Cities over 50,000 may have a General Registrar and assistants to keep open an additional registration place at City Hall.

Time: One day, on thirtieth day before November elections. Cities and towns, 3 Tue. May in addition. Registrar may receive names at any previous time. Registration closes in cities of 50,000 or more 15 days before any special or primary election.

Term: Permanent.

Refusal: Any voter denied registration may appeal to county circuit court or municipal corporation court, and thence to Supreme Court, without costs.

Purging: Registrar, of own motion, on demand of 3 voters, or on order of County Electoral Board at least once in 6 years, or a court on demand of 3 voters. Hearing on 10 days' notice before registrar; appeals as under "Refusal."

Primary Regulations

Status: Primaries held at public expense; officered by party officials.

Scope: Optional for parties polling one-quarter of total State vote at preceding presidential election. Nominates candidates or elects party officers according to the party authority in respective state, district, county, or municipal jurisdictions.

Time: 1 Tue. Aug. preceding a November election; 1 Tue. April preceding a June election.

Election Procedure

Time: All but certain judicial and municipal officers: 1 Tue. after 1 Mon. Nov. Remaining judicial and most municipal officers: 2 Tue. June.

Ballots: Official only. Names put on by primary or other methods. Voter must scratch out at least three-quarters of each unwanted name. Time limit: two and one-half minutes, if other voters waiting.

Officers: Three-member Electoral Board per county or city, appointed by Circuit or Corporation Court (in turn appointed by Governor); one new appointment each year. Electoral Board appoints 3 judges and 2 clerks per polling place, for one year; giving representation to two highest parties; 2nd highest party nominates one judge.

Voters' Tests: Voters identified through tax and registration lists.

Challenges: Any elector or judge may challenge. Judges explain suffrage qualifications to challenged party, and may examine him as to same. If challenged party insists he is qualified, he is sworn. May still be rejected if judges are not satisfied by the record or other legal evidence.

Sources:

V. the most recent constitutions and code compilations in the general bibliography.

As to "white primary rules"—

For Mississippi, no evidence is available save the unanimous agreement of every one, white and black, interviewed by the writer in that State. Citations for the others are as follows:

Alabama Official and Statistical Register for 1907, p. 262; and "Notice of Democratic Primary Election . . . 12 August 1930," printed slip filed with Secretary of State, Montgomery.

Supreme Court of Arkansas, brief of Robinson *vs.* Holman, 1928, p. 11.

Local primary call of Pensacola Democratic Committee, Pensacola (Florida) Journal, 16 March 1928; and testimony of Representative Clark of Florida, Census Hearings 1921, pp. 186-87.

"Rules and Regulations of the Democratic Executive Committee of Georgia," pamphlet, 1928, p. 6, par. II.

State primary call, Louisiana, 1928, typewritten sheet from the office of the secretary of the Democratic party, in the writer's possession.

Texas Almanac, 1904, p. 35; later renewal cited in 27 Fed. Rep. (2) 942.

Virginia Election Laws, 1928, published by the Secretary of the Commonwealth, Appendix, p. 98.

"Rules of the South Carolina Democratic Party," pamphlet, 1928, p. 2, par. 7.

Where these rules are given as part of an election call, they are renewed every year.

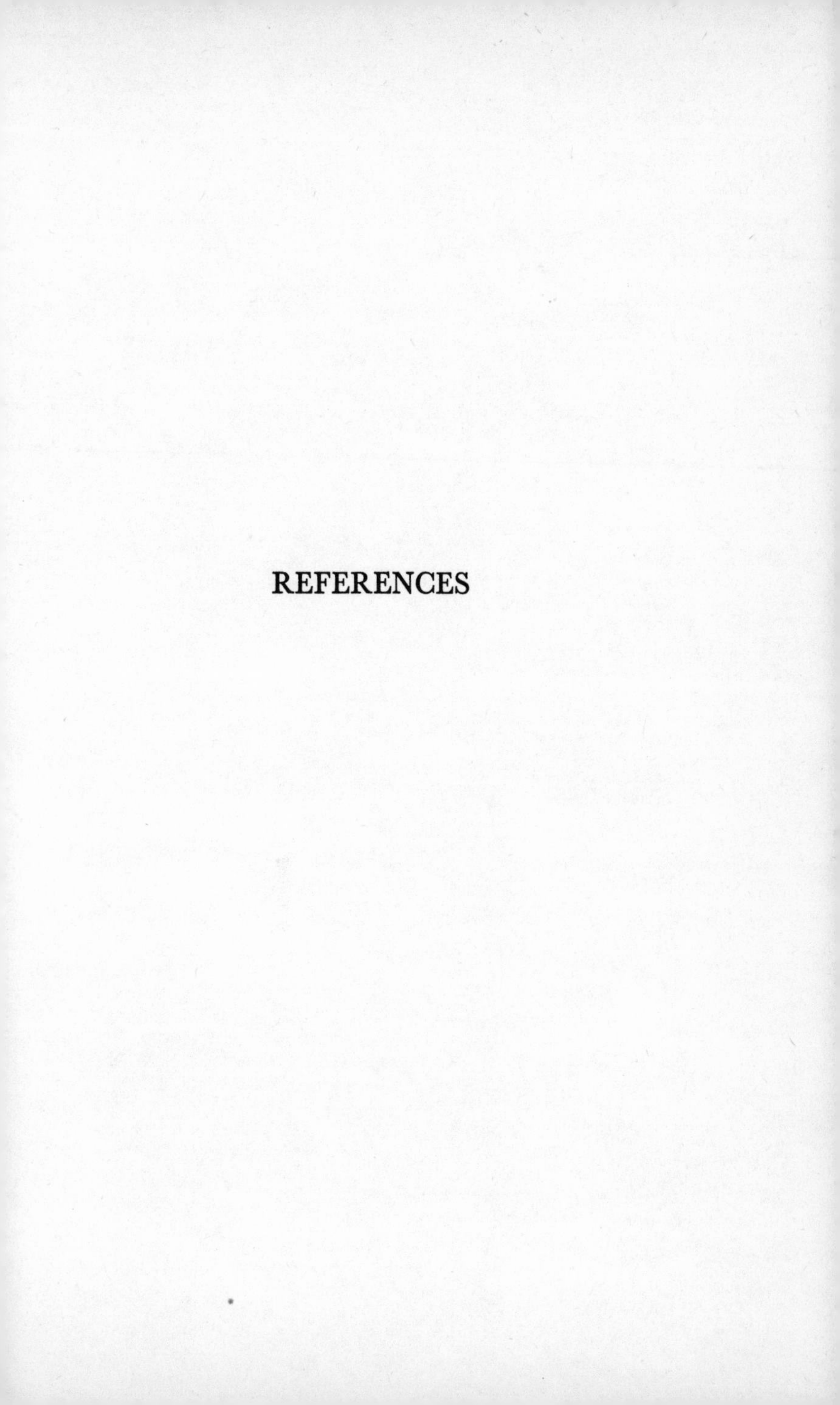

REFERENCES

CHAPTER I

1. It has been deemed unnecessary to document in detail so summary an account as that undertaken in this chapter. A few direct quotations have been specifically credited. The general bibliography will indicate the general sources. The following volumes, especially, should be cited: Ambler, "Sectionalism in Virginia"; Beveridge, "Abraham Lincoln," especially the chapters on abolitionism and the reaction of the South; Buck, P. H., "The Poor Whites"; Cairnes, "The Slave Power"; Carpenter, "The South as a Conscious Minority"; Chandler, "Representation in Virginia" and "Suffrage in Virginia"; Cole, "The Whig Party in the South"; Dew, "Essays on Slavery" (the Southern view); Fitzhugh, "Sociology for the South"; Helper, "The Impending Crisis" (the only articulate complaint from the poor-white viewpoint); Jack, "Sectionalism and Politics in Alabama"; Owsley, "Defeatism in the Confederacy"; Norton, "The Democratic Party in Ante-Bellum N. C."; Olmstead, "Journey in the Back Country"; Phillips, "American Negro Slavery" and "The Southern Whigs"; Porter, "Suffrage in the U. S."; Schaper, "Sectionalism in South Carolina"; Shryock, "Georgia and the Union"; Spero and Harris, "The Black Worker," and Wesley, "Negro Labor in the U. S." (early chapters on Negro-white competition before 1860); Weeks, "Anti-Slavery Opinion in the South." The whole intra-Southern sectional conflict is clearly described in a book issued after this chapter had been formulated: F. M. Green, "Constitutional Development in the South Atlantic States, 1776-1860."

2. Cole, 104; and maps at end.

3. Ibid., 70 note.

4. Ibid., 69.

5. Ibid., 69 note, quoting from "Life of Wise."

6. V., e.g., the petition of the Virginia Burgesses to the King in 1772, asking permission to prohibit the slave trade; Howard, 251.

7. Cole, 72-73.

8. Ambler, 193; v. also Shryock, 36-37, e.g.

9. Fitzhugh, 83-84.

10. Dew, 77; and passim; v. also Fitzhugh.

11. Owsley, 4, e.g. V. also below, Chapter II, pp. 20-22, 25-27.

CHAPTER II

1. V. Fleming, "Sequel"; Dunning, "Reconstruction"; the Reconstruction monographs. For accounts of want among the once wealthy, v. Fleming, "Sequel," 17; Mayes, 117 ff., Chapter XI, especially letters from members of the Lamar family. The Atlanta Daily Intelligencer printed appeals for charity towards war widows and orphans, e.g., 30 August, 23 December 1865. The most recent summary is also one of the best: Nevins, Chapter I.

2. Texts in MacDonald, 457 ff., 494. There was some technical difficulty

about the application of the Proclamation in Tennessee, North Carolina, and Louisiana, where the beginnings of "loyal" reorganization went back to 1862, thus *prima facie* exempting these States from its operation. In the Louisiana Convention of 1864, a die-hard element opposed the incorporation of emancipation in the new constitution, and tried to hold out at least for compensation for the old owners. V. La. Convention Debates 1864, 142, 153-56; and below, pp. 28-29.

3. Census Bureau, "Negro Population in the U. S., 1790-1915," 51.

4. Graphic description in Fleming, "Alabama," 271; confirmed for Georgia, C. M. Thompson, 43 note 1. For a complaint as to city conditions, v. an editorial in the Atlanta Daily Intelligencer, 27 August 1865. The colored soldiers of the Federal armies sometimes added their misbehavior to that of the Negro civilians; ibid., 30 August 1865, e.g.

5. Text in MacDonald, 470 ff.

6. Arkansas: Staples, 21; Virginia: Morton, 15; Louisiana: Convention Debates 1864; Tennessee: Dunning, "Reconstruction," 14-15, Herbert, 173 ff. President Johnson's recognition was accorded in May 1865; Fleming, "Sequel," 74.

7. See below, page 39.

8. Dunning, "Reconstruction," 36, 39. Text of the first proclamation in MacDonald, 491 ff.; for North Carolina, where Lincoln's efforts had proved nugatory.

9. McPherson, 9-10.

10. Texas in 1865-66, Convention Journal; the others in the Spring, Summer, and Fall of 1865: North Carolina Convention Journal, 1865-66; the same for Florida and South Carolina, 1865; Georgia Confederate Records, vol. iv; Vicksburg, Miss., Daily Herald for August 1865.

11. Texas, whose first new State election was held in June 1866; Herbert, 352.

12. In the Louisiana and Arkansas convention elections, e.g. held before the final collapse of the Confederacy, about 12,000 voters took part, as against more than 50,000 in the last election before the war. In Alabama, where the election came after Appomattox, 56,000 ballots were cast. In Tennessee, because of the divided loyalty of the State, the first elections were a succession of farces so far as representative character was concerned; Rhodes, vol. v, 47; Fleming, "Alabama," 358; Fertig, 47-48, e.g.

13. Fleming, "Sequel," 29, 30; "Documents," vol. i, 51 and 53. Schurz and Grant to President Johnson, who had asked them to report to him on conditions in the South.

14. Stephenson, N. W., 91.

15. Missouri passed through somewhat the same struggles as those to be sketched in the text. For an account, see Barclay. We have not included Missouri, Maryland, and Delaware in this study.

16. The account of events in Kentucky follows Coulter.

17. Herbert, 216-22.

18. On separation, Fertig, 25, 26, 29; 48, 76-77; on the activities of the Union Party of East Tennessee, ibid., 55-59; Herbert, 187-88; Dunning, "Reconstruction," 41; MacDonald, 498-99.

19. McPherson, 47 note.

20. 1865: Fleming, "Sequel," 26; Herbert, 271.

21. Not all of the Border States enacted all of these restrictions. For Kentucky, v. Coulter, 140-41; for Tennessee, Fertig, 66, 67; Herbert, 179; for West Virginia, 265-67, 270; and Ambler.

22. Coulter, 140, 280.

23. Tennessee loyalty test: Fertig, 65-66, 73-76, 186; text of the earlier measure in the Nashville Daily Press and Times, 6 June 1865. West Virginia oath: Herbert, 268.

24. Centralized canvassing: Herbert, 200-01; Fertig, 73.

25. They were always violently debated: v., e.g., reports of the suffrage debates in Tennessee, Nashville Daily Press and Times, May 1865; also Ambler, for West Virginia.

26. The examples are from Tennessee (Fertig, 65-66), West Virginia (Herbert, 282-84), and Kentucky (Coulter, 150).

27. Truman to President Johnson, April 1866; J. T. Trowbridge, "The South," 1865, p. 239; both cited in Fleming, "Documents," vol. i, 98 and 81, respectively.

28. Coulter, 258, 261.

29. V. Coulter, 291-94, 303 ff. Proscription of ex-Confederates of course ceased.

30. Fleming, "Documents," vol. i, 311; from Laws of 1865-66. The administration paper called it "a bill to reëstablish slavery" (Nashville Daily Press and Times, 31 May 1865).

31. Herbert, 260; Porter, 159.

32. Johnson to a fellow-Tennessean seeking advice, McPherson, 40.

33. McPherson, 257.

34. Herbert, 269, 276; Ambler, 179.

35. Fleming, "Alabama," 766-67.

36. Stephenson, N. W., 118-19, 169-71; v. Ch. XI, "Disintegration," passim.

37. Fleming, "Sequel," 13-15.

38. Staples, 12-15, 34, 72. The Fishback speech is to be found in the Little Rock Gazette, 3 April 1892. It was made in October 1863, and was reprinted to keep Fishback from the gubernatorial nomination in 1892, when memories of Reconstruction made Confederate loyalty seem the highest of virtues.

The election of 1866 returned the Conservative Party to office in such strength that a Confederate pension bill was passed over the governor's veto (Staples, 109-11). Meanwhile, the Fourteenth Amendment had been going the rounds of the States, the national Civil Rights bill had become law, and the Radical element in Congress had held an inquisition on the "loyalty" of the State.

39. Louisiana Convention Debates 1864, 190.

40. McConnell, 46.

41. Fleming, "Alabama," 342-43, 364-65.

42. Text in Charleston Daily Courier, 29 September 1865. There were similar disputes before the 1864 Convention in Louisiana; Ficklen, 46, 67.

43. As in Alabama: Fleming, "Alabama," 398.

44. Speech at Crawfordsville, Ga., 1864; "South in the Building of the Nation," vol. ix, 406.

45. There was a great lack of faith in the Negro as a free laborer, attested both by contemporary reporters and present-day historians: v. Hamilton, 307; C. M. Thompson, 130, 279-304; Fleming, "Documents," vol. i, 45, 54, 75, 78, e.g. Projects to form Emigration Companies to bring white labor to the South came to naught; v. Charleston Daily Courier, 3, 12 October 1865; C. M. Thompson, 92; Nevins, 17, and note 2, cites laws to encourage immigration in Virginia, Texas, and Georgia.

46. C. M. Thompson, 130.

47. Louisiana Debates 1864, 142, Mr. Abell; Georgia Confederate Records, vol. iv, 343-44. The attempt in Georgia to bring the convention to a rash and impolitic commitment was tabled.

48. The account of the Freedmen's Bureau here followed is that of Peirce, save where a citation to some other source is given. For the Freedmen's Bureau Acts, v. McPherson, 149-151, 349 ff. and 378; and McDonald, 488 ff.

49. Sidney Andrews in 1865; cited in Webster, 145.

50. Webster, 146, quoting the assistant commissioner in South Carolina: "The planters came forward and upheld my policy throughout, and are panic-stricken at the very idea of the removal of the Bureau." Nevins, 18, says that lowland Tennessee, the seat of slavery before the war, coöperated with the Bureau, while Eastern, poor-white Tennessee was "malevolent."

51. Eliot Report, 8.

52. Charleston Daily Courier, 27 December 1865.

53. Eliot Report, loc. cit.

54. Journal, 60. V. attempt to revive expatriation schemes, as in Texas (Convention Journal 1866, 119).

55. Fleming, "Sequel," 94.

56. Full summaries are given in McPherson, 29-44; summaries and a discussion in Stephenson, G. T., 35-66; and excerpts in Fleming, "Documents," vol. i, 274-311. They are also taken up State by State in the respective Reconstruction monographs. Not all the States enacted all the provisions of the composite picture in the text. The eight States were Mississippi, Georgia, Alabama, South Carolina, Florida, Virginia, Louisiana, and Tennessee. North Carolina provided for the apprenticing of freed minors to their old masters wherever possible. The most stringent codes were those passed early in Reconstruction, before the storm of disapproval which soon rose in the North (Fleming, "Sequel," 97). Alabama's first legislature repealed her code under the influence of such criticism (Fleming, "Alabama," 484). Georgia is said to have enacted comparatively mild regulations for the same reason (C. M. Thompson, 157). The Federal military commanders in South Carolina and Virginia ordered the non-enforcement of the codes in those two States (McPherson, 34-36, 41 ff.). In some States, masters were required to give bond to secure humane treatment of their apprentices and the provision of food, clothing, medicine, and education in the three R's and in their trades.

57. Georgia Confederate Records, vol. iv, 361-62. The gentleman was, however, pessimistic: "We may succeed if we are . . . animated [by these high considerations]. If we do not, the experiment will only prove to be a failure; and I fear it will be a failure. But let us make the experiment in good faith."

58. Woolley, 21. "To demand that Georgia, stricken and menaced as she was, should pass by the needs of the present and enter upon a vague scheme

of philanthropy, was unreasonable. It was just as unreasonable to conclude . . . that the black race would be forever held down." (22)

59. See the references for the Black Codes, note 56 above, and Johnson.

60. Selma, Ala., Times, 30 December 1865; quoted by Fleming, "Documents," vol. ii, 177. Cf. other quotations, 178-81.

61. Charleston Daily Courier, 4 July 1865.

62. Louisiana Debates 1864; 161, 143 (Mr. Abell), 501-2 (Mr. Sullivan), respectively.

63. "Reconstruction," 213.

64. C. M. Thompson, 124; of Georgia. The author quotes General Howard of the Freedmen's Bureau in support.

65. Hamilton, 318; see his Ch. VII for North Carolina's attitude towards the Bureau in matters of education. V. also the chapter on the Bureau in Fleming, "Documents," vol. ii.

66. Arkansas: Staples, 33; Louisiana: 1864 Convention Debates, 244-45; Virginia: Morton, 15; North Carolina: Porter, 159; Alabama: 1865 Convention Journal; South Carolina: 1865 Convention Journal, 79; Georgia: Confederate Records, vol. iv, 275; Florida: 1865 Convention Journal, 69; Mississippi: Vicksburg Daily Herald, 17-24 August 1865; Texas: 1866 Convention Journal, 187. Tennessee, under exceptional circumstances, enacted Negro suffrage in 1867; v. above, p. 25.

67. For the first two, Charleston Daily Courier, 6 July 1865; the others in "South in the Building of the Nation," vol. iv, 588.

68. Louisiana Debates 1864, 250, 210, respectively. The permissive clause for a qualified extension of the suffrage was written into the Constitution, but not acted upon; Ficklen, 79.

69. Florida Convention Journal 1865, 81.

70. The letter was made public at the time; v. Charleston Daily Courier, 1 June 1865.

71. McPherson, 18-20; cf. Garner, "Mississippi": the suggestion did not "receive any attention whatever" from the convention; "It is highly probable that the unanimous sentiment of the convention was against the idea of political rights for the Negro in any form" (109).

72. Vicksburg Daily Herald, 12 July, 12 August 1865, e.g.

73. The literature of invective and exposition on this point is too extensive for citation here. A random sampling of the pages of such convention debates as are available, or the Southern newspapers of the period, will disclose any number of examples. Some are quoted or referred to in Chapter V below, section II.

74. McPherson, 40; Johnson to a fellow-Tennessean seeking advice.

75. Fleming, "Alabama," 387-88; italics mine.

76. Fleming, "Documents," vol. i, 234.

77. Op. cit., vol. i, 95; v. also his similar speeches of 1867, 421; and as late as 1876, 411.

78. Charleston Daily Courier, 8 March 1865; v. also note 74 and text above.

79. Charleston Daily Courier, 16 September 1865; South Carolina Convention Journal 1865, 14.

80. Already in 1863, Congress had passed a bill, vetoed by Lincoln, under

which the readmission of "reclaimed" States would have depended on Congressional consent. The President, in his veto message, declared himself unwilling to commit the nation to any single plan of reconstruction, or to undo the good work already begun in Arkansas and Louisiana (MacDonald, 482-87). In 1864, the Radical group—although not yet dominant—succeeded in putting off the readmission of Louisiana and Arkansas.

81. It will be remembered that the Confederate groups returned to office even in the Border States in a few years after the close of the war, and in each case during or before the period of Congressional Reconstruction legislation.

82. Dunning, "Reconstruction," 42; Rhodes, vol. vi, 200-01.

83. McPherson, 72. During Johnson's administration, Reconstruction measures were without exception passed over the presidential veto.

84. McPherson, 102-03. The Confederate debt was also finally repudiated, and the States forbidden to assume it.

85. Rhodes, vol. vi, 13.

86. McPherson, 191-94. Tennessee, already readmitted, did not fall within the scope of this legislation.

87. Senator Wilson, Rhodes, vol. vi, 34.

88. Fleming, "Sequel," 223. Estimated disfranchisement in Georgia was 7000 to 10,000 (C. M. Thompson, 188); North Carolina, 12,000 (Rhodes, vol. vi, 82); South Carolina, 8000 (ibid.). In Virginia, General Schofield, unable to find sufficient "loyal" whites to manage the elections, made the grossly exaggerated estimate of 70,000 (Morton, 30).

89. Garner, "Mississippi," 158-59; Charleston Daily Courier, March-April 1867. Congress, to make assurance doubly sure, finally passed a bill denying the court jurisdiction.

90. Reynolds, 51 f., 499; Fleming, "Documents," vol. i, 238-40; Charleston Daily Courier, 15 February 1867.

91. Morton, 31, e.g. See accounts of the Committee of Nine in Virginia, headed by A. H. H. Stuart. Its pacific manifesto was at first refused publication in three Richmond newspapers, so strong was feeling against any compromise (Robertson, 267-71; Richmond Daily Whig, 2 March 1874; Morton, 64). Governor Patton of Alabama gave out an address of similar import (Fleming, "Alabama," 303-04). V. also Hamilton, 399-400, etc.

92. Notably in the white counties of North Carolina (Hamilton, 245), Arkansas (Staples, 389 ff.), South Carolina (Reynolds, 143), and Georgia (Woolley, 95-96).

93. Herbert, 37. For the formation and early activities of Moderate Republican groups, v. Woolley, 87; Hamilton, 245; Morton, 39, 72; C. M. Thompson, 172-74; Garner, "Mississippi," 237. Complaint of a Moderate Republican of ill-treatment, South Carolina Convention Proceedings 1868, 523-24.

94. See his "Notes on the Situation," written during the pendency of the Reconstruction Acts, Hill, 730-811; and the Davis Hall, Bush Arbor, and New York speeches, op. cit., 294-331.

95. Staples, 254; quoted from a leading Democratic (Conservative) organ.

96. See below, Chapter III, pp. 50-51, 54.

97. Charleston Daily Courier, 19 May 1867; General Clanton to a meeting

of Negroes in Montgomery, Ala. The General spoke in reply to a Radical plea from Senator Wilson, touring the South for the Republican policies. V. similar editorials, 26 March ("There is within the limits of this Commonwealth no necessity for any antagonism," etc.), 10, 29 April 1867; report of presidential Governor Johnson's speech to the freedmen, 15 April 1867, etc.

98. Herbert, 41; Peirce, 166-67. Among the higher Bureau officials to use their position for political purposes were General Wager Swayne, commissioner for Alabama, a candidate for the Senate in 1868; and General R. K. Scott, commissioner for South Carolina, later one of the most notoriously corrupt of Reconstruction governors.

99. The military authorities had great difficulty in finding natives who were qualified to sit on the registration boards or to replace "disloyal" officers of the Presidential governments. See Garner, "Mississippi," 172; C. M. Thompson, 177; Fleming, "Alabama," 370, 488, 495. The "iron-clad oath," obligatory for Federal office since 1862, made the local Federal patronage, too, a hunting ground for carpetbaggers.

100. Fleming, "Alabama," 488; Garner, "Mississippi," 187; e.g.

101. V. the tables in Rhodes, vol. vi, 83, 85.

102. Quoted in Hamilton, 256.

103. Herbert, 369, quoting provisional Governor Pease to the Texas Convention of 1868.

104. McPherson, 408-09.

105. Op. cit., 335-36.

106. Op. cit., 337, 573 ff.

107. Op. cit., 399. For the legislative history of the Amendment, v. Mathews.

108. Virginia, Mississippi, Texas, and Georgia (McPherson, 409, 610).

109. All summarized in Fleming, "Documents," vol. ii, 108-28. Passed in May 1870 (McPherson, 546-50); February 1871 (MacDonald, 554-59); April 1871 (ibid., 560-64). The provisions for the use of Federal troops against franchise conspiracies were directed against the KuKlux Klan; v. below, Chapter III, sec. III. The first Civil Rights Act also was reaffirmed in 1870, and in 1871 another explicitly extended the ban on discrimination to public conveyances, places of amusement, and hotels, and to juries.

110. New Orleans Commercial Bulletin, 1 November 1867.

111. Quoted in Fleming, "Sequel," 228. South Carolina was an extreme case throughout Reconstruction.

The Negro legislators and officials were of course in many instances illiterate and untrained; v. Garner, "Mississippi," 269; Herbert, 54; and Chapter III, sec. I, below. On the other hand, many others gave evidence of capacity and intelligence which Southerners have not always been willing to admit; see, e.g., Staples, 220; Taylor, "South Carolina," 156-58.

CHAPTER III

1. Rhodes, vol. vi, 88, 92, 173-74. Arkansas, e.g., disfranchised and disqualified all persons who had violated oaths of allegiance to the United States, armed enemies of the United States, and persons who had aided and encour-

aged the same, and all persons who were disqualified from office by the Fourteenth Amendment (Convention Debates 1868, 878). V. also any of the Reconstruction monographs.

2. Virginia: Chandler, "Representation," 77-78; South Carolina: Reynolds, 126, 243; e.g.

3. Alabama: Fleming, "Alabama," 742. Mobile suffered three purges.

4. Some of these laws are summarized in Reynolds, 397-98; Staples, 281-82; Herbert, 399-400 (Louisiana), 144 (Florida), 300-01 (Arkansas); cf. Dunning, "Reconstruction," 211-12. V. also above, Chapter II, pp. 21-22, for the Radical election laws in the Border States.

5. Texas: Herbert, 370-73; Arkansas: ibid., 297; Tennessee: ibid., 192, 196-97, 202-03; South Carolina: Reynolds, 114, 119, 144-45; e.g. Pope County, Arkansas, was for three years under military rule enforced by the State militia; v. Staples, 368.

6. Herbert, 141, 155, 301; C. M. Thompson, 206; Fleming, "Documents," vol. ii, 81, 86, 87; e.g.

7. C. M. Thompson, 217-19.

8. V. the letter from the Negro ex-Senator Revels to Lucius Lamar, Mayes, 311-12.

9. V., e.g., Fleming, "Documents," vol. ii, 39-68; "Alabama," 739-40, Reynolds, 121-25, 177-78, 293; Staples, 365; Chamberlain, 477-78; Hamilton, 656 note; on inefficiency, irresponsibility, corruption, extravagance, and fraud. The subject may be pursued in any of the Reconstruction monographs, in Dunning, "Reconstruction," etc.

10. The figures in what follows are from Fleming, "Documents" and "Sequel"; Dunning, "Reconstruction," and the respective State Reconstruction monographs. A few are from Herbert, but his figures are to be taken with caution; the book, prepared as a Democratic campaign document in 1890 (Fleming, "Sequel," 305-06), has been caught in exaggerations; v. Skaggs, 73.

11. Reynolds, 116, e.g.

12. Staples, 245.

13. Hill, 387.

14. Garner, "Mississippi," 285; Reynolds, 291; Fleming, "Documents," vol. ii, 285-88; e.g.

15. Reynolds, 344-47; Woolley, 61-62; Fleming, "Alabama," 789-90, 793, 794; Garner, "Mississippi," 328-29; e.g.

16. The Klan was organized, seemingly as a lark, in Pulaski, Tennessee, in the Autumn of 1865 (see Lester and Wilson, Introduction, 15-44; Fleming, "Sequel," 243-64). It spread from State to State, and was federated in May 1867. In the lower South, the more powerful federated organization was known as the Knights of the White Camelia. There were numerous independent bodies everywhere, some operating under the name of one or another of the major organizations.

17. Lester and Wilson, Intro., 24; Fleming, "Alabama," 660. Dunning claims that KuKlux disorders of the worse sort were restricted to the white counties ("Reconstruction," 213).

18. Dunning, "Undoing," 438; C. M. Thompson, 366; Fleming, "Alabama," 688; e.g.

19. Fleming, "Documents," vol. ii, 349, 352.

20. V., e.g., Hamilton, 250-52; Morton, 46-49; Reynolds, 100-01; Fleming, "Alabama," 536-37; Robertson, passim.

21. Interview in Philadelphia, quoted in Charleston Daily Courier, 19 January 1868.

22. Mayes, 242, 243.

23. Morton, 41-42; cf. 76, on Negro demands for office.

24. With their help, a Conservative interregnum broke into the Radical supremacy in Alabama for one term, from 1870 to 1872 (Fleming, "Alabama," 750-55); and Georgia Conservatism made gains both in the State legislature and at Washington (C. M. Thompson, 184).

25. Herbert, 140, 411; Staples, 373; v. also Reynolds, 143; C. M. Thomp son, 201-02; Morton, 70; Lonn, "Louisiana," Chapters IV-VII; e.g.

26. Florida: Herbert, 146-47; Louisiana: Dunning, "Reconstruction," 215; Lonn, loc. cit.

27. Fleming, "Documents," vol. ii, 381, 382; Dunning, "Undoing," 453.

28. This was the Third Force Bill (MacDonald, 560-64). Grant did send troops to nine South Carolina counties (Reynolds, 182-211).

29. U. S. Treasury Dept., "Repudiation of State Indebtedness," 27 ff., for a glimpse at the protests in Minnesota. As to the South, indeed, we learn that "Not all the blame for this perverted legislation [issuing guaranteed bonds, etc.] should be placed on the corrupt legislators . . . for the lawyers who saw the bills through were frequently Southern Democrats representing supposedly respectable Northern capitalists" (Fleming, "Sequel," 235-36).

30. Dunning, "Reconstruction," 184, 247, 248, 267; "Undoing," 438, 440; Fleming, "Documents," vol. ii, 381; Weeks, 690; Herbert, 378-9. Details of the methods employed in some of these States are to be found, e.g., as follows: Georgia: Woolley, 96-99; North Carolina: Hamilton, 499-507, 521, 534, 536, 537-57, 593, 604; Arkansas: Staples, 391; Florida: Herbert, 166.

31. Florida was restored with these three States in 1876, as part of the compromise settling the Hayes-Tilden presidential contest.

32. For detailed accounts, v. Mayes, 249-64; Garner, "Mississippi," 372-414. This account follows the latter.

33. Herbert, 421-27.

34. Reynolds, 355-59.

35. Fleming, "Documents," vol. ii, 413.

36. Reynolds, 375-91.

37. Op. cit., 399-460.

38. Dunning, "Undoing," 445.

39. Dunning, "Undoing," 445-46; Fleming, "Documents," vol. ii, 382-83, 431-32; "Sequel," 305-06.

40. The vacillating attitude of the United States Supreme Court towards the Reconstruction legislation in general is the subject of Chapter XVI in Dunning's "Reconstruction," q.v. For citations and analyses of the cases under the Fifteenth Amendment, v. Mathews.

The position here described was in part developed in cases arising under the later "disfranchising" constitutions of six Southern States (v. Chapter V below); and represents the judicial status of the Negro as a voter till as late as 1930.

41. G. T. Stephenson, 111.

CHAPTER IV

1. Summary in G. T. Stephenson, Chapters VI-IX; digests and dates in Johnson.

2. On the Negro in court, see G. T. Stephenson, Chapter X.

3. Johnson, 53.

4. V. passim Dowd, DuBois, and Reuter, especially Chapter XI.

5. Especially "local option" campaigns when prohibition became an issue. Use of Negro votes was charged to the "liquor interests." V. Augusta Chronicle, 6 June 1907; and Atlanta Constitution, 15 August 1907—Mr. Hines' reminiscences on the floor of the legislature.

6. Natchez Democrat, 17 July 1890; this arrangement was reported to have been "working well" for ten years. Negroes sat in the South Carolina legislature as late as 1890, sometimes as Democrats; Taylor, "South Carolina," 292 ff.

7. Jacksonville Times-Democrat, 8 May 1885; the writer seems to have been a recent arrival from the North. V. Little Rock Gazette, 21 February 1891, wherein a Negro Representative is reported as protesting against Jim Crow proposals.

8. Knoxville Daily Journal, 8 January 1890; v. also, e.g., ibid., 2 January 1890; Simkins, 16 note, for charges made in the South Carolina elections of 1880.

9. Dunning, "Undoing," 444.

10. Morton, e.g., 129, 132-33, 145.

11. Chandler, "Suffrage," 73.

12. Harris, 193.

13. Chandler, "Representation," 79-82; Morton, 123.

14. Richmond Daily Whig, April 1874; Morton, 92.

15. Morton, 92-93; v. Weeks, 692.

16. Richmond Dispatch, 3, 7 March 1894; 4 November 1894 gives provisions in full. Weeks, 698; Morton, 133-34. This was the "Walton Law."

17. Morton, 134.

18. Weeks, 694-95, for this and other South Carolina legislation; v. also Simkins, 15 note. Passage and provisions in Charleston News and Courier, 23, 27, 28 January 1882.

19. Details may be found for the several States as follows: North Carolina: Hamilton, 560, 568, 570, 608, 643; Raleigh News and Observer, 1 March 1899; Tennessee: Weeks, 693, 698; Louisiana: Weeks, 692, 701; Florida: Weeks, 692, 694; Jacksonville Times-Democrat, 2 August 1885; Georgia: Weeks, 693; Alabama: Weeks, 696, 703; Arkansas: Weeks, 692, 697; Little Rock Gazette, 28 February, 22 September 1892.

20. Weeks, 695.

21. Grady, 244.

22. Dunning, "Undoing," 445-46.

23. Mayes, 394; written of Greenback-beleaguered Mississippi in 1879; the writer added that this was still true in 1896.

24. The general account of the agrarian depression in this and the two following paragraphs is based on Buck and Arnett, especially Buck, 19-22, 102, 104, 106-110; and Arnett, 66, 68-71.

25. Arnett, 29-32; Simkins, 8-12.
26. Kendrick, 269.
27. Hill, 344.
28. Johnson, G. W.—"Behind the Monster's Mask," Survey, April 1923.
29. Kendrick, 270-71.
30. Simkins, as cited in note 25.
31. Arnett, as cited in note 25.
32. In Virginia, it appears that the normal antagonism between east and west, "new Bourbon" and agrarian radical, was first given a vent through differences over the State debt. V. Morton, 81-126. Early redeemed, Virginia had sufficient Independents in her General Assembly by 1877 to permit one William Mahone, a none-too-scrupulous politician, to organize the "Readjuster" party, which combined the repudiation issue with other platform material suitable to the agrarian discontent. The Readjusters drew on the Negroes for support at the polls, the regular Democracy retaliated in kind, and ballot frauds and race friction harried the State until the enactment of the Walton Law in the nineties (v. above, p. 66, note 16). Divisions among the whites and mutual recriminations were not allayed until the turn of the century, with the enactment of a new constitution designed to relieve politics of the Negro.
33. Weeks, 693. It was finally reënacted in 1890. The 1890 measure—the Dortch Act—was not passed until after much airing of poor-white fears (Knoxville Daily Journal, January-March 1890). This measure included not merely a poll-tax requirement, but enacted also a complicated nonpartisan ballot, a time-limit on marking, etc.
34. Weeks, 698.
35. Jacksonville Times-Democrat, 5 August 1885.
36. Charleston News and Courier, 3, 8 December 1881, 21 January 1882, e.g. The editor pointed out that one-fifth of all the illiterates in the State were white; 18 January 1882.
37. V., e.g., Richmond Dispatch, 4 December 1893.
38. Morton, 145-46; present author's italics.
39. Weeks, 696.
40. White, 110; from a Populist manifesto.
41. Simkins, 116, 123; for Louisiana, e.g., v. "South in the Building of the Nation," vol. iii, 171.
42. Simkins, 21; Martin Gary to a county convention of Democrats in South Carolina, 1880. V. also Charleston News and Courier, 21 January 1882: complaint of the "young Democracy" of North Carolina, "similar to that of young Democrats in several other Southern States, that all the honors and emoluments go to the old stagers, and the young men of the party are left out in the cold . . ."
43. Hill, 317.
44. Skaggs, 103.
45. Hill, 821-22.
46. Harris, 99; v. also 124-25, 126, 130.
47. Arnett, 37, 68-71, 80; Buck, 25, 27, 70; Simkins, 16-17.
48. Buck, 111-19; Arnett, 76-77 for the Southern branch of the movement; Simkins, Chapter IV, 70-102, for South Carolina.

49. Arnett, 130-40; Buck, 132-53.

50. V., e.g., the Little Rock Gazette, September 1892; Atlanta Constitution, 13 August 1907, Mr. Massingale on the elections of 1892; Raleigh News and Observer for 1899-1900; and below, especially Chapter V, section IV.

51. Charleston News and Courier, 6 November 1882.

52. Ibid., 29 October 1882.

53. Brewton, 249, 263, 264.

54. Arnett, 122-23; Simkins, 134.

55. Arnett, 153. V., e.g., Watson's bid for Negro support for the Georgia independents, Brewton, 157; Haskell's for the South Carolina regulars, Simkins, 129; the use of Negroes during the Mahone episode in Virginia, note 32 above.

56. Little Rock Gazette, 6 February 1892.

57. Arnett, 153-55.

58. White, 13-14.

CHAPTER V

1. Garner, "Studies," 243.

2. White, 12.

3. Brewton, 305-06; Simkins, 206. Personal political ambitions may have had some share in bringing about such coalitions.

4. Natchez Democrat, 27 September 1890. McGehee indignantly denied his authorship; ibid., 3 November 1890.

5. New constitutions were passed in South Carolina and Louisiana in 1895, North Carolina (two series of amendments) in 1900 and 1905, Alabama and Virginia in 1901, Georgia in 1908, and Oklahoma in 1910. The Virginia convention may be followed in the published debates, the others in contemporary newspapers. Earlier attempts at constitutional restrictions had been made in South Carolina in 1892 (Simkins, 112, 141), and in Georgia in 1897 (Atlanta Constitution, 14 August 1907). Maryland made an attempt in 1905 (Porter, 245), and there was talk of another in Florida in 1907 (Augusta Chronicle, 18 June 1907).

6. G. T. Stephenson, 322 ff.; tables showing voting requirements in the United States; below, Appendix III.

7. V. the extraordinary list of crimes and petty misdemeanors proposed as bars to the suffrage in the North Carolina legislature, Raleigh News and Observer, 7 January 1899.

8. Reports of the Secretary of State to the Governor: 1898, 26-27; 1900, 25-27. The 1898 Report gives the figures as of 1 January 1897.

9. Virginia Debates 1901-02, 599.

10. Birmingham Age-Herald, 20 March 1901; report of the constitutional convention debates.

11. Arkansas Debates 1868, 115. V. also, e.g., Fleming, "Documents," vol. i, 457 (Alabama); Birmingham Age-Herald, 24 July 1901; Virginia Documents 1867-68, 196; Virginia Debates 1901-02, vol. i, 20; vol. ii, 2952; etc.

12. T. V. Smith, 343-45; Phillips, "Slavery," 344, e.g.

13. Dowd, 150; DuBois, 16; "Negro Population 1790-1915," 403-04.

14. See lists of such institutions, Dowd, 163; Reuter, 284-87. Some of them dated back to the Reconstruction era; Nevins, 16.

15. "Negro Population 1790-1915," 526.

16. Ibid., 461.

17. Vicksburg Daily Herald, 12 July, 12 August 1865.

18. V., e.g., Arkansas Debates 1868, 515; Virginia Documents 1867-68, 196 ff.; Virginia Debates 1867-68, 472 (Mr. Marye); Birmingham Age-Herald, 9 January (Senator Morgan), 20 March 1901; Arnett (Georgia), 43, 45; Raleigh News and Observer, 12 February 1899 (Representative, later Senator, Simmons); Natchez Democrat, 9 March 1890; etc.

19. Birmingham Age-Herald, 5 June, 12, 17 July 1901.

20. Virginia Debates 1901-02, vol. ii, 2965 (Mr. Thoms), 3068 (Mr. Watson), respectively. The "threat" of Negro literacy was presented to the Alabama convention in a curious fashion. Here, there was to be a "grandfather" exemption for illiterates; a delegate pointed out that since few or no Negroes could qualify under the grandfather clause, they would be encouraged to acquire literacy in order to vote; the whites, meanwhile, resting on their inherited right of suffrage, would neglect to educate themselves. "Followed to its logical conclusion, this deplorable law might easily result in the end in raising up a majority of Negro voters in Alabama" (Birmingham Age-Herald, 9 July 1901; Mr. Roden).

21. Sinclair, 196.

22. Augusta Chronicle, 24 January 1908.

23. Virginia Debates 1901-02, vol. ii, 2972-73 (Mr. Thoms), and 3076-77 (Hon. Carter Glass), respectively. V. also Dunning, "Undoing," 448, on the South Carolina discussions of 1895; symposium of State senators, Raleigh News and Observer, 12 January 1899; proposals to disfranchise "natives of Africa or Asia or their descendants," Atlanta Constitution, 3 August 1907; Natchez Democrat, 18 July 1890; e.g.

24. Virginia Debates 1901-02, vol. ii, 3079; Mr. Blair. V. also Mr. Williams, during thc Alabama discussions: pointing out that many white men after the Civil War had not the means to acquire an education, he asked "Would you disfranchise these white men on account of their misfortune?" (Birmingham Age-Herald, 26 July 1901).

25. Birmingham Age-Herald, 7 July 1901; Virginia Debates 1901-02, vol. ii, 3004; Porter, 147; Raleigh News and Observer, 12 February 1899; Atlanta Constitution, 14 August 1907; e.g.

26. Garner, "Studies," 241: White, 19; Porter, 210-13.

27. Wells, H. G., "Future in America," 270.

28. Arkansas Debates 1868, 515 and 363, respectively.

29. Fleming, "Documents," vol. ii, 352; from the ritual of the Knights of the White Camelia, 1869.

30. Arnett, 48, and Harris, 127, respectively.

31. V., e.g., cartoon in the Raleigh News and Observer, 7 July 1900, showing white and Negro drunkards tippling from a bottle, with a caption stating "on the best of authority" that the Republican candidate for the governorship "had Cheatham and several other Negroes in his room, and was

drinking and fraternizing with them"; also the controversy in Georgia between Governor Brown and candidate Hoke Smith over similar charges (Atlanta Constitution, 28 May 1908).

32. Arkansas Debates 1868, 627.

33. Harris, 99 and 127, respectively.

34. Virginia Debates 1901-02, vol. ii, 3064.

35. Harris, 191; present author's italics.

36. Charleston News and Courier, 3 December 1881. Cf. Morton, 126.

37. Virginia Debates 1901-02, vol. ii, 3032. V. also 2960, 2966, Mr. Thoms; 2998, McIlwaine; 3015, Dunaway; 3074, Hancock.

38. Atlanta Constitution, 13 August 1907.

39. Major Handley, in the Birmingham Age-Herald, 26 July 1901; v. also Mr. Burke: "... forced to maintain white supremacy by methods they abhorred," 4 August 1901; etc. In North Carolina charges of corruption were bandied about right and left during the debates on disfranchisement; v. almost any issue of the Raleigh News and Observer for 1899 and 1900.

40. Senator L. Q. C. Lamar of Mississippi.

41. Virginia Debates 1901-02, vol. ii, 2961.

42. Birmingham Age-Herald, 3 May 1901. V. also Senator Watson's declaration in Georgia, that he would swing his agrarian following back to Democracy, if the regulars would promise Negro disfranchisement, so that the whites could divide "without fear of a Negro umpire" (Arnett, 220; Brewton, 305-06).

43. The Republican remnants who depended on the Negro vote for whatever influence they retained were of course also in opposition. Thus one: "I feel it to be a duty I owe to my conscience, to my constituents, and to the people of the entire State, and the United States, to enter my protest against any and every movement towards the disfranchisement of any of the citizens of the State, as being wrong and unlawful" (Virginia Convention Debates 1901-02, vol. ii, 3046). Another couched his warning in terms which might easily have been employed by some irregular Democrat: "How many voters will be deprived of the right of suffrage [by the understanding clause] ... no one can tell. It is as elastic as a rubber band and can be adjusted to any voter to suit the desire of a partisan registration board ... It will not do to claim that men will not take advantage of a law so loosely drawn" (ibid., 3012).

44. Natchez Democrat, 30 January, 3 July, 23 September, 4, 8 October 1890.

45. Atlanta Constitution, 29 July 1907; letter from Wm. J. Neel.

46. Natchez Democrat, 30 January 1890. The editor even conceded that where a "fusion" plan for the division of local offices gave certain minor posts to Republicans and Negroes, harmony between the races had been promoted, and the Negro officials found efficient (17 July 1890). It is highly significant that the regular Democracy was thus willing to divide and rule with the despised Negro party, and that an independent newspaper should prefer such an arrangement to further disfranchising legislation.

47. Augusta Chronicle, 16 June 1907; editorial.

48. Atlanta Constitution; Mr. Neel's letter (v. note 45).

49. Birmingham Age-Herald, 20, 21, 24 May, 2 June 1901; etc.

50. Raleigh News and Observer, 12, 13 January 1899; e.g. Twelve loyal Democrats put up a thousand-dollar bond that the proposed suffrage amendment would disfranchise no whites.

51. Natchez Democrat, 18 September 1890. "Fraudulent" of course meant "in violation of the spirit of white solidarity against the Negro."

52. Atlanta Constitution, 3 August (Mr. Hall), 31 July (Senator Taylor) 1907; respectively.

53. Birmingham Age-Herald, 16, 11 July 1901 (speeches); 20, 21 May, 2 June 1901 (editorials).

54. Ibid., 7 July 1901.

55. Atlanta Constitution, 13 August 1907; Mr. Hall. In Virginia there was a long debate over the incorporation of a clause in the new constitution requiring bipartisan election boards. This the regular Democrats insisted was a useless safeguard, that might compel the appointment of "incompetents." It was finally agreed that not more than two members of a local board should be of the same party (Virginia Debates 1901-02, vol. ii, 3030-32).

56. Raleigh News and Observer, 8, 10, 21 July 1900; 18 March 1899; respectively.

57. Morton, 155; Natchez Democrat, 31 October, 1, 2 November 1890. The regular organization in Virginia had good reason to fear rejection of the disfranchising code. When the convention call was submitted to plébiscite in 1900, the thirty-two counties west of the Blue Ridge—the stronghold of white Republicanism and agrarian independency—were all but seven against the holding of a convention. The plébiscite must therefore have gone for a convention in the counties which had the larger Negro population, "although it was a foregone conclusion that the Negro would be disfranchised if a convention were called," and the Democrats had pledged themselves not to disfranchise white voters (ibid., 147-49). This points to the double conclusion that the Negroes did not vote freely in the black counties, and that the whites in the politically heretical counties were afraid of disfranchising measures.

An influential clique in Tillman's South Carolina agrarian party tried to sabotage their leader's plans for a disfranchising convention (Simkins, 203-28).

58. Richmond Dispatch, 18 June 1894, quoting the Richmond Times. The Dispatch added accusingly: "What do the people of the black counties think of this coming from a Democratic newspaper?"

59. Birmingham Age-Herald, 31 March, 21 July 1901. V. also 26 April, 6 May; quotation from the Geneva Reaper, e.g., and reports of the debates, 15 July 1901.

60. Fleming, "Alabama," 767; v. also "Sequel," 47-48, quoting Truman's report to Johnson; and C. M. Thompson, 130.

PART II—INTRODUCTION

1. V. also the debates over the segregation of "Gold-Star Mothers" on their government-subsidized trips to the graves of their sons in France; N. Y. Times, May-June 1930.

2. V., e.g., statements of Southern governors, in reply to direct questions,

in the New York World, 21 February 1926; and the testimony of Representative Larsen of Georgia, Hearings before the Committee on the Census on H. R. 14498, etc., (1921), p. 56. Hereafter cited as Census Hearings, 1921.

3. A number of questionnaire replies give the information on disfranchisement; the population figures are for 1930—U. S. Census Bulletin, 2nd series, for Tennessee.

4. Questionnaire return.

CHAPTER VI

1. For denials, v. Introduction above, p. 102 and note 2. For admissions, v. statements of Senators George of Georgia and Glass of Virginia, in Liberty, 21 and 28 April 1928; and a quotation from Senator Blease of South Carolina, in the Congressional Record, 28 February 1928, p. 3827. The matter is further pursued below, pp. 108-109.

2. For some tabulations of Negro registration and voting, see Appendices I and II.

3. Questionnaire replies.

4. Registrar in Georgia and Virginia, respectively, to the writer.

5. One heard of registrars being replaced if the Negro vote increased. In Virginia, a local judge had ordered many colored applicants registered over the head of the local registration officer, ruling out of court extreme questions asked under the "understanding" clause. Later, he became much more lenient in allowing such questions, when protests against them continued to be brought to his court by a local Negro attorney. It was thought in the community that the political powers-that-be had warned him of too great liberality. Such stories, of course, cannot be verified.

6. The occupation figures are from the Census of 1920, vol. iv, ch. vii, Table 1. The "unskilled" group it is impossible to calculate because of the manner of tabulation. It is unquestionably very large. These figures do not include West Virginia, because of the large number of Negro mine workers. Literacy has been calculated from the 1920 Census Abstract, p. 433. The "white" averages given are derived from the three Census classifications "native white of native parentage," "of foreign parentage," and "foreign white." The home ownership figures are derived from the 1920 Census, vol. ii, p. 1285; they include "encumbered" and "free" ownership.

7. 2 March 1927; Congressional Record, vol. 68, no. 69, pp. 5388-9.

8. Census Hearings 1921, p. 213.

9. Montgomery Advertiser, 13 February 1927.

10. Birmingham Age-Herald, 12, 13, 17, 18, 20 October 1925; Birmingham News, 9, 10, 11, 15 October 1929; N. Y. Times, 27 October 1929; interviews in Birmingham; letter from a Birmingham newspaper man. Needless to say, there are no Negro policemen in Birmingham.

During the Alabama senatorial campaign of 1930, one of the points made by Senator Heflin against his opponent Bankhead was the latter's acceptance of a Negro juror at the trial of a white man—N. Y. Times, undated clipping, November 1930.

11. The chairman of the Alabama Anti-Smith Committee (of bolting

Democrats) went so far as to assert that Smith had promised Commissioner Morton a cabinet office—N. Y. Times, 7 October 1928. V. also ibid. 28 October 1928. On the other hand, the regular State Democratic Committee in North Carolina sent out 80,000 copies of an order issued by Hoover as Secretary of Commerce abolishing racial segregation in his department— N. Y. Times, 22 September 1928.

A statement signed by many prominent Negroes declared that not since the Civil War had there been so much appeal to race feeling as in the 1928 national campaign (N. Y. Times, 26 October 1928); a condition deplored also in a manifesto issued by a group of forty-five prominent white Southerners, lay and clerical (N. Y. Times, 21 and 28 October 1928).

12. Waco (Texas) News-Tribune, 27 October 1928, e.g., for the former attitude; for the latter, Senator Harrison in the Montgomery Advertiser, 4 November 1928; editorial in the Jasper (Fla.) News, 2 November 1928; Raleigh News-Observer, 27 October 1928; Vicksburg Post, 6 November 1928.

The president of the National Woman's Law Enforcement League wrote to the "Woman Voter": "Will you be good enough to ask Governor Smith to deny that he believes in equality among blacks and whites . . . a point which is important to Southern women and their children. We understand that [he is] counting on Negro support because he does believe in . . . equality." Quoted in N. Y. Times, 10 July 1928.

13. The lily-white movement is considered in detail below, Chapter VIII, sections II-IV.

14. For the admission of Negroes, v. below, Chapter VII, sec. IV; of white Republicans, Chapter VIII, p. 179 and note 43.

15. The exceptions were in the Border States, whose legislatures always contained a number of Republicans; and in certain Republican enclaves in otherwise solidly Democratic States, such as the Ninth Congressional District of Virginia. In these enclaves, it should be borne in mind, there were very few Negroes.

16. For a brief sketch of this and the later legal development, see Merriam, "Primary Elections," pp. 9, 14, 19, 22, 32, 34, 35, 51.

17. Atlanta Constitution, 29 July 1907.

18. See Appendix III, Table of Election Laws.

19. For these exceptions, see next chapter, pp. 138-143.

20. For the action of the Supreme Court, see next chapter, pp. 155-156.

21. The exceptions in certain other States are interesting only as exceptions. They are fully treated below, Chapter VII, section IV.

22. For a full statement of Southern election laws, see Appendix III.

23. Questionnaire replies.

24. Louisville (Ky.) News (Negro), 8 March 1924, reported at the time that suit for registration was brought. There was another case in 1926; v. Birmingham Age-Herald and N. Y. World, 20 January 1926.

25. Census Hearings 1921, pp. 40-41; v. affidavits of similar import, pp. 166-8, especially nos. 5, 6, and 7.

26. Constitution of 1902 as amended 1928, sec. 20.

27. For further samples of questions of this sort, asked under the "understanding" clause, see the report of several test cases in Norfolk in the Norfolk Journal and Guide (Negro), 6 November 1920. The registrar himself, on

cross-examination in the court, failed to answer some of his own questions correctly.

28. For the allegations of white disfranchisement recently made in Virginia, v. below, Chapter VIII, pp. 177-178.

29. Census Hearings 1921, 166-8, e.g.

30. Questionnaire reply. In Birmingham, it was once openly proposed that a selected group of Negroes be recommended for registration by a joint conference of white and Negro leaders; quoted in Census Hearing 1921, p. 70.

31. V. testimony of Walter White on this point, Census Hearings 1921; pp. 43, 44, 47, 49, 61-67, 187-8, 190-2 show that intimidation was also common.

32. Except in Alabama, Louisiana, and Virginia, where no costs are assessed in suits over registration and voting.

33. The quotations are all from questionnaire replies, originating in various parts of the South. The N. A. A. C. P's 1930 lynching Report included one case of a Negro "being active in politics." (N. Y. Times, 28 December 1930).

34. The foregoing quotations are again from questionnaire replies.

35. The 1928 elections sent two Negro Republicans to the State Legislature; one a woman elected to succeed her deceased husband. Between 1914 and 1929 there were, at various times, six Negroes in the State House of Representatives (N. Y. Times, 20 February 1928; Atlanta Independent, 23 March 1929). The State had for some years maintained a Bureau of Negro Welfare and Statistics, in charge of a Negro Director.

36. V. an article on "The Rehabilitation of a Commonwealth" (N. C.), American Historical Review, vol. xxxvi, no. 1, October 1930; esp. pp. 55-56.

37. See below, Chapter VIII, pp. 186, 189-190.

38. Pinchbeck, p. 115.

39. DuBois, in "The College-Bred Negro," gives 3856 as the *total* number of Negroes graduated from colleges between 1820 and 1909 (45). There were, in 1926, 17,506 Negroes enrolled in colleges, universities, and normal schools for the country as a whole; that is, 15 per 10,000 population among Negroes as compared with 90 per 10,000 among whites. In 1928, there were only fifty-four colored holders of the Ph.D. degree in the United States. (Johnson, "Negro in American Civilization," pp. 292, 294.)

The writer assembled lists of Negro graduates of higher institutions of learning (including technical schools) for a questionnaire in 1929-30, from the leading schools, and from the principal professional associations. The number of names yielded for all Southern and Border States except West Virginia was about 10,000; had all the women been included, this figure might have been raised to about 25,000.

The 1920 Census gave the South about 55,000 professional men and women in the colored group, over half of whom, it can be shown, were school teachers and clergymen (U. S. Census, 1920, vol. iv, Ch. vii, Table 1; cf. U. S. Census, "Negro Population . . . 1790-1915," pp. 510-11).

40. This dilemma of the Negro leader is well summarized in M. W. Ovington, "Portraits in Color," especially the chapters devoted to Dr. DuBois and Dr. Moton. "Whoever is familiar with the Negro world, knows of its conservative and radical groups, those who believe that the cause of the black man is best served by demanding his full rights . . . and those who believe it is best

to ask for what there is some chance of getting in the near future . . . At the extreme of one group are the fanatics, at the extreme of the other, the time-servers. And it is the lot of the conservative that if he works with the oppressor he cannot escape suspicion" (p. 72). V. also pp. 71, on Moton's popularity among the whites, and 83-4, on DuBois.

CHAPTER VII

1. Questionnaire reply.
2. Interviews.
3. V. Dutcher, 21 ff., e.g.
4. V. Dutcher, on "Negroes serving Negroes," p. 50, e.g.
5. Many questionnaire replies attested to the comparative ease with which "educated," "respectable" Negroes might be registered. There were also quite a few, however, which said that the "Uncle Tom" Negro fared better.
6. Individual questionnaire replies indicated in various localities that "persistence" might eventually win registration for the same reason.
7. The reality of Church's power over local Federal appointments was clearly brought out in the Hearings of a subcommittee of the Senate Committee on Post Offices and Post Roads, 70th Congress, 2nd session, 1929, especially pp. 4, 7, 11, 40, 46, 50, 62-63, 65, 97-112. Senator Heflin's poem is on p. 117.
8. Crump, curiously enough, came to Memphis from the Mississippi Black Belt.
9. Interviews.
10. V., e.g., N. Y. Times, editorial correspondence, 10 August 1930, recalling the events of 1928 in connection with the current election.
11. N. Y. Times, 8 June, 20 July, 3 and 10 August 1930. Crump had unsuccessfully opposed Horton in 1926 and 1928.
12. Account of G. W. Lee, Church's lieutenant, in the N. Y. Messenger (Negro), February 1928, pp. 30-1. The following, put in evidence at the Memphis Postmastership Hearings, is also significant. It is the text of a pledge which Church required of an aspirant to Federal office, as a condition of Church's support: ". . . If any colored person passes the examination for clerkship or is eligible I will recommend his immediate appointment on your recommendation . . . I will remove or demote any employee upon your request who is not giving a square deal to his subordinates . . ." (p. 47).
13. Indeed, as the writer has it on good authority, it was probably due to the Negro vote that he was once retained in office against a recall campaign.
14. Andrews, R. M.—"John Merrick."
15. Letter from a business associate of O'Kelly's.
16. U. S. Census 1930, Population Bulletins, 2nd series; Georgia.
17. In this, Davis followed the precedent of the colored Republican leader he succeeded, Henry Lincoln Johnson. For Johnson's efforts to secure Negro registration, through the publication of a pamphlet "Stepping Stones to Registration," and the prosecution of suits against registrars, v. Census Hearings 1921, pp. 119-20.
18. V., e.g., the Houston Sentinel (Negro), 18 July 1930, for accounts of

an attempt to break into the Democratic State primaries; and the Norfolk Journal and Guide (Negro), 9 November 1929, for accounts of the organization of a local body to test certain aspects of "understanding" questions in the local courts. It is worth noting that the New Orleans campaign referred to in the text had the support of Walter Cohen, Negro Republican State chairman.

19. City-manager cities are listed in "The Story of the City-Manager Plan," National Municipal League pamphlet, N. Y., 1930, pp. 26-9; the commission figure is from U. S. Census Bureau, Financial Statistics of Cities, 1927, pp. 10-11.

20. Interviews. The writer was told that there is a recurrent agitation in Roanoke for a return to nonpartisan city elections.

21. Interviews.

22. The Norfolk figures are those of the city registrar, confirmed by Negroes in a position to know. The registrar, who gave the impression of great unfriendliness towards the Negro "out of his place," added that all city employees, including Negro unskilled and day laborers, were "encouraged" to keep up their registration. The figures from Portsmouth and Newport News were given the writer with great exactitude, and in the former case with a copy of the official list, by local Negro leaders active in nonpartisan political clubs, public forums, etc.

23. The Lynchburg News carried a story of the Newport News city election in its issue of 25 April 1920: to date twenty-five candidates had offered for the five available Council positions, and a Negro meeting had been held to pick the five it would recommend for support at the polls.

24. Interviews in Dallas, Galveston, Fort Worth, Houston, and San Antonio.

25. Census Hearings 1921, p. 39; Representative Beer.

26. Interviews.

27. Interviews.

28. William ("Goose-neck Bill") McDonald.

29. This story was told to the writer over and over again by Negroes not only in Atlanta, but elsewhere; the details were given by a white man in a strategic position for information on Atlanta interracial matters.

30. The Atlanta Independent (Negro) for 3 February 1921 called upon Negroes editorially to support the issue, citing the promise of the mayor and several councilmen to give specific shares to the Negro school system: $350,000 for a high school, $150,000 for a new grammar school, etc.

31. Failure to keep such promises were not uncommon; v., e.g., Houston Informer (Negro), 9 October 1926.

32. Interviews. V. Louisville Courier-Journal, August, September, and November 1927.

33. Interviews; and undated clipping from the Courier-Journal in the Tuskegee Institute files. V. the Courier-Journal for October and November 1925. The subsequent reorganization of the University of Louisville prevented the keeping of this promise, until 1930, when a municipal college for Negroes was organized.

34. Athens, Ga., Banner, 2 November 1920.

35. Respectively, Atlanta Constitution, 17 April 1922, 25 May 1927; Birmingham Reporter (Negro), 11 November 1922; Tampa Times, 8 October 1920.

36. Atlanta Georgian, undated clipping of March 1919 in Tuskegee files.

37. E.g., Houston Informer, 8, 15 April, 6 May, 18 November 1922; Savannah Tribune, 4, 11 May 1922; Birmingham Reporter, 13 May 1922.

38. In the Louisville municipal election of 1922, William Warley, Negro Republican leader and editor of the Louisville News, supported one Harris, a Democrat, hoping to increase the power of the Negro vote by a show of independency. For this he was reviled by the Negro leadership of the city, and even threatened with personal injury. The Negro electorate stuck to its Republican tradition, and helped elect Mayor Quinn. Warley remained a Democrat, or at least an independent, working for Smith in 1928. He claimed to have increased the municipal Democratic vote among Negroes in Louisville to 8000 by 1929—probably a much exaggerated number. He admitted to the writer that Negro independency was on the whole remote.

39. V., e.g., the appeal of a candidate for the Tennessee State Senate, for the Negro vote of Knoxville; East Tennessee News, 20 July 1922.

40. But in Winston-Salem, in the midst of this region, a Negro Democratic club organized by a local restaurant keeper in behalf of Smith in 1928 was frowned out of existence.

There is some reason to believe that a number of Negroes habitually voted in the primaries of Roanoke, Va.

41. In strict accuracy, Florida should be added to this list, but in fact Negroes, save in thoroughly exceptional circumstances, were as effectively barred by the rules of the city and county party committees.

42. The secretary of the Columbia Democratic Club agreed in his testimony with several Negroes of the place that there were in 1930 twelve duly qualified Negro Democrats in the city. Several of the writer's questionnaire returns indicate an occasional vote in the primary.

The writer has been unable to verify the story that between 1916 and 1920 Columbia was the scene of hard-fought municipal primary campaigns between one Griffiths and all comers, in which a group of Negro voters figured until their presence in his behalf brought about his defeat, through a revulsion of white feeling. The result was supposed to have been greater vigilance in the local enforcement of the "Hampton rule."

43. Charleston News and Courier, 2 April 1929.

44. The writer was asked not to name the city, lest the State committee, which had several times remonstrated with the local party authority, carry out its threat of invalidating the whole county's primary returns, and take steps to bar all Negroes in the future.

45. Questionnaire returns; e.g., ". . . a few Negroes (favorite cringers) vote in the Democratic primary unmolested." The principal of a Negro institution in Alabama showed the writer a letter from a white lawyer asking for the names and addresses of Negro primary voters in order to circularize them in behalf of a candidate.

46. Houston Sentinel, 18 July 1930; the counties were DeWitt, Jefferson, McLennan, and Zavalla. The N. Y. Times also included Val Verde County (20 July 1930).

47. Editorial, 4 February 1930. This was also the viewpoint of the judge of a Portsmouth (Va.) court who had been instrumental in securing fair registration conditions for Negroes. In so conservative a place as Vicksburg,

Miss., the admission of Negroes to the municipal primary was from time to time discussed, albeit academically, by local business men; an observer hazarded the guess that each faction in city politics was merely waiting for the other to take the first step.

48. N. Y. Times, 31 May 1930. The regular Democratic organization, opposed as it was to Senator Simmons' renomination, was well advised if it did admit Negroes to this primary. Simmons was greatly disliked by North Carolina Negroes because of his connection with the disfranchising laws, and his repeated use of appeals to race feeling in his later political life. Bailey won the nomination and the election.

49. V. above, Chapter III, p. 59. Only the "grandfather clauses" were ever invalidated by the U. S. Supreme Court.

50. In Florida and Arkansas, there have been white primary cases in the State courts, but the decisions were adverse to the Negro plaintiffs, and up to the time of writing no appeals had been taken to the Federal judiciary. The Florida case, Goode vs. Johnson, Riera, and Bell, election officials, arose in Pensacola, was thrown out of the Escambia County Court in September 1928 (Houston Informer, 15 September 1928), and then went on the calendar of the State Supreme Court (Atlanta Constitution, 13 October 1929). A similar case in Tampa was dropped by plaintiff (Atlanta Constitution, 8 September 1929). The Arkansas case originated in Little Rock. On 26 November 1928, the judge of the Arkansas Circuit Court, 2nd division, issued an order restraining Little Rock primary election officials from keeping Negro Democrats from the polls under the party rule. At a hearing to make this order permanent, held on 8 December, the Pulaski County Chancery Court dismissed the case, dissolving the injunction. This ruling was appealed to the State Supreme Court, which upheld it in the following language: "Nowhere is there to be found any provisions in the statutes of Arkansas requiring any political party to hold primary elections. The acts mentioned [in the Negro brief] are applicable only in the event a political party does hold a primary election. The State of Arkansas has passed no law depriving . . . qualified electors . . . on account of color . . . of the right to vote. The party rule quoted above is merely a rule of the Democratic party . . . The State has nothing to do with the primary . . . appoints no officers . . . does not pay the costs . . . A voluntary political organisation . . . the Democratic party had the right to prescribe . . . the qualifications of membership . . . The fact that [its] nominees are always elected . . . does not alter the situation. Neither does the fact that appellants are Democrats . . ." (Arkansas Democrat, 24 March 1930.)

51. The statute is in General Laws of Texas, 2nd extra session of 1923, p. 74. The case arising out of it was Nixon vs. Herndon, 273 U. S. 536. Justice Holmes wrote: "The State of Texas in the teeth of [the Fourteenth Amendment] assumes to forbid Negroes to take part in a primary election the importance of which we have indicated, discriminating against them by the distinction of color alone. States may do a good deal of classifying that it is difficult to believe rational, but there are limits, and it is too clear for extended argument that color cannot be made the basis of a statutory classification affecting the right set up in this case." The possible loophole in this decision, as will be seen, is in the expression "*statutory* classification."

52. The new permissive statute is in General Laws of Texas, extra session

of 1927, ch. 67, p. 193. The party rule is quoted in Grigsby vs. Harris, 27 Fed. Rep. (2) 942. This rule was annually renewed in the party conventions.

53. Grigsby vs. Harris (cited above; also described in the N. Y. Times, 25 July 1928); Nixon vs. Condon, 34 Fed. R. (2) 464; and a suit instituted by Luther Wiley, colored, against the Bexar County Democratic Committee, N. Y. Times, 20 July 1930. Grigsby vs. Harris provided the precedent on which the Arkansas primary case of 1930 was decided; for the full logic of this position, see note 50 above.

54. The enabling statute was of the same type as the latest Texas law; Michie's Virginia Code, 1924, sec. 228. The party rule may be found in "Virginia Election Laws," issued by the Secretary of the Commonwealth, 1928, p. 98. The District Court case was Bliley et al. vs. West, on appeal from the Richmond Court of Law and Equity, 33 Fed. Rep. (2) 177 (newspaper accounts in N. Y. Times, 6 June and 25 October 1929). The appeal taken by the primary election officials to the Circuit Court was decided against them at Asheville, N. C., 13 June 1930 (N. Y. Herald-Tribune, 14 June 1930). As a result of the decision in Bliley vs. West, at least one further suit was entered in the same U. S. Court, by J. S. Briggs of Newport News (Norfolk Journal and Guide, 17 and 31 August 1929).

55. The leader of a local Negro political forum and vote-encouraging organization told the writer that 230-odd Negroes voted in the 1929 State primary in Portsmouth. He had been warned that three out of five city wards were under orders to refuse Negroes. Taking one case to a friendly court, he secured a favorable decision under the U. S. District Court opinion. Thereupon, to avoid the unpleasant publicity attendant upon continued violation of this opinion, the party authorities passed down the word to admit all Negro primary aspirants in the city.

56. A petition for review of the Arkansas case was filed before the U. S. Supreme Court in July 1930 (Houston Informer, 26 July 1930), but was denied. Funds for carrying Nixon vs. Condon to the U. S. Circuit Court of Appeals—the first step in getting before the highest court—were sent to Texas by the N.A.A.C.P. in 1929 (Norfolk Journal and Guide, 9 November 1929).

57. State officials and others in Virginia with whom the writer discussed the matter in the Autumn of 1929 were sure that revision of the primary law, placing the nominating machinery in the hands of the party as a private organization, would be undertaken at the next session of the General Assembly. V. also the Miami Herald, 17 July 1929, shortly after the West decision: "Some other means . . . must be discovered . . .," etc.

58. The run of questionnaire returns confirmed this impression; v. also the quadrennial rise in Negro registration in Louisiana, as shown in the Biennial Reports of the Secretary of State to the Governor.

59. Where there was a lily-white faction, the Negro party leaders often encouraged Negro voting and other activity in order to get the weight of numbers behind the "black-and-tan" organization in case of a contest for convention seats, patronage control, etc. Voluntary Negro primaries were sometimes held for the same reason.

60. Gossip in Georgia and Alabama had it that Mr. Hoover would have carried them too if the votes had been counted as they were cast. In Alabama, it was said, the Hoovercrat organization was prepared to contest the returns,

but did not because of the overwhelming victory of their candidate in the nation as a whole.

61. N. Y. Times, 17 July 1928, e.g. The writer discussed this change of front with McDonald; it was due to recognition of the lily-white faction in Texas at the 1928 Republican convention.

62. In Columbia, capital of South Carolina, the writer heard of friendly visits paid Negroes by Klansmen in behalf of the white, Protestant, and Nordic Hoover.

63. The returns were: Anderson (lily-white), 67,116; Mitchell ("lily-black"), 5230; Trinkle (Democrat), 141,481. The Negro leaders in this campaign believed that many Negroes voted for Trinkle. Interviews furnished the material for this diagnosis of the election and its results. The returns are from the World Almanac, 1925, p. 853.

64. The primary call is in the Atlanta Constitution, 6 August 1929. Alexander's name first appeared in the same paper on 6 September 1929, in connection with a speech in which he asked that the "whispering campaign" against him be stopped. The "whispers" concerned at least in part his efforts to get Negro support for the November election. His charges against the "ring" appeared incidentally in the issue of 25 September 1929, in the report of a speech in rebuttal by his opponent. Palmer's name first appeared 11 September 1929; his "machine-control" charges, 28 September 1929.

65. Atlanta Constitution, 8 and 25 September 1929.

66. Atlanta Constitution, 25 and 27 September and 1 October 1929. Fulton County is Atlanta and suburbs, with an estimated Negro vote of 5000.

67. Atlanta Constitution, 2 October 1929; unofficial returns.

68. The conclusion is drawn from interviews in Atlanta in the winter following the election. As to the Negro voter's strength in Atlanta, v. above, pp. 143-144, 150-151, 160-162.

In Mobile, Ala., in 1912, shortly after the adoption of a commission government, the municipal election was contested beyond the primary. The issues aroused much excitement: one candidate was branded as a hangover from the corrupt aldermanic machine, the "tool of the corporations," and opposed to certain improvements of port and terminal facilities. He was defeated by 143 votes. More recently, the official Negro registration of Mobile was 159. Had it been less in 1912, there would still be every reason to believe the stories current in the city that both candidates quietly solicited Negro help at the ballot box (interviews; Mobile Register, 3 September 1912, 14 April 1926). The writer saw in Mobile several letters appealing for the influence of a Negro leader, variously dated, and signed by various candidates for commissionerships.

The special election without a preliminary primary also brought the Negro occasionally into politics where his influence otherwise was nil. Thus, in Vicksburg, Miss., the death of the Mayor in 1926 necessitated an unexpected campaign in which the polls were open to all registrants. The election was expected to be close, and the 75 to 100 Negro voters of the town found themselves sought after. It was won by 135 votes; the Negro bloc, therefore, was worth considering. (Interviews; Vicksburg Herald, 9 June 1926.)

69. Such a case was reported to the writer, from highly credible sources, in the matter of a sheriff's election in Macon County, Georgia, in 1928.

CHAPTER VIII

1. The date, that is, by which the new Southern constitutions had fixed a new norm of Negro voting.

2. A careful study of election returns showed this to be true. Wherever possible, the returns for Congressional, State legislature, and gubernatorial elections were examined, in the variously named State Manuals, Directories, and Official Registers, and the Congressional Directory, from 1900 to 1930, and the figures compared with the Negro-white population ratio of the counties affected.

3. For Congress, cf. Congressional Directory, 71st Congress, pp. 149 ff., and N. Y. Times, 9 November 1930.

4. Of course, the bare fact of the Hoover victory remains; it is safe to say that no Quaker Republican could have won the South from even a Catholic Democrat in 1880. The 1928 election showed what was possible—not what was immediately probable. This was the view of most Southerners, at least after the 1929 elections. For example, Julian Harris, editorial correspondent for the N. Y. Times in Georgia, wrote: "The simple truth is that the South is at heart and by tradition Democratic, and the Hoover vote was a sort of hysteria that had its basis not in politics, but in a sort of religious crusade, in which sentiment for prohibition and against Catholicism aroused to a frenzy many persons who already took their politics seriously." (22 June 1930.)

5. New Republic, 31 October 1928. The five Southerners were Senators Caraway (Ark.), Harrison (Miss.), and Glass (Va.), Governor Dan Moody of Texas, and Josephus Daniels of North Carolina.

6. Hare, pp. 92 ff., 150, 153, 197.

Other manifestations of lily-whitism included: Alabama—a State ticket run in 1906, carried Chilton and Winston counties (Off. and Stat. Register 1906, pp. 246-7, 287); Arkansas—Came to a head in 1924, then relaxed (interviews); Florida—injunction sought to prevent Negroes from holding a State Convention (New York Times, 30 December 1919), attempt to capture 1920 national convention delegation (Census Hearings 1921, p. 129), formation of "Independent Republican Party" to eliminate Negroes (Montgomery, Ala., Advertiser, 23 July 1922); Georgia—national convention disputes 1920 (Atlanta Independent, 18 April 1929), State convention contests (Atlanta Constitution, 3 April, 1 June 1924); North Carolina—Negro address to State chairman charging lily-whitism (Greensboro Daily News, 15 September 1924); Texas—Creager, present lily-white leader, powerful since gubernatorial candidacy in 1916, official announcement of lily-whitism 1919, Creager national committeeman 1920, patronage referee 1922 (Postmastership Hearings 1930, pp. 216, 784, 818); Republican primary held (Texas Almanac, 1927, p. 97); Virginia—first official lily-white announcement 1921 (Norfolk Virginian-Pilot, 25 October, 14-15 July 1921). In Alabama, Arkansas, and Texas, early lily-white organizations attempted to come between the warring Democratic factions during the Agrarian Revolt; v. Nashville Daily American, 11 April 1889, and Little Rock Gazette, 14, 15 April, 1892.

7. Editorial Research Reports, 14 June 1927, pp. 466, 469 ff.

8. N. Y. Times, 20 May 1928.

9. Ibid., 20 November 1928.
10. Ibid., 7 June 1928.
11. Ibid., 30 May 1928.
12. New Orleans Times-Picayune, 7 May 1929; Howard was permitted resign but very plainly under administration pressure.
13. N. Y. Times, 6 and 9 June 1928.
14. Ibid., 7 June 1928; v. also below, pp. 173 and 176, and notes 16 and 33.
15. For a discussion of the Mann organization and influence from the Negro point of view, v. the Norfolk Journal and Guide, 16 November 1929.
16. Tennessee: Memphis Postmastership Hearings 1929, pp. 66, 77. Texas: interviews in Ft. Worth; v. also Postmasterships Subcommittee Report 1930, pp. 22 ff.
17. E.g., statement of Henry Anderson, Virginia lily-white, after a conference with the president-elect, N. Y. Times, 4 February 1929.
18. N. Y. Times, 27 March 1929.
19. N. Y. Times, 1 and 14 April 1929; 6 August 1930.
20. N. Y. Times, 11 March 1929.
21. E.g., Detroit Free Press, 29 July 1929; Norfolk Journal and Guide, 21 September 1929.
22. N. Y. Times, 7 August 1930.
23. N. Y. Times, 12 and 24 August 1930.
24. It was widely believed that many Northern (as well as Southern) Negroes voted for Smith in 1928 because of the evidence of lily-whitism in the Hoover nomination and campaign machine; this, and the effective row made by Negroes over the proposal of Judge Parker for the Federal supreme bench, gave pause to the party strategists. The Negroes opposed Parker's confirmation (which eventually failed) because of anti-Negro suffrage speeches which he had made in North Carolina. For the nature of the protest, v. an article by Walter White, "The Negro and the Supreme Court," Harpers Magazine, January 1931.
25. N. Y. Times, 7 March, 6, 20, 21 April 1930; Atlanta Constitution, 28 March 1929; Norfolk Journal and Guide, 21 September 1929.
26. Norfolk Journal and Guide, 21 September 1929; New Orleans Times-Picayune, 7 May 1929; Greenwood (Miss.) Commonwealth, 18 April 1929.
27. Charleston News and Courier, 2 April 1929.
28. For Louisiana, v. N. Y. Times, undated clipping, April 1930. After these lines had been written, Cohen's death was announced, N. Y. Times, 29 December 1930.
29. Interviews.
30. Undated clipping, N. Y. Times, February 1929.
31. Postmasterships Report 1930, 13 ff.; for Texas, 19 ff.
32. V. an article by Owen P. White, in Colliers Weekly, 22 June 1929; also Postmasterships Hearings 1929, pp. 883 ff.
33. For McDonald's feelings, see his letter to the Houston Sentinel (Negro), 18 July 1930. The rancorousness of the factional feeling between Creager and Wurzback is fully documented in the Postmasterships Report 1930, pp. 22 ff., and in the hearings preceding the same, parts 4 and 5 of which are almost wholly given over to disputes among Texas witnesses and their partisans on the Committee. "T. R. B.," the Washington correspondent of the New Re-

public, discredits the whole "clean-up" movement in his letters in the issues of 22 and 29 April 1931.

34. There was no lily-whitism in West Virginia or Kentucky; there was in Tennessee. In all three of these States, Republicanism was a genuine fighting opposition to the generally prevailing Democracy. Perhaps lily-whitism made little or no headway on the border because an active Republicanism, winning elections from time to time and here and there, felt that it could not afford to cut loose from Negro support. In Tennessee, moreover, Robert Church's black-and-tan Republicanism had the support of the Crump Democracy; v. above, Chapter VII, pp. 138-141.

35. The Anderson lily-white vote was 67,116; a Negro protest ticket polled 5230; Trinkle won with 141,481 votes. Anderson polled the largest Republican vote in Virginia since Reconstruction days. V. World Almanac, 1925, p. 853.

36. Norfolk Virginian-Pilot, 23 October 1921, e.g.; N. Y. Times, 16, 18 June 1929, e.g., respectively.

37. Norfolk Virginian-Pilot, 14 and 15 July 1921, 25 October 1921.

38. Except for sporadic charges in a few places during the heat of campaigns. In this connection, it is interesting to note that North Carolina in 1920 repealed her poll-tax registration requirement—the first Southern State so to do since the adoption of the new constitutions (N. C. Public Laws of 1920, Ch. 93, confirmed by plébiscite, November 1920).

39. This statement of the "new" Republican platform of Virginia is derived from two speeches of Col. Anderson, "The Solid South" (1927), and address to the Republican State Convention in Richmond (1929). Additional references on particular points are: complete 1921 platform—Norfolk Virginian-Pilot, 15 July, 25 October 1921; complete 1929 platform—N. Y. Times, 30 July 1929; "ring" charges—N. Y. Times, 4 February 1929; solicitation of absentee ballots—Roanoke Times, 4, 5 November 1929; election law changes demanded—Roanoke Times, 4 November 1929 (advertisement), Norfolk Virginian-Pilot, 18 November 1929 (editorial in a Democratic newspaper), a [Republican] Petition of Right before the Virginia General Assembly, 1927; charges of white disfranchisement—interviews, but no cases definitely established; the "short-ballot" constitution—described, N. Y. Times, 17 June 1928, as an issue, Roanoke Times, 4 November 1929, N. Y. Times, 3 November 1929; the oyster, labor, and aristocracy controversies, N. Y. Times, 3 November 1929. There were other issues in the 1929 campaign: the alleged "wetness" of the regular Democrats and their connection with "Raskobism" and Tammany on the one side; and the apostasy of the anti-Smith bolters, the DePriest issue, and the Negro-domination question on the other.

40. E.g., the following returns, from the World Almanac, 1931, p. 896:

For Governor:			*For Senator:*		
	Dem.	Rep.		Dem.	Rep.
1928	362,009	289,415	1926	218,934	142,891
1924	294,441	185,627	1924	294,404	184,393
1920	308,151	230,175	1920	310,504	229,343
1916	167,761	120,157	1918	143,542	93,697
1912	149,975	43,625 (R.); 49,930 (Ind.)	1914	121,342	87,101

Compare this showing with that of the Republicans in Virginia, ibid., p. 906. In 1916 and 1918, the Virginia Republican party offered no Senatorial candidate; in 1920, its Senatorial candidate polled 18,000 votes; in 1922, 43,000; in 1924, 50,000; and in 1928 there were 436 "scattering" votes against the Democrat.

41. The white counties were not, strictly speaking, "lily-white." Other exceptions have been unimportant. Thus, in 1906, a lily-white convention met in Birmingham, Ala., nominated a State ticket and carried two counties by small majorities (Ala. Off. and Stat. Register 1906, pp. 246-7, 287); in Texas, Mr. Creager headed a State ticket in 1916 (Postmasterships Hearings 1929, p. 818). Negro Republicans have nominated Negro tickets from time to time as protests against lily-whitism: in Virginia in 1921 (above, Ch. VII, p. 159), in South Carolina in 1918 and 1920 for Congress as a counter to lily-white influence in Federal patronage circles (Columbia State, 23 November 1918; 24, 25 November 1920). Black-and-tan groups have also held voluntary primaries in order to hold their own at national conventions by a show of popular support (interviews in New Orleans and questionnaires). A Negro municipal ticket was put in the field in Raleigh in 1919 to exhibit the local Negro voting strength for the sake of future concessions from white candidates (Raleigh Independent [Negro], 29 March, 26 April 1929).

42. Alabama: a candidate for the State legislature barred from the primary ticket because of his support of Hoover (N. Y. Times, 12 August 1928); the primary candidacies of Hoover supporters barred by the State Democratic Committee, pursuant to the form of the primary call (Charleston News and Courier, 17 December 1929); ruling upheld by the attorney-general (Charlotte Observer, 24 December 1929); an injunction unsuccessfully sought by ex-Hoovercrats which would enable them to run in Democratic primaries (Mobile Register, 29 April 1930). V. also N. Y. Times, 28 December 1929; 3, 15 January, 23 February, 18 April 1930. The result was the formation of the abortive "Jeffersonian party," running Thomas Heflin for the U. S. Senate and Hugh Locke for the governorship (N. Y. Times, 19 April, 5 July, 10 August 1930).

Arkansas: Demand of the anti-Smith leader for reinstatement of Hoovercrats to full Democratic privileges (Baton Rouge State Advocate and Times, 20 February 1930); cf. rule barring "disloyal" Democrats in general terms, Rules of the Democratic party of Arkansas 1922-26, sec. 3.

Florida: Attorney-General rules that Hoovercrats are barred from candidacy in Democratic primaries (N. Y. Times, 28 January 1930).

Georgia: Representative Upshaw barred from candidacy in the Democratic primaries as a Hoovercrat (N. Y. Times, 11 August 1928).

Mississippi: Two counties plan to bar Hoovercrats from *voting* at Democratic primaries (N. Y. Times, 23 May 1930).

North Carolina: Attorney-General rules that no questions can be asked of primary candidates or voters such as had been hoped might bar Hoovercrats (N. Y. Times, 7 May 1930).

Tennessee: Democratic State chairman welcomes Hoovercrats back to the fold, lest the party lose the State (New Orleans Times-Picayune, 19 February 1930).

Texas: Bill permitting bar on Hoovercrats through State-committee action passed by legislature; believed to be aimed at Hoovercrat *candidacies* rather than *votes* (N. Y. Times, 17 March 1929). Vetoed by governor (ibid., 3 April 1929). Attorney-General rules no such bar possible in absence of law (Atlanta Journal, 30 January 1930). Senator T. J. Love, Hoovercrat and aspirant for governorship, charges Democratic State Committee with intention of barring Hoovercrat candidates and voters anyway (Houston Post-Dispatch, 3 February 1930). Love gets his name on Democratic primary ballot by order of State supreme court (N. Y. Times, 19 May 1930).

Virginia: the 1929 election discussed above, Ch. VII, pp. 159-160, Ch. VIII, pp. 178-179. The anti-Smith element quit the regular Democratic organization because the latter planned to nominate a "Raskobian" and "Tammany" candidate. No one in Virginia quite knew what these epithets meant.

43. Apart from the author's interviews, the following may be cited: From Florida: "Well-informed Democrats have known for the last five years that thousands of Republicans [white] have been participating in Democratic primaries as the only means of exercising their suffrage" (N. Y. Times, 23 September 1928; v. also 18 November 1928). From Tennessee: "According to report, many Republicans make it a practice to vote in Democratic primaries when they believe there is no chance of the election of their own party nominees" (N. Y. Times, 24 September 1928). Both these reports are unnecessarily cloaked in an atmosphere of rumor. V. also the statements of witnesses from Tennessee (a Republican speaking), and from Texas, Postmasterships Hearings 1929, p. 1165, and Memphis Postmastership Hearings 1929, pp. 75-76.

In Georgia, the Republican patronage referee for the 12th Congressional district declared that he supported the local Democratic ticket and the Democratic congressional nominee, voted in the Democratic primary, helped his "friends" in their primary races, and finally—what is probably exceptional—was five times elected sheriff of his county in the Democratic primary. Nevertheless, he made regular contributions to Davis' black-and-tan Republican organization (Postmasterships Hearings 1929, pp. 111-13).

44. Atlanta Constitution, 1 September 1929, Greenwood (Miss.) Commonwealth, 18 April 1929, respectively.

45. E.g., advertisement of the Norfolk City Democratic Committee in the Virginian-Pilot, during the campaign. This paper editorially took the same stand as the advertisement.

46. E.g., N. Y. Times, 7 July, 3 November 1929; Roanoke Times, 2, 4 November 1929. The DePriest incident was an issue in the Virginia State campaign of 1929.

47. Negro protest and failure to confirm were not necessarily cause and effect; v. reference above, note 24.

48. Perhaps most startling of all was the use of the title "Mr." as a prefix to Howard's name in one of these letters.

49. Interviews; v. also New Orleans Times-Picayune, 7 May 1929; Postmasterships Report 1930, pp. 3 ff.; and especially 8-10; Postmasterships Hearings 1929, pp. 365-6, 368, 387-9.

50. There is only one case on record in Mississippi: Postmasterships Hearings 1929, p. 356.

51. See Postmasterships Hearings, 1929, as follows, e.g.: for Georgia, pp. 39, 47, 51-2, 79-80, 178-85, 186; for South Carolina, pp. 266, 270, 301, 620, 626, 1324; for Mississippi, 356.

52. We write "not necessarily corruptly"—it is not meant to imply that there was no corruption. It was testified from South Carolina, e.g., that "politics made no difference, it was simply a question as to who bids the most" (Postmasterships Hearings 1929, p. 297).

53. Quoted from his correspondence to the Chicago Inter-Ocean, Hare, p. 93.

54. But Anderson had as associate Bascom Slemp, whose reputation was not that of a constructive statesman and unselfish public servant, however correct his actions undoubtedly were. And in Texas, as has been said, the Creager organization had been sharply criticized for its patronage dealings by the Senate investigating committee of 1929-30, and was widely suspected of commitments to a corrupt Democratic machine in southwest Texas.

55. Before the Credentials Committee of the 1892 Republican Convention, quoted in Hare, p. 197.

56. V. an extremely interesting article by Judson King, "Crisp County (Ga.) Bucks the Utilities," in the New Republic, 29 October 1930; and its sequel, N. Y. Times, 26 March 1931.

57. Two eminent Southern historians, once active in Virginia politics, secured the defeat of a member of the Page family, one hundred per cent Virginian, for a local office, by stressing the fact that among his supporters was a man whose ancestors in Reconstruction days cast their lot with the moderate Republicans instead of the Conservative "white man's party."

58. The Martin-Swanson organizations in Virginia were the most marked exceptions; less so an important group of Democrats in North Carolina.

59. The occasion was Blease's bolt from Smith in 1928. V. N. Y. Times, 27 and 28 August and 10 September 1930.

60. Again, the occasion was Heflin's failure to support Smith in 1928. V. above, note 42. The existence of such a faction within the Democratic party, be it noted, was a distinct handicap to the "new" Republicanism.

61. E.g., Natchez Democrat, 1 August 1923.

62. This account of the Whitfield régime is drawn from interviews in Mississippi, and from the Mississippi press of 1923, supplemented by a summary in the Mississippi Official and Statistical Register for 1924-28, pp. 59-60. See also Hobbs, G. A.

63. For further light on the views and public life of Bilbo, Long, and Graves, see, respectively: Hobbs, G. A., and N. Y. Times, 20 April 1930; N. Y. Times, 24 June 1928, 30 July and 31 August 1930; the Birmingham Age-Herald and the Montgomery Advertiser for July and August 1926—especially, on the Negro question, the former for 2 August, the latter for 1 August 1926.

64. Interviews. For the Liberal Democratic election law proposal, v. the Virginian-Pilot for 18 November 1929 (editorial). In the matter of election law reform, as in several other points, the Liberal Democrats stole considerable thunder from Anderson's lily-white Republicanism; v. above, pp. 176-178.

65. Interviews; v. also N. Y. Times, 9 June 1930. The occasion for the retirement of Simmons was his anti-Smith stand in 1928.

66. Virginia (reapportioned in 1922) and Alabama (1926).

CHAPTER IX

1. V. Hobbs, S. H., pp. 185, 252, 257, 304, 382, 388, for these and similar figures, and Negro wealth, mortality, crime, and literacy statistics which go to show that the North Carolina Negroes were still a depressed class. V. also Chapter IV, p. 62, and note at foot of page, above; and Chapter VI, p. 108.

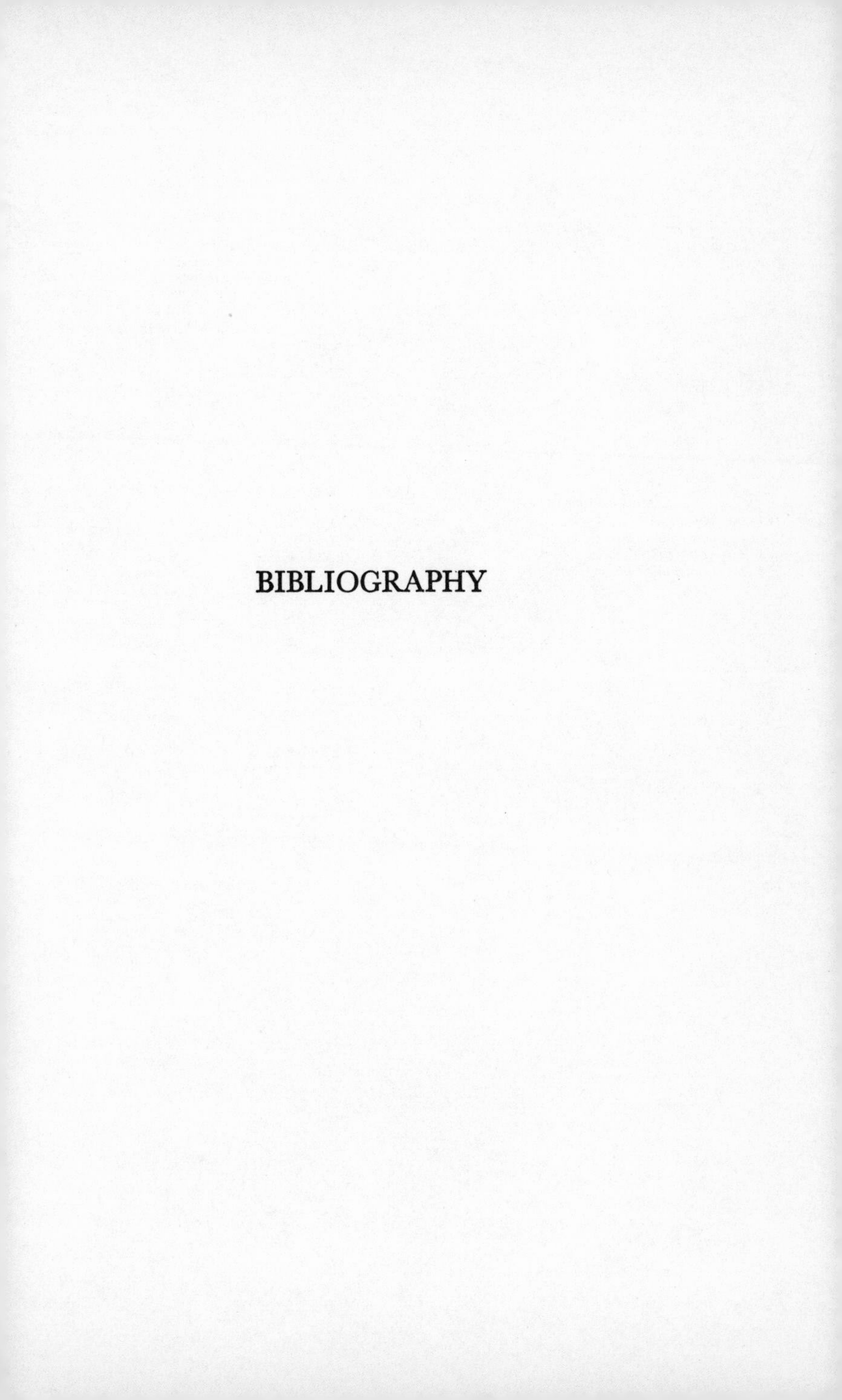

BIBLIOGRAPHY

OFFICIAL DOCUMENTS AND LAWS

Alabama—Convention Journal, 1865; Montgomery, 1865.
Alabama—Michie's Code of 1928; Charlottesville, 1928.
Arkansas—Convention Debates and Proceedings, 1868; Little Rock, 1868.
Arkansas—Digest of Statutes 1921; Little Rock, 1921.
Castle's Supplement; St. Louis, 1927.
Congressional Record, *passim*.
Eliot, T. D.—House Report of the Committee on Freedmen's Affairs, 10 March 1868; Washington, 1868.
Fleming, W. L.—"Documentary History of Reconstruction," 2 vols.; Cleveland, 1906-07.
Florida—Compiled General Laws, 1927; Atlanta, 1929.
Florida—Convention Journal, 1865; Tallahassee, 1865.
Georgia—Confederate Records of the State of Georgia, vol. iv; Convention Journal, 1865; Atlanta, 1910.
Georgia—Michie's Code of 1926, and Supplement, 1928; Charlottesville, 1926 and 1928.
Kentucky—Carroll's Statutes and Baldwin's Supplement; Louisville, 1922 and 1929.
Louisiana—Constitution of 1921; Indianapolis, 1921.
Wolff's Code of 1920; Indianapolis, 1920.
Acts of Legislature, 1920-28 (biennial); Baton Rouge.
Convention Debates, 1864; New Orleans, 1864.
Report of the Secretary of State, 1895-1928 (biennial); Baton Rouge.
Mississippi—Hemingway's Code of 1927; Indianapolis, 1927.
General Laws, regular and special session of 1928; Jackson, 1928.
Moores, M.—Contested Election Cases, U. S. House, 1901-1917; Washington (Government Printing Office), 1917.
National Association for the Advancement of Colored People, files—Matter in cases of Robinson *vs.* Holman, Nixon *vs.* Herndon, Nixon *vs.* Condon, West *vs.* Bliley.
North Carolina—Consolidated Statutes, 1919; Raleigh, 1920.
Same, revisions and additions, 1924; Raleigh, 1924.

Public Laws and Resolutions of the General Assembly, 1921, 1923, 1924, 1925, 1927; Raleigh, 1921-25, Charlotte, 1927.

Convention Journal, 1865-66; Raleigh, 1866.

Rowell, Chester—Contested Election Cases, U.S. House, 1789-1901; Washington (Government Printing Office), 1901.

South Carolina—Code of Laws, 1922; Columbia, 1922.

Acts of the Legislature, 1922, 1924, 1925, 1927, 1928.

Convention Journal, 1865; Columbia, 1865.

Convention Proceedings, 1868; Charleston, 1868.

Tennessee—Thompson's Shannon's Code, 1918; Louisville, 1918.

Same, Supplement, 1926; Indianapolis, 1926.

Texas—Convention Journal, 1866; Austin, 1866.

Revised Civil Statutes, 1925; Austin, 1925.

Penal Code, 1925; Austin, 1925.

General and Special Laws, 40th Legislature, regular and 1st called sessions.

United States Census, 1920, 1930.

United States Census Bureau—"Negro Population in the U.S., 1790-1915"; Washington, 1918.

United States House of Representatives, 66 Congress, 3d session—Hearings before the Committee on the Census on H.R. 14498, 15021, 15158, 15217; Washington, 1921.

United States Senate Subcommittee of the Committee on Post Offices and Post Roads, 70 Congress, 2d session—Influencing Appointments to Postmasterships, Hearings, pts. 1-5, and Report; Washington, 1929, 1930.

United States Senate Subcommittee of the Committee on Post Offices and Post Roads—Hearings on the Nomination . . . to the Memphis Postmastership, pts. 1-2; Washington, 1929.

Virginia—Convention Debates, 1867, vol. i; Richmond, 1868.

Convention Documents, 1867, vol. i; Richmond, 1867.

Convention Debates, 1901-02, 2 vols.; Richmond, 1906.

Michie's Code of 1924, and Supplement of 1928; Charlottesville, 1924 and 1928.

Petition of Right Before the General Assembly (Republican demand for suffrage revision); Richmond, 1927.

State Directories, Official and Statistical Registers, Manuals, etc., under various names, 1890-1929.

NEWSPAPERS

Alabama—Birmingham Age-Herald, 1900-01.
Arkansas—Little Rock Gazette, 1891-92.
"Crisis"—Organ of the National Association for the Advancement of Colored People, New York.
Florida—Jacksonville Times-Democrat, 1884-85.
Georgia—Atlanta Constitution, 1907-08.
 Atlanta Daily Intelligencer, 1865.
 Augusta Chronicle, 1907-08.
Louisiana—New Orleans Commercial Bulletin, 1867.
Mississippi—Natchez Daily Democrat, 1890.
 Vicksburg Herald, 1865.
North Carolina—Raleigh News and Observer, 1899-1900.
Oklahoma—Oklahoma City Oklahoman, 1906-07.
"Opportunity"—Organ of the National Urban League, New York.
South Carolina—Charleston Daily Courier, 1865, 1867.
 Charleston News and Courier, 1882.
Tennessee—Knoxville Journal, 1889-90.
 Nashville American, 1889-90.
 Nashville Daily Press and Times, 1865.
Virginia—Richmond Daily Whig, 1874.
 Richmond Dispatch, 1894.

Clipping Files at Tuskegee Institute, Ala.

New York Times.

BOOKS AND ARTICLES

Adams, J. T.—"Provincial Society," History of American Life, vol. iii; New York, 1928.
Ambler, C. H.—"Disfranchisement in West Virginia"; Yale Review, May-Aug. 1905.
 "Sectionalism in Virginia"; Chicago, 1910.
Anderson, H. W.—"The Solid South," address; Charlottesville, 1927.
 Speech to Republican State Convention; Richmond, 1929.

Andrews, R. M.—"John Merrick"; Durham, 1920.
Annals, American Academy of Political and Social Science—"The American Negro"; Nov. 1928.
Annals, American Academy of Political and Social Science, vol. cvi; "Primary Laws"; March 1923.
Archer, Wm.—"Through Afro-America"; London, 1910.
Arnett, A. M.—"The Populist Movement in Georgia"; Columbia University Studies in History, Economics, and Public Law, vol. civ; New York, 1922.
Baker, R. S.—"Following the Color Line"; London, 1909.
Barclay, T. S.—"The Liberal Republican Movement in Missouri, 1865-71"; Columbia, Mo., 1926.
Beard, C. A.—"Contemporary American History"; New York, 1924.
Beveridge, W.—"Abraham Lincoln"; Boston, 1928.
Bowers, C.—"The Tragic Era"; New York, 1929.
Boyd, W. K.—"Memoirs of W. W. Holden."
Brawley, B. G.—"A Short History of the American Negro"; New York, 1913.
Brewton, W. W.—"Life of Thomas E. Watson"; Atlanta, 1926.
Buck, P. H.—"The Poor Whites of the Ante-Bellum South"; American Historical Review, vol. xxxi, no. 1, 41-54.
Buck, S. J.—"The Agrarian Crusade," Chronicles of America, no. 45; New Haven, 1920.
Caffey, F. G.—"Suffrage Limitations at the South," Political Science Quarterly, vol. xx, p. 53; 1905.
Cairnes, J. E.—"The Slave Power"; London, 1863.
Carpenter, J. T.—"The South as a Conscious Minority"; New York, 1930.
Carson, Wm.—"Financing the Production . . . of Cotton"; Federal Reserve Board, Washington, 1923.
Chamberlain, D. H.—"Reconstruction in South Carolina"; Atlantic Monthly, vol. lxxxviii, p. 473; April 1901.
Chandler, J. A. C.—"Representation in Virginia"; Johns Hopkins Studies in Historical and Political Science, 14th series, nos. vi-vii; Baltimore, 1896.
"History of Suffrage in Virginia"; *ibid.*, 19th series, nos. vi-vii; Baltimore, 1901.
Cole, A. C.—"The Whig Party in the South"; Washington, 1913.

Coody, A. S.—"Biographical Sketches of J. K. Vardaman"; Jackson, Miss., 1922.

Coulter, E. M.—"Civil War and Readjustment in Kentucky"; Chapel Hill, N. C., 1926.

Davis, W. W.—"Civil War and Reconstruction in Florida"; New York, 1913.

Dew, T. R.—"Essays on Slavery"; Richmond, 1849.

Dodd, W. E.—"The Cotton Kingdom"; Chronicles of America, no. 27; New Haven, 1919.

Dowd, J.—"The Negro in American Life"; New York, 1926.

DuBois, W. E. B.—"College-Bred Negro"; Atlanta, 1909.

DuBois, W. E. B., and Dill, A. G.—"The Common School and the Negro American"; Atlanta, 1911.

Dunaway, L. S.—"Jeff Davis, His Life and Speeches"; Little Rock, 1925.

Dunning, W. A.—"Reconstruction, Political and Economic"; American Nation Series, vol. 22; New York, 1907.

"The Undoing of Reconstruction"; Atlantic Monthly, vol. lxxxviii, p. 437; October 1901.

Dutcher, D.—"Negro in Modern Industrial Society"; Lancaster, Penna., 1930.

Felton, R. L.—"Country Life in Georgia"; Atlanta, 1919.

Fertig, J. W.—"The Secession and Reconstruction of Tennessee"; Chicago, 1898.

Ficklen, J. R.—"The History of Reconstruction in Louisiana"; Johns Hopkins Studies in History and Political Science, 28th series, no. 1; Baltimore, 1910.

Finot, J.—"Race Prejudice"; London, 1906.

Fitzhugh, G.—"Sociology for the South"; Richmond, 1854.

Fleming, W. L.—"Civil War and Reconstruction in Alabama"; New York (Columbia University), 1905.

"The Sequel to Appomattox"; Chronicles of America, no. 32; New Haven, 1919.

Foster, Roger—"Commentaries on the Constitution of the United States"; London, 1896.

Garner, J. W.—"Reconstruction in Mississippi"; New York, 1901.

Grady, H. W.—"The New South"; New York, 1890.

Green, F. M.—"Constitutional Development in the South Atlantic States, 1776-1860"; Chapel Hill, 1930.

Hall, G. D.—"The Two Virginias"; pamphlet; Glencoe, Ill., 1915.

Hamilton, J. G. de R.—"Reconstruction in North Carolina"; New York, 1914.

Hare, M. C.—"Norris Cuney Wright"; New York, 1913.

Harris, J. C.—"Life of Henry W. Grady," including his writings and speeches; New York, 1890.

Harris, J. P.—"Registration of Voters in the U. S."; Washington, 1929.

Hart, A. B.—"Realities of Negro Suffrage"; American Political Science Association Proceedings, 1905.

Helper, H. R.—"The Impending Crisis"; New York, 1857.

Herbert, H. A.—"Why the Solid South?"; Baltimore, 1890.

Hesseltine, W. B.—"The Underground Railway"; Publications of the E. Tenn. Historical Society, no. 2, 1929.

Hill, B. H., Jr.—"Senator B. H. Hill of Georgia; Life, Speeches, and Writings"; Atlanta, 1891.

Hobbs, G. A.—"Bilbo, Brewer, and Bribery in Mississippi"; Memphis, 1918.

Hobbs, S. H.—"North Carolina, Economic and Social"; Chapel Hill, 1930.

Hosmer, J. K.—"Outcome of the Civil War," American Nation Series, vol. 21; New York, 1907.

Howard, G. E.—"Preliminaries of the American Revolution," American Nation Series, vol. viii; New York, 1905.

Ingle, Edward—"Southern Sidelights"; New York, 1896.

Jack, T.—"Sectionalism and Politics in Alabama"; Menasha, 1919.

Jacobson, C.—"Life Story of Jeff Davis"; Little Rock, 1925.

Johnson, C. A. (ed.)—"The Negro in American Civilisation"; New York, 1930.

Johnson, F.—"Development of State Legislation Concerning the Free Negro"; New York, 1919.

Kendrick, B. B.—"The Agrarian Discontent in the South, 1880-90"; Report of American Historical Association for 1920; Washington, 1925.

Kent, F. R.—Articles on Southern politics, *Baltimore Sun*, June-July, 1926.

Lester, J. C., and Wilson, D. L.—"The KuKlux Klan, Its Origin, Growth, and Disbandment"; 1884; republished with In-

troduction by W. L. Fleming, New York and Washington, 1905.
Locke, A. L. —"The New Negro"; New York, 1925.
Lonn, E.—"Reconstruction in Louisiana"; New York, 1918.
"Desertion During the Civil War"; New York, 1928.
McConnell, W. J.—"Social Cleavages in Texas"; Columbia University Studies; New York, 1925.
McDonald, Wm.—"Documentary Source Book of American History," 3rd edition; New York, 1926.
McGregor, J. C.—"The Disruption of Virginia"; New York, 1922.
McPherson, E.—"Political History of the United States during the Period of Reconstruction," 3d edition; Washington, 1880.
Martin, A. E.—"Anti-Slavery Movement in Kentucky to 1850"; Cornell University (thesis), 1918.
Mathews, J. M.—"Legislative and Judicial History of the Fifteenth Amendment"; Johns Hopkins University, Baltimore, 1909.
Mayes, E.—"L. Q. C. Lamar, Life and Speeches"; Nashville, 1896.
Merriam, C. A.—"Primary Elections"; Chicago, 1928.
Meyer, E. C.—"Nominating Systems"; Madison, Wis., 1902.
Mims, Edwin—"The Advancing South"; New York, 1926.
"The Independent Voter in the South"; South Atlantic Quarterly, vol. v, p. 1; January 1906.
Moffat, R. B.—"Disfranchisement of the Negro from a Lawyer's Standpoint"; Journal of the American Social Science Association, no. 42, 1904.
Moore, A. B.—"Conscription and Conflict in the Confederacy"; New York, 1924.
Morton, R. L.—"The Negro in Virginia Politics"; University of Virginia, 1919.
Murphy, E. G.—"The Basis of Ascendancy"; New York, 1910.
Nevins, A.—"The Emergence of Modern America"; History of American Life, vol. vii, New York, 1927.
Norton, C. C.—"The Democratic Party in Ante-Bellum North Carolina"; Chapel Hill, 1930.
Odegard, P. H.—"Pressure Politics"; New York, 1928.

Olmstead, F. L.—"A Journey in the Back Country"; London, 1860.

Ovington, M. W.—"Portraits in Color"; New York, 1927.

Owsley, F. L.—"Defeatism in the Confederacy"; N. C. Historical Review, July 1926.

Peirce, P. S.—"The Freedmen's Bureau"; University of Iowa Studies in Sociology, Economics, Politics, and History, vol. iii, no. 1; Iowa City, 1904.

Phillips, U. B.—"American Negro Slavery"; New York, 1918. "The Southern Whigs, 1834-1854," in Turner Essays on American History; New York, 1910.

Pinchbeck, R. B.—"The Virginia Negro Artisan and Tradesman"; Richmond, 1926.

Poe, C. H.—"Suffrage Restrictions in the South"; North American Review, vol. clxxv, p. 534; 1902.

Poole, W. F.—"Anti-Slavery Opinion before 1800"; Cincinnati, 1873.

Porter, K. H.—"A History of Suffrage in the United States"; Chicago, 1918.

Ramsdell, C. W.—"Reconstruction in Texas"; Columbia University Studies, no. 95; New York, 1910.

Reuter, E. B.—"The American Race Problem"; New York, 1927.

Reynolds, J. C.—"Reconstruction in South Carolina"; Columbia, S. C., 1905.

Rhodes, J. F.—"History of the United States"; vols. iv-vii; New York, 1920.

Robertson, A. F.—"Alex Hugh Holmes Stuart"; Richmond, 1925 (?).

Rose, J. C.—"Negro Suffrage; the Constitutional Point of View"; American Political Science Review, vol. 1, no. 1; 1906.

Schaper, W. A.—"Sectionalism and Representation in South Carolina"; American Historical Association Report, 1901.

Shannon, F. A.—"The Organisation and Administration of the U. S. Army"; Cleveland, 1928.

Shepard, W. J.—"The Theory of the Nature of the Suffrage"; Proceedings of the American Political Science Association, 1912.

Shryock, R. H.—"Georgia and the Union in 1850"; Durham, 1926.

Simkins, F. B.—"The Tillman Movement in South Carolina"; Durham, N. C., 1926.
Sinclair, W. A.—"The Aftermath of Slavery"; Boston, 1905.
Skaggs, W. H.—"The Southern Oligarchy"; New York, 1924.
Smith, E. C.—"The Borderland in the Civil War"; New York, 1927.
Smith, T. V.—"Slavery and the American Doctrine of Equality"; Southwestern Political and Social Science Quarterly, vol. vii, no. 4, March 1927.
"South in the Building of the Nation"—Richmond, 1909.
Spero, S., and Harris, A.—"The Black Worker"; New York, 1931.
Stanwood, E.—"A History of the Presidency"; Boston, 1928.
Staples, T. S.—"Reconstruction in Arkansas"; New York, 1923.
Stephenson, G. T.—"Race Discriminations in American Law"; New York, 1910.
Stephenson, N. W.—"The Day of the Confederacy"; Chronicles of America, no. 30; New Haven, 1919.
Taylor, A. A.—"The Negro in the Reconstruction of Virginia"; Washington, 1926.
"The Negro in South Carolina during Reconstruction"; Washington, 1924.
Thompson, C. M.—"Reconstruction in Georgia"; Columbia University Studies, vol. lxiv, no. 1; New York, 1915.
Thompson, H.—"The New South"; Chronicles of America, no. 42; New Haven, 1919.
Turner, E. R.—"The Negro in Pennsylvania, 1639-1861"; Washington, American Historical Association, 1911.
United States Treasury Department—"Repudiation of State Indebtedness"; (mimeographed) Washington, 1925.
Webster, L. J.—"The Operations of the Freedmen's Bureau in South Carolina," Smith College Studies in History, vol. i, nos. 2, 3; Northampton, 1916.
Weeks, S. B.—"Anti-Slavery Opinion in the South"; Southern Historical Association Publications, ii, 1898.
"History of Negro Suffrage"; Political Science Quarterly, vol. ix, p. 671; December 1894.
Wells, H. G.—"The Future in America"; London, 1906.
Wesley, C. H.—"Negro Labor in the United States"; New York, 1927.

White, M. J.—"Populism in Louisiana during the Nineties"; Mississippi Valley Historical Review, vol. v, no. 1, p. 3; June 1918.

Woolley, E. C.—"The Reconstruction of Georgia"; Columbia University Studies; New York, 1901.

INDEX

INDEX

History and Political Science

Carr, E. H. *Studies in Revolution* UL-171
Friedrich, Carl J. (Ed.) *Totalitarianism* UL-167
Kissinger, Henry A. *A World Restored* UL-170
Lippmann, Walter *The Good Society* UL-3
Mathiez, Albert *The French Revolution* UL-169
Mosse, George L. *The Crisis of German Ideology* UL-173

Literature, Criticism, Drama, and Poetry

Chekov, Anton *Nine Plays of Chekov* UL-59
cummings, e.e. *50 Poems* UL-66
Deutsch, Babette *Poetry Handbook* UL-126
Edel, Leon *The Modern Psychological Novel* UL-174
Eleven Plays of the Greek Dramatists UL-38
Hoagland, Kathleen (Ed.) *1000 Years of Irish Poetry* UL-140
Ibsen, Henrik *Four Plays* UL-31
James, Henry *French Poets and Novelists* (Intro. by Leon Edel) .. UL-164
Lukacs, Georg *Studies in European Realism*
(Intro. by Alfred Kazin) UL-166
McLaughlin, Richard and Slack, Howard E. (Eds.)
1000 Years of European Poetry UL-152
O'Faolain, Sean *The Vanishing Hero* UL-43

Psychology

Cohen, Elie A. *Human Behavior in the Concentration Camp* UL-100
Lundberg, Ferdinand and Farnham, Marynia
Modern Woman: The Lost Sex UL-46
Meerloo, Joost A. M. *The Rape of the Mind* UL-118
Stekel, Wilhelm *Compulsion and Doubt* UL-142
——— *The Interpretation of Dreams* UL-127
Wittels, Fritz *Freud and His Time* UL-34

Titles of General Interest

Biancolli, Louis (Ed.) *The Mozart Handbook* UL-132
Blacker, Irwin R. and Rosen, Harry M.
Conquest: The Dispatches of Cortez from the New World UL-145
Collaer, Paul *A History of Modern Music* UL-148
Denney, Reuel *The Astonished Muse*
(Intro. by David Riesman) UL-165
Colum, Padraic *Myths of the World* UL-50
Eastman, Max *Reflections on the Failure of Socialism* UL-137
Gross, Gerald *Editors on Editing* UL-147
Hamilton, Edith *Mythology* UL-93
Kuncewicz, Maria (Ed.) *The Modern Polish Mind* UL-162
Koestler, Arthur *The Sleepwalkers* UL-159
Lowenthal, Marvin (Ed.) *The Diaries of Theodor Herzl* UL-128
Lynes, Russell *The Tastemakers* UL-54
Perruchot, Henri *Cézanne* UL-149
Protter, Eric (Ed.) *Painters on Painting* UL-156
Trotsky, Leon *My Life* UL-72
Wright, Frank Lloyd *On Architecture* UL-70